2nd edition

Korean Made Easy for Everyday Life

Korean Made Easy for Everyday Life 2nd edition

Author	Seung-eun Oh
Translator	Michael Park, Isabel Kim Dzitac
Proofreader	Isabel Kim Dzitac

First Published	August, 2008
Second Edition	November, 2022
Publisher	Kyu-do Chung
Editor	Suk-hee Lee, Hyeon-soo Lee, Da-heuin Baek
Design	Na-kyoung Kim, Mi-jeong Yoon
Illustrator	Moon-su Kim
Voice Actor	So-yun Shin, Rae-whan Kim, Word Cameron Lee
Sources of photos	p. 266, 2020 부산국제영화제 포스터, 부산국제영화제 제공 p. 266, 2023 광주 비엔날레 포스터, (재)광주비엔날레 제공 p. 266, 2019 보령 머드축제 포스터, Boryeong Festival Tourism Foundation 제공

DARAKWON Published by Darakwon Inc.

Darakwon Bldg., 211, Munbal-ro, Paju-si, Gyeonggi-do, Republic of Korea 10881
Tel: 82-2-736-2031 (Sales Dept. ext.: 250~252; Book Publishing Dept. ext. 420~426)
Fax: 82-2-732-2037

Copyright©2022, 2008, Seung-eun Oh

Price: 18,000 won (Free MP3 Download)

ISBN: 978-89-277-3303-4 14710
　　　 978-89-277-3272-3 **(set)**

http://www.darakwon.co.kr
http://koreanbooks.darakwon.co.kr

※ Visit the Darakwon homepage to learn about our other publications and promotions and to download the contents of the book in MP3 format.

Korean made easy
for Everyday Life

2nd edition

Seung-eun Oh

🐘 DARAKWON

Preface

〈Korean Made Easy〉 시리즈는 제2언어 혹은 외국어로서 한국어를 공부하는 학습자를 위해 집필되었다. 특히 이 책은 시간적·공간적 제약으로 인해 정규 한국어 교육을 받을 수 없었던 학습자를 위해 혼자서도 한국어를 공부할 수 있도록 기획되었다. 〈Korean Made Easy〉 시리즈는 초판 발행 이후 오랜 시간 독자의 사랑과 지지를 받으며 전 세계 다양한 언어로 번역되어 한국어 학습에 길잡이 역할을 했다고 생각한다. 이번에 최신 문화를 반영하여 예문을 깁고 연습 문제를 보완하여 개정판을 출판하게 되어 저자로서 크나큰 보람을 느낀다. 한국어를 공부하려는 모든 학습자가 〈Korean Made Easy〉를 통해 효과적으로 한국어를 공부하면서 즐길 수 있기를 바란다.

시리즈 중 〈Korean Made Easy for Everyday Life〉는 한글을 익히고 시제와 같은 기본적인 학습을 마친 학습자(학습 시간 150~400시간)를 대상으로, 한국에서 살면서 겪을 수 있는 다양한 상황을 중심으로 자연스럽게 한국어를 사용할 수 있도록 고안되었다. 따라서 이 책에서는 학습자가 일상생활에서 자주 접하는 대화를 먼저 제시하고, 그 대화 맥락에서 공부할 수 있는 어휘나 문법과 같은 언어적 요소를 익혀, 궁극적으로는 문법과 대화를 확장하면서 의사소통을 향상시키는 데 초점을 두었다. 한국 생활이나 한국 문화에 대한 설명도 학습자가 한국에서 생활하면서 한국 사회 문화를 더 잘 이해할 수 있도록 고려하였다.

〈Korean Made Easy for Everyday Life〉는 크게 Part 1과 Part 2로 구성되어 있다. Part 1은 실생활에서 자주 사용되는 50개 표현을 10개 과로 제시하였다. 각 상황별로 다섯 가지 유용한 표현을 선정하여 제시하는데, 한국인이 어떤 맥락에서 이런 표현들을 사용하는지 자세한 설명을 덧붙여 학습자의 이해를 돕고 대화 연습을 통해 실제 생활에서 바로 적용할 수 있도록 하였다. Part 2는 여행, 일, 공부 등으로 한국에서 생활하는 6명의 외국인을 설정하여 한국에서 직접 겪을 만한 대화 상황을 24개의 장면으로 구성하였다. 각 장면에서 제시된 대화의 어휘와 발음, 문법, 문화적 정보는 학습자가 한국인과 의사소통하는 데 적극적으로 사용할 수 있도록 하였다.

이 책은 많은 분의 관심과 도움으로 출간하게 되었다. 먼저, 초판에서 필자의 의도가 이 책에 충실히 반영될 수 있도록 명확한 번역과 교정을 해 주신 번역가 Michael Park 씨께 감사 드린다. 자신의 가르친 경험을 토대로 조언을 해 준 동료 교사 오승민 선생님과 자신의 한국어 학습 경험으로 조언하고 초판 교정을 꼼꼼하게 봐 주신 Tauri Gregory 씨, Brian Yang 씨께도 깊은 감사를 드린다. 이 책의 개정판에서 번역과 교정을 훌륭하게 해 주신 Isabel Kim Dzitac 씨께도 진심으로 감사드리고 싶다. 또한 한국어 교육에 많은 애정과 관심을 보여 주시는 ㈜다락원의 정규도 사장님과 좋은 책을 만들고자 여러모로 애써 주신 한국어출판부의 편집진들께도 진심으로 감사의 말씀을 전한다. 마지막으로, 언제나 곁에서 저를 격려해 주시는 어머니께, 그리고 하늘에서 큰딸을 응원해 주시는 아버지께 이 책을 바치고 싶다.

오승은

The *Korean Made Easy* series is written for learners who are studying Korean as a second language or a foreign language. In particular, this book was designed so that learners who cannot receive regular Korean language education due to time and space limitations can study Korean independently. The *Korean Made Easy* series has been loved and supported by learners for a long time since the publication of the first edition and has been translated into various languages around the world, serving as a guide to learning Korean. I feel very rewarded as the author to publish a revised version that adds example sentences and practice questions that reflect the latest cultural trends. I hope that all learners who want to study Korean can enjoy their learning experience while studying Korean effectively through *Korean Made Easy*.

Korean Made Easy for Everyday Life was designed to help learners use Korean naturally, focusing on various situations you may experience while living in Korea. It is aimed at learners (150~400 hours of study time) who have mastered hangeul and have completed learning the basics of tenses. In this book, the learner is first acquainted with conversations frequently encountered in daily life, presented with linguistic elements such as vocabulary and grammar that can be studied in the context of the conversation, and introduced to grammatical and linguistic features that improve communication. Korean life and Korean culture are also explained so that learners can better understand Korean society and culture while living in Korea.

Korean Made Easy for Everyday Life is composed of two parts: Part 1 and Part 2. Part 1 presents 50 expressions frequently used in real life in 10 scenes. Five useful expressions are selected and presented in each situation, and detailed explanations of the context in which Koreans use these expressions are added to help learners not only understand but also apply them in real life through conversation practice. Part 2 consists of 24 Scenes of conversations that 6 foreigners who live in Korea for travel, work, and study experience. The vocabulary, pronunciation, grammar, and cultural information of the conversations presented in each Scene were carefully selected so that learners can similarly communicate actively with Koreans.

This book was published thanks to the interest and help of many people. First of all, I would like to thank Michael Park for translating, proofreading, and conveying my thoughts in the first edition. I would also like to express my deepest gratitude to my colleague Seungmin Oh, who gave advice based on her teaching experience, and Tauri Gregory and Brian Yang who carefully reviewed the first edition while providing advice based on their Korean learning experience. I would also like to express my heartfelt thanks to Isabel Kim Dzitac for her excellence in translating and proofreading this revised edition. In addition, I would like to express my sincere gratitude to the President of Darakwon, Kyu-do Chung, who has shown great affection and care about Korean language education, and to the editors of the Korean Publishing Department, who worked hard to create a good book. Finally, I would like to dedicate this book to my mother, who has always stood by my side and encouraged me along the way, and to my father, who has been supporting her eldest daughter from heaven.

Seung-eun Oh

How to Use This Book

Part 1 | Part 1 consists of 50 of the most essential everyday expressions in 10 different situations and puts each of them into conversation practice in three different settings.

50 Useful Expressions

It introduces five of the most essential everyday expressions in 10 different units. Each expression is recorded twice by professional male and female voice actors so that learners may learn the correct pronunciation and natural accents of native Koreans. You can listen via MP3 or QR code.

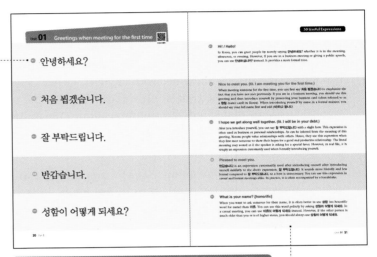

The Actual Meaning and Use of Useful Expressions

The actual meaning and use of useful expressions are explained in detail. This explanation shows in what contexts you can use useful expressions and how the useful expressions are used differently depending on the context of their use and their relationship to the participants of the conversation.

Conversation

This section shows how five expressions are used in real-life conversations. Each conversation can be heard via MP3 or QR code.

Try it Out

This section is for practicing each expression through role-play. Learners can speak as a given character in a specific situation and check their answers via the MP3 sound file. You can listen via MP3 or QR code.

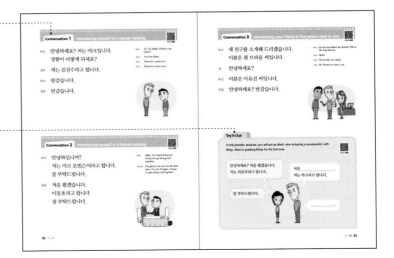

Part 2

Part 2 consists of 24 episodes from six foreigners in six different situations. Each foreigner experiences four short stories about living in Korea, applying essential grammar and practical vocabulary in each Scene in order to learn how to communicate with Koreans.

Scene

This indicates the location and situation of the conversation, explaining the background of each Scene.

Action

This indicates the main action in the conversation, explaining the primary objective. It also helps learners know where and when to actively participate in real-life conversation.

Title

This shows the main focus of each Scene, explaining its grammar and practical use.

Characters

This introduces the characters in each Scene explaining learners understand the background of the story more easily.

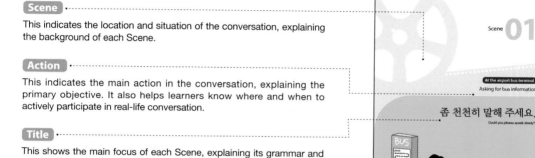

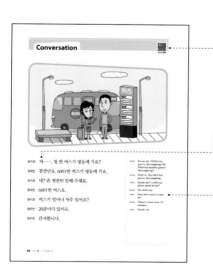

Listening Material

The conversation is recorded as an MP3 file in two versions. One is a slow recorded version that is easy for learners to understand, and the other is recorded at a speed that can be heard in real life. MP3 files can be heard via MP3 or QR code.

Conversation

This section visually presents a conversation situation that the learner may encounter.

English Translation

This section is the English translation of the conversation. The translation is focused on a natural presentation rather than a literal, word-to-word translation. Literal translations are marked with parentheses.

New Vocabulary

This section introduces new vocabulary with English translations.

New Expressions

This section shows new expressions with English translations.

Close-Up

This section explains the specific grammatical points or parts that need further explanation from the main conversation.

Flashback

This section reviews the essential points from *Korean Made Easy for Beginners*, which have not been selected as part of the learning objectives in this book.

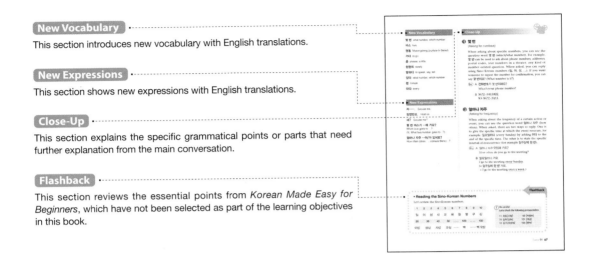

Grammar in Focus

This section explains the main grammar point in detail, showing its meaning, pattern, and usage. Various examples will help learners understand the grammar more easily.

The ★ indicates irregular form.

Grammar Chart

This indicates the page containing a detailed grammar pattern table in the appendix.

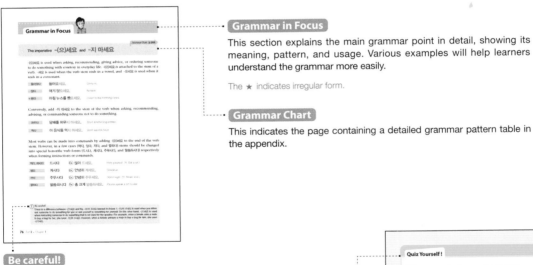

Be careful!

This section helps learners understand difficult grammar points and how to correct common mistakes.

Quiz Yourself!

This section is for practicing grammar points, with various exercises ranging from easy to difficult.

★ Answers for the quiz are in the appendix.

Grammar Rehearsal

This section is designed for learners to practice and expand upon the grammar they have learned as a learning objective. Through Grammar Rehearsal, learners can practice using grammar that can be used in conversations and other situations beyond the use of grammar limited to conversational situations. Grammar Rehearsal is recorded as an MP3, and you can listen to the audio via MP3 or QR code.

Additional Vocabulary

This section introduces supplemental vocabulary selected for each scenario.

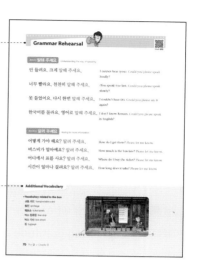

Conversation Rehearsal

This section expands on the previously presented conversation by introducing additional conversations. As such, the learner can continue practicing conversations via MP3 or QR code.

Pronunciation Tip

This section explains the specific rules of pronunciation for hard-to-pronounce words in the conversation. Each word is recorded twice for learners to repeat the pronunciation via MP3 or QR code.

Coffee Break

This section introduces helpful real-life information regarding the given conversation situation.

Director's Commentary

This section introduces practical information about life in Korea and helps learners familiarize themselves with the unique cultural perspective of the Korean people.

Contents

Part 1 | 50 Useful Expressions

Part 2 | 24 Scenes in Everyday Life

Chapter 1 Beginning your journey in Korea

Chapter 2 Preparing the necessary items for living in Korea

Table of Contents Part 1

Unit	Topic	Expressions	Conversation
06	**Expressions at the dinner table**	• 맛있게 드세요. Enjoy your meal. (lit. Please eat it deliciously.) • 잘 먹겠습니다. Thank you for the food. / Bon appetit. (used before having a meal. lit. I will eat well.) • 잘 먹었습니다. Thank you for the food. (used after a meal. lit. I ate well.) • 아니요, 괜찮아요. No, thank you. (lit. No, it's alright.) • 초대해 주셔서 감사합니다. Thank you for inviting me.	• Before eating • After finishing the meal • Leaving a party
07	**Congratulating, consoling, and encouraging**	• 축하합니다. Congratulations. • 제가 한턱낼게요. I'll treat you. / It's on me. / I'll get it (the bill). • 힘드시겠어요. It must be difficult for you. • 걱정하지 마세요. Don't worry. • 힘내세요. Cheer up. (lit. Please have more strength.)	• Congratulating someone • Consoling a person who is having trouble • Cheering up a worried person
08	**Talking on the telephone**	• 여보세요? Hello? • 지금 통화 괜찮으세요? Are you available now? (lit. Is it all right to call now?) • 실례지만, 누구세요? Excuse me, who is this? • 잠깐만요. Hold on a minute. / Just a minute. • 전화 잘못 거셨어요. You've called the wrong number.	• Making a call • Looking for a person on the phone • Responding to a wrong number
09	**Asking someone to repeat**	• 네? Excuse me? / I'm sorry? • 뭐라고 하셨어요? Pardon me? (lit. What did you say?) • 못 들었어요. I couldn't hear you. • 다시 한번 말해 주세요. Please, say it one more time. • 잘 안 들려요. I can't hear you well.	• When you couldn't hear what others are saying • When asking others to repeat what was said • When you can't hear well during a telephone call
10	**Saying goodbye**	• 주말 잘 보내세요. Have a nice weekend. • 안녕히 가세요. Goodbye. • 내일 봐요. See you tomorrow. • 몸조리 잘 하세요. Take care of yourself. • 연락할게요. I'll contact you.	• Saying goodbye at the end of the week • Saying goodbye when leaving early • Saying goodbye to a sick person

	Scene	Action	Title	Grammar in Focus	Flashback	Additional Vocabulary	Coffee Break	Director's Commentary
Chapter 3		Making appointments with friends in Korea : Sam Brown						
09	Over the telephone	Making an appointment by phone	우리 같이 영화 볼까요? Do you want to see a movie together?	-(으)ㄹ까요? Shall we...?	Reading the time	**Vocabulary related to appointments**	Confirming an appointment	Korean popular culture
10	On a video call	Inviting a friend	내일 친구들하고 영화를 보려고 해요. I'm going to see a movie with my friends tomorrow.	-(으)려고 하다 be going to...	Vocabulary related to places	**Vocabulary related to calling on the phone**	How to say goodbye when ending a phone call	Special foods on special occasions
11	At the meeting place	Changing the meeting place	사람이 많아서 유진 씨가 안 보여요. I can't see you, Yujin, because there are too many people here.	-아/어서 because	Frequently used conjunctions	**Expressions often used when making excuses**	When you can't hear someone on the phone well	Street food in Korea
12	At a café	Ordering coffee	죄송합니다. 지금 빵이 없습니다. Sorry. There is no bread right now.	The formal form -(스)ㅂ니다	Counting words	**Vocabulary related to stores**	Some expressions to say to store employees	Scenery from a Korean cafe
Chapter 4		Adapting to life in Korea : Susan Peters						
13	At an electronics store	Comparing electronics	더 싼 거 있어요? Is there anything cheaper?	The comparative 보다 더 and the superlative 제일, 가장	Adjectives with opposite meanings	**Vocabulary related to products**	Useful expressions for shopping	Korean pronunciation of English words
14	At a beauty salon	Getting a haircut	너무 짧지 않게 잘라 주세요. Please, cut it so that it is not too short.	-게 Changing an adjective into an adverb	Irregular verbs 1: ㅇ and ㄹ	**Vocabulary related to the hair salon**	Expressions for styling hair	K-beauty
15	At a gym	Asking for information	토요일에 하지만 일요일에 쉽니다. We are open on Saturdays but closed on Sundays.	-지만 but	Days of the week	**Vocabulary related to exercise**	Expressions for periods	Holidays in Korea
16	At the post office	Sending a parcel	비행기로 보내시겠어요? Would you like to send it by plane?	Expressing intent: -겠- and -(으)ㄹ게요	Reading dates	**Vocabulary related to the post office**	Registered mail: 등기	Korea's fast delivery service culture

	Scene	Action	Title	Grammar in Focus	Flashback	Additional Vocabulary	Coffee Break	Director's Commentary
Chapter 5		Working out problems : *Mei Chang*						
17	At a hospital	Explaining symptoms	열도 있고 콧물도 나요. I have a fever and a runny nose.	-고 and	Words for parts of the body	**Vocabulary related to symptoms**	Titles for doctors and nurses	K-Quarantine: Korea's medical services and medical insurance system
18	At a clothes store	Asking for other clothes	옷이 조금 크니까 한 치수 작은 사이즈로 주세요. The clothing is a little big, so could you give me one size smaller?	Explaining reasons: -(으)니까	Words for colors	**Vocabulary related to clothing**	Questions about service	The collective culture of Korean people
19	At home	Explaining a problem	이따가 출발할 때 연락해 주세요. Please contact me when he leaves later.	-(으)ㄹ 때 When	Adverbs with opposite meanings	**Vocabulary related to repairs**	A simple problem situation expression	A Korean culture that emphasizes hierarchical order
20	At the Lost-and-Found	Describing a lost item	가방을 잃어버렸는데 어떻게 해야 돼요? I lost my bag, what should I do?	Explaining a situation: -(으)ㄴ/는데	Frequently used question words	**Vocabulary related to one's belongings**	Expressions that can be used in urgent situations	Useful services
Chapter 6		Traveling in Korea : *Paul Smith*						
21	At a hotel	Checking into a hotel	방을 예약했는데 확인해 주시겠어요? Could you please confirm the room that I reserved?	-아/어 주시겠어요? Would/Could you please...?	Expressing time throughout the day	**Vocabulary related to accommo-dations**	Expressing the duration of a trip with : O박 O일	Temple stay: Enjoy meditation at a Korean temple
22	At the ticket booth	Buying a ticket	돌아오는 배가 몇 시에 있어요? What time is the return ship?	-는 The noun modifier	Irregular verbs 2: ㄹ omission	**Vocabulary related to money**	When asking about the first service and the last service	Korea's topography
23	At the travel destination	Receiving must-eat restaurant recommendations	'바다' 식당에 가 보세요. Go to the restaurant 'Bada'.	-아/어 보세요 You should...	Irregular verbs 3: Omission of ㄷ and ㅂ	**Vocabulary related to travelling**	Taking pictures with Koreans	Means of transportation when traveling domestically
24	While talking to a friend	Talking about travel experiences	한국에서 여행해 봤어요? Have you traveled in Korea?	-아/어 봤다 I have done...	Vocabulary expressing emotions	**Vocabulary related to frequency**	Sentences with a common question and answer	Famous Korean festivals

Main Characters

야마다 유키코 (일본)
Yukiko Yamada (Japan)

- Started studying Korean because she is interested in Korean food.
- Visiting Korea for 3 nights and 4 days.

마크 로빈슨 (미국)
Mark Robinson (USA)

- Came to work in a Korean company.
- Has been in Korea for six months.

샘 브라운 (영국)
Sam Brown (United Kingdom)

- Started studying Korean because he is interested in Korean movies.
- Foreign exchange student at a Korean university.

수잔 피터스 (호주)
Susan Peters (Australia)

- Teaches English in Korea.
- Has lived in Korea for more than 2 years.

장메이 (중국)
Mei Chang (China)

- Started studying Korean to study abroad at a Korean university.
- Currently studying for admission to a Korean university.

폴 스미스 (캐나다)
Paul Smith (Canada)

- Started studying Korean as a hobby.
- Loves to travel so he travels every weekend.

김진수 (한국)
Jinsu Kim (Korea)

- A university student who gets along well with foreign friends.
- Studying to prepare for a job.

이유진 (한국)
Yujin Lee (Korea)

- A university student who is studying English through a language exchange with her foreign friend.
- Preparing to study abroad.

Part 1

50 Useful Expression

01 안녕하세요?

02 처음 뵙겠습니다.

03 잘 부탁드립니다.

04 반갑습니다.

05 성함이 어떻게 되세요?

01   **Hi! / Hello!**

In Korea, you can greet people by merely saying 안녕하세요? whether it is in the morning, afternoon, or evening. However, if you are in a business meeting or giving a public speech, you can use 안녕하십니까? instead. It provides a more formal tone.

02   **Nice to meet you. (lit. I am meeting you for the first time.)**

When meeting someone for the first time, you can first say 처음 뵙겠습니다 to emphasize the fact that you have not met previously. If you are in a business meeting, you should use this greeting and then introduce yourself by presenting your business card (often referred to as a 명함 (name card) in Korea). When introducing yourself by name in a formal manner, you should say your full name first and add (이)라고 합니다.

03   **I hope we get along well together. (lit. I will be in your debt.)**

After you introduce yourself, you can say 잘 부탁드립니다 with a slight bow. This expression is often used in business or personal relationships. As can be inferred from the meaning of this greeting, Korean people value relationships with others. Hence, they use this expression when they first meet someone to show their hopes for a good and productive relationship. The literal meaning may sound as if the speaker is asking for a special favor. However, in real life, it is simply an expression customarily used when formally introducing yourself.

04   **Pleased to meet you.**

반갑습니다 is an expression customarily used after introducing oneself similarly to the above expression, 잘 부탁드립니다. It sounds more friendly and less formal compared to 잘 부탁드립니다, so a bow is unnecessary. You can use this expression in casual and formal meetings alike. In practice, it is often accompanied by a handshake.

05   **What is your name? [honorific]**

When you want to ask someone for their name, it is often better to use 성함 (an honorific word for name) than 이름. You can use this word politely by asking 성함이 어떻게 되세요. In a casual meeting, you can use 이름이 어떻게 되세요 instead. However, if the other person is much older than you or is of higher status, you should always use 성함이 어떻게 되세요.

Conversation 1 — Introducing oneself in a casual meeting

track 002

마크   안녕하세요? 저는 마크입니다.
       성함이 어떻게 되세요?

진수   저는 김진수라고 합니다.

마크   반갑습니다.

진수   반갑습니다.

Mark	Hi. I'm Mark. What's your name?
Jinsu	I'm Kim Jinsu.
Mark	Pleased to meet you.
Jinsu	Pleased to meet you.

Conversation 2 — Introducing oneself in a formal meeting

track 003

마크   안녕하십니까?
       저는 마크 로빈슨이라고 합니다.
       잘 부탁드립니다.

동호   처음 뵙겠습니다.
       이동호라고 합니다.
       잘 부탁드립니다.

Mark	Hello. I'm Mark Robinson. I hope we get along well together.
Dongho	I'm glad to see you for the first time. I'm Lee Dongho. I hope we get along well together.

track **004**

마크	제 친구를 소개해 드리겠습니다.
	이분은 샘 브라운 씨입니다.
샘	안녕하세요?
마크	이분은 이유진 씨입니다.
유진	안녕하세요? 반갑습니다.

Mark — Let me introduce my friend. This is Mr. Sam Brown.

Sam — Hello.

Mark — This is Ms. Lee Yujin.

Yujin — Hi. Pleased to meet you.

Try it Out

In this practice exercise, you will act as Mark, who is having a conversation with Minju. Mark is greeting Minju for the first time.

track **005**

안녕하세요? 처음 뵙겠습니다.
저는 최민주라고 합니다.

처음 _____.
저는 마크라고 합니다.

잘 부탁드립니다.

_____.

01 감사합니다.

02 별말씀을요.

03 죄송합니다.

04 괜찮아요.

05 실례합니다.

01 Thank you.

When politely expressing gratitude, you can say 감사합니다. It is much politer when accompanied by a slight bow. However, if you use it with people who are close to you, such as friends or family members, it will sound too formal. It is better to use the more friendly expression 고마워요 to give thanks to close people instead.

02 Don't mention it.

When someone says 감사합니다, you can say 별말씀을요 to convey respect. Literally, it means that there is no need for special mention and is used as a polite response to a thank you. This expression will sound humble and modest. If you find the pronunciation too tricky, you can simply say 아니에요 instead.

03 I'm sorry.

When politely expressing regret, generally you can say 죄송합니다. If the other person is older than you or of higher status, you can report it with a slight bow. In casual relationships such as with acquaintances or co-workers in a company, you can use 미안합니다 instead.

04 It's all right.

When responding to an apology, you can say 괜찮아요 to express that there is no problem. This expression can be used in several ways. For example, you can use it to ask about another's condition, expressing your concern by asking 괜찮아요? (Are you all right?) with a rising tone at the end. You can also use it to calm down others by saying 괜찮아요 (It is all right) with a slightly declining tone at the end.

05 Excuse me.

When politely asking to be excused or calling for attention from someone, you can say 실례합니다 which sounds very formal and courteous. In daily life, 저... is often used to attract another person by making sounds because Korean don't use "you" when calling others.

마크   저……, 길 좀 가르쳐 주세요.

한국인   이쪽으로 가세요.

마크   감사합니다.

한국인   별말씀을요.

Mark	Excuse me, could you please show me which way I should go?
Passerby	Go this way.
Mark	Thank you.
Passerby	Don't mention it.

마크   정말 죄송합니다.

한국인   아니에요.

마크   괜찮으세요?

한국인   네, 괜찮아요.

Mark	I'm really sorry.
Korean	It's all right. (lit. You don't need to be sorry.)
Mark	Are you all right?
Korean	Yes, I'm all right.

마크	실례합니다.
한국인	네?
마크	좀 지나가겠습니다.
한국인	아, 죄송합니다.

Mark	Excuse me.
Bystander	Yes?
Mark	I'd like to get past.
Bystander	Oh, I'm sorry.

Try it Out

In this practice exercise, you will act as Mark, who is having a conversation with Minju. Mark is asking Minju for water.

track 010

저……, 물 좀 주세요.

여기 있어요.

별말씀을요.

_____.

01 알겠습니다.

02 잘 모르겠는데요.

03 아니요, 잘 못해요.

04 저도 그렇게 생각해요.

05 그럽시다.

01 **I see. / I understand. / Yes, sir.**

알겠습니다 has three meanings in common usage. One is to politely express that you know politely what the person is trying to say, as is done with the English phrase "I see." The second is to show that you understand the subject discussed when concluding a discussion, as in "I understand." The last use is to confirm that you have understood and will carry out another person's request as in "Yes, Sir." When replying to customers or senior staff in a company, you can use this expression. In closer relationships, it is better to use the more friendly form 알겠어요.

02 **I don't understand. / I don't know. / I'm not sure.**

This expression also has three meanings. One is to politely express that you don't understand the subject discussed, as in English, "I don't understand." The other is to explain that you do not have the detailed information that the person is asking about, as in "I don't know." The last use is to explain that you do not know something for sure, as in, "I'm not sure." This expression is used in everyday conversation.

03 **No, I'm not very good at it.**

When complimented on one of your abilities, such as speaking a foreign language or cooking, you can respond humbly by saying 아니요, 잘 못해요. In Korea, being humble and modest about one's ability has traditionally been considered polite and courteous. So even if you know that your performance excels, it is crucial that you do not express overly positive opinions about yourself.

04 **I think so too.**

When agreeing with another person's opinion in colloquial conversations, you can say 저도 그렇게 생각해요. If you disagree, you can express disagreement indirectly by using 그렇게 생각 하세요? (Do you think so?)

05 **Let's do that.**

그럽시다 is used when discussing an idea with another person and agreeing to the final proposal proposed. This expression gives off a strong sense of formality and is used more often by men than by women when talking to co-workers. In the case of close relationships, you can say 그래요.

track **012**

유진 저……, 부탁 하나 해도 돼요?

마크 말씀하세요.

유진 이거 좀 진수 씨한테 전해 주세요.

마크 네, 알겠어요.

Yujin	Excuse me, I have a favor to ask.
Mark	Go ahead.
Yujin	Please give this to Jinsu.
Mark	OK, I will.

track **013**

마크 덕수궁이 어디에 있어요?

유키코 프라자 호텔 알아요?

마크 글쎄요, 잘 모르겠는데요.

유키코 그럼, 시청 알아요?

마크 네, 알아요.

유키코 덕수궁은 시청 앞에 있어요.

Mark	Where is Deoksugung Palace?
Yukiko	Do you know the Plaza hotel?
Mark	Um, no, I don't know it.
Yukiko	Then do you know City Hall?
Mark	Yes, I know where that is. (lit. Yes, I know.)
Yukiko	Deoksugung Palace is in front of City Hall.

track **014**

한국인 한국어 정말 잘하시네요.

마크 아니요, 잘 못해요.

한국인 무슨 말씀을요. 잘하시는데요.

마크 아직 멀었어요.

Korean	You speak Korean well.
Mark	No, I'm not very good at it.
Korean	What do you mean? You speak really well.
Mark	I still have a long way to go.

Try it Out

In this practice exercise, you will act as Mark, who is having a conversation with Minju at the reception desk for a seminar. Mark is explaining that he doesn't know the person whom Minju is asking. Then they are going to greet the person together.

track **015**

저분이 누구세요?

글쎄요, _____.

그럼, 같이 가서 인사할까요?

_____.

track **016**

01 좋아요.

02 맞아요.

03 그럼요.

04 아, 그래요?

05 정말이에요?

01　OK. / That's great.

When accepting another person's proposal in everyday life, you can say 좋아요. To make it sound formal, you can say 좋습니다 instead. Conversely, when turning down someone's proposal, you can say 미안해요 to apologize and then go on to explain the reasons for your refusal.

02　That's right. / That's correct.

When answering affirmatively to another person's question on the validity of certain information, you can say 맞아요. When responding negatively, you can use 틀려요 (That's wrong / That's incorrect). If you want to check if you are right, you can ask 맞아요? as a question with a rising intonation at the end. It commonly uses to confirm information that has been discussed, such as telephone numbers or appointment times.

03　Of course. / Sure.

When expressing that something is just the way you would expect it to be or is a given, you can use 그럼요. In a formal relationship such as in a company meeting, it is better to use 물론입니다 instead.

04　Is that so? / Really?

When learning new information or coming to understand a particular situation, you can respond, by saying 아, 그래요 with a rising tone at the end. It is most often used in colloquial conversations. You can also use it when showing interest in another's story or if you are uncertain of how to respond to it.

05　Is that true? / Really?

When it is hard to believe a story that someone has told you or when you are really shocked at the news that you have just heard, you can respond with 정말이에요. It can be inappropriate to use this expression with elder people, so it is better to use it only within close relationships.

Conversation 1 Accepting another's proposal

track 017

유키코 내일 시간 있어요?

마크 네, 있어요.

유키코 그럼, 내일 같이 영화 봐요!

마크 좋아요. 그래요.

Yukiko	Do you have some free time tomorrow?
Mark	Yes, I do.
Yukiko	Then let's go see a movie together tomorrow!
Mark	OK, let's do that.

Conversation 2 Confirming information

track 018

유키코 몇 시에 만나요?

마크 1시간 후에 봐요.

유키코 그럼, 3시 30분 맞아요?

마크 네, 맞아요.

Yukiko	What time should we meet?
Mark	Let's meet in an hour.
Yukiko	So, at 3:30. Right?
Mark	Yes, that's right.

track **019**

유진	불고기 좋아해요?
마크	그럼요. 정말 좋아해요.
유진	저는 고기를 못 먹어요.
마크	아, 그래요?

Yujin	Do you like bulgogi?
Mark	Of course. I like it a lot.
Yujin	I can't eat meat.
Mark	Ah, really?

Try it Out

In this practice exercise, you will act as Mark, who is having a conversation with Minju. They are making an appointment to go hiking together.

track **020**

내일 등산 같이 가요!

7시 반

아침 7시 반에 만나요!

네, 맞아요. 그때 봐요!

_____.

7시 30분 _____?

01 잘 지내셨어요?

02 오랜만이에요.

03 요즘 어떻게 지내세요?

04 덕분에 잘 지내요.

05 수고하셨습니다.

01 How have you been? (lit. Have you been doing well?)

When meeting acquaintances, you can use 잘 지내셨어요 to ask how they have been recently. It can be used with people you have not met for a long time and with people you meet regularly. To reply to this question, you can say 잘 지냈어요 (I have been doing fine). If you happen to meet someone that you know, you can say 안녕하세요 first and then ask 잘 지내셨어요. By doing so, you will begin a conversation smoothly.

02 It's been a long time.

To express how glad you are to meet someone you have not met for a long time, you can say 오랜만이에요 or 오래간만이에요. These expressions are often used in everyday life. To respond, you can say 네, 정말 오랜만이에요 (Yes, it has been a long time).

03 How are you doing these days?

When asking your acquaintance about how they have been recently, you can use 요즘 어떻게 지내세요. It is often used in colloquial conversation but not with people you meet regularly. To reply, you can say 잘 지내요 (I am doing fine), or you can explain your current situation. Between people who have not met for some time, this expression allows one to begin a conversation by letting the other person know about recent life changes.

04 Thanks to you, I'm doing fine.

This expression means that you owe your good fortune or right circumstances to the other person's care or concern. It derives from an Oriental mindset in which one's well-being is connected with the people around you in your life. It is a common expression in Korea, so feel free to use it.

05 Good job. / I appreciate your hard work. (lit. You have made a great effort.)

수고 means putting in the effort on a specific task. So when you say 수고하셨습니다, it means that you appreciate the effort that someone has settled into a job. It is used to give thanks to someone who has provided a service to you. You can say 수고하셨습니다 when paying for the service. It can also apply to thanking co-workers when leaving your office for the day.

track **022**

마크	잘 지내셨어요?
유키코	네, 잘 지냈어요. 마크 씨도 잘 지내셨어요?
마크	네, 저도 잘 지냈어요.

Mark   How have you been?

Yukiko I've been doing fine.
       How have you been, Mark?

Mark   I've been doing fine too.

track **023**

마크	오랜만이에요.
메이	네, 정말 오랜만이에요.
마크	요즘 어떻게 지내세요?
메이	덕분에 잘 지내요.

Mark   It's been a long time.

Mei   Yeah, it's been a really long time.

Mark   How are you doing these days?

Mei   Thanks to you, I'm doing fine.

마크	여기에 놓아 주세요.
기사	네, 알겠습니다.
마크	수고하셨습니다.
기사	감사합니다.

Mark	Please put it here.
Driver	Yes, sir.
Mark	Thanks for your good work.
Driver	Thank you.

Try it Out

In this practice exercise, you will act as Mark, who is having a conversation with Yujin. Mark is asking Yujin how she has been doing recently.

오랜만이에요.

_____?

안녕하세요?

덕분에 잘 지내요.
마크 씨는요?

_____.

01 맛있게 드세요.

02 잘 먹겠습니다.

03 잘 먹었습니다.

04 아니요, 괜찮아요.

05 초대해 주셔서 감사합니다.

01 Enjoy your meal. (lit. Please eat it deliciously.)

When presenting food to guests, you can say 맛있게 드세요. You will often hear this expression when you are invited to dinner parties or when you receive your order in a restaurant. It sounds friendly and is a common expression used in everyday life. You can also use a similar phrase 많이 드세요 (Help yourself. lit. Please eat a lot). Feel free to use these expressions when you are offering people something to eat.

02 Thank you for the food. / Bon appetit. (used before having a meal. lit. I will eat well.)

To show gratitude to the person who is providing food, you can say 잘 먹겠습니다. It means that you will be eating well. You can also use it to give thanks to someone who pays for your meal. It is customarily used when responding to the expression 맛있게 드세요. You can use these expressions in both everyday life and formal situations alike.

03 Thank you for the food. (used after a meal. lit. I ate well.)

When you finish a meal, you can say 잘 먹었습니다. It is customary to show gratitude to the person who provided the food. You can also use it when paying the owner of a restaurant. This expression can be used in both everyday life and formal situations alike.

04 No, thank you. (lit. No, it's alright.)

Koreans believe that offering more than enough food is a way of demonstrating 정 (warm affection and generous concern for people) and showing proper courtesy. So they will often provide more food even after you have finished a whole dish. To decline politely, you can say 아니요, 괜찮아요. Still, they may insist that you have more food because it is customary to repeat the offer three times. If you are sure that you can not eat anymore, then you can say 아니요, 많이 먹었어요 (lit. No, I have eaten a lot).

05 Thank you for inviting me.

When leaving a party or event, you can say 초대해 주셔서 감사합니다 (Thanks for inviting me). The host can respond by saying 와 주셔서 감사합니다 (Thanks for coming). If you want to leave in the middle of a meeting or party, you can politely say 그만 가 볼게요 (I will have to go). If it is a formal meeting, then it is better to use 그만 가 보겠습니다 instead.

Conversation 1 Before eating

한국인 맛있게 드세요.

마크 잘 먹겠습니다.

(after tasting) 정말 맛있네요.

한국인 그래요? 많이 드세요.

마크 네.

Korean	Enjoy your meal (lit. Please eat it deliciously.)
Mark	Thank you for the food. *(after tasting)* It's really delicious!
Korean	Really? Help yourself.
Mark	OK.

Conversation 2 After finishing the meal

마크 잘 먹었습니다.
정말 맛있었어요.

한국인 조금 더 드릴까요?

마크 아니요, 괜찮아요.

한국인 알겠어요.

Mark	Thank you for the food. It was really delicious.
Korean	Would you like some more?
Mark	No, thank you.
Korean	OK.

Conversation 3 Leaving a party

track 029

마크   초대해 주셔서 감사합니다.

한국인 와 주셔서 고마워요.

마크   안녕히 계세요.

한국인 안녕히 가세요. 또 놀러 오세요.

Mark	Thanks for inviting me.
Korean	Thanks for coming.
Mark	Goodbye.
Korean	Goodbye. Please come again.

Try it Out

In this practice exercise, you will act as Mark, who is having a conversation with Yujin. Mark has been invited to Yujin's party.

track 030

맛있게 드세요.   _____.

(after finishing the meal)

음식은 어땠어요?

정말 맛있었어요.
_____.

01 축하합니다.

02 제가 한턱낼게요.

03 힘드시겠어요.

04 걱정하지 마세요.

05 힘내세요.

01 Congratulations.

When congratulating someone, you can use 축하합니다. You can name the occasion first such as 생일 (birthday), 승진 (promotion), 합격 (passing an entrance exam), and add 축하합니다 to the end. You can use it in formal and informal situations alike. To respond to this phrase, you can just say 감사합니다.

02 I'll treat you. / It's on me. / I'll get it (the bill).

When there is an occasion to celebrate in Korea, it is customary for the person who is celebrating to buy food in a restaurant or invite close friends to have dinner together. You can say 제가 한턱 낼게요 to make a promise to treat others. Even when there is no particular occasion to celebrate, when people dine together in Korea, it is customary for one person to pay for the group's food. This culture is because Korean people feel uneasy about paying separate bills, so they take turns covering the bill.

03 It must be difficult for you.

When consoling a person who is going through a tough time, you can say 힘드시겠어요. Unlike in English, you should not use 미안해요, because Korean use 미안해요 only when apologizing for something you have done. If you want to express your feeling of regret or pity for an unfortunate circumstance for which you are not to blame, you can say 유감입니다 (It is unfortunate. lit. It is regrettable) to express your disappointment.

04 Don't worry.

When trying to calm down people who are worried or stressed about something, you can say 걱정하지 마세요. This expression may sound a little rude to people from other cultures. However, Koreans use it often because they think it is essential to show concern for people who are in trouble. You can use 걱정 마세요 as the shortened form of 걱정하지 마세요.

05 Cheer up. (lit. Please have more strength.)

When encouraging people who are worried or disappointed, you can say 힘내세요. The English loanword 파이팅! (Fighting!) is also used, especially for supporting athletes and crowds right before a game. When accompanied by a clenched fist gesture, it will feel like giving strength to them.

track **032**

마크	승진 축하합니다.
동호	감사합니다.
마크	정말 잘됐어요.
동호	제가 한턱낼게요.

Mark   Congratulations on your promotion.

Dongho   Thank you!

Mark   I'm really glad for you.
(lit. It really turned out well.)

Dongho   I'll treat you (to a meal/drink etc. to celebrate).

track **033**

마크	힘드시겠어요.
한국인	네.
마크	제가 도울 일이 있으면 언제든지 말해 주세요.
한국인	고맙습니다.

Mark   It must be difficult for you.

Korean   Yes.

Mark   Just let me know if there's anything I can do.

Korean   Thank you.

Conversation 3 Cheering up a worried person

메이	결과가 걱정돼요.
마크	걱정하지 마세요. 잘될 거예요.
메이	네, 고마워요.
마크	힘내세요. 파이팅!

Mei	I'm worried about my results.
Mark	Don't worry. Everything is going to be fine.
Mei	OK, thank you.
Mark	Cheer up. Fighting!

Try it Out

In this practice exercise, you will act as Mark, who is having a conversation with Minju. Mark is congratulating Minju on her birthday and making an appointment to have dinner together.

track **035**

01 여보세요?

02 지금 통화 괜찮아요?

03 실례지만, 누구세요?

04 잠깐만요.

05 전화 잘못 거셨어요.

01   **Hello?**

여보세요 is the customary greeting used in telephone conversations regardless of age and status. You can use this expression in a casual and formal settings alike. When politely saying goodbye at the end of a call, you can say 안녕히 계세요. You can also say 끊을게요 in an informal setting.

02   **Are you available now? (lit. Is it all right to call now?)**

When asking whether the person is available to speak at the moment, you can ask 지금 통화 괜찮아요. This expression is commonly used with people in a business relationship or people with whom you have a little or no acquaintance and shows general courtesy. When responding, you can say 네, 괜찮아요 (Yes, it is all right). Or if you are busy at that moment, you can say 제가 다시 전화할게요 (I will call you back).

03   **Excuse me, who is this?**

This expression is used to ask for the identity of the caller politely. When you cannot be sure of who is calling or visiting you, you can ask 실례지만, 누구세요. You can also use it with people who wish to speak to someone else during a phone call or are looking for someone else at your place. It is a polite expression, so when you use it, you should say it in a slightly low tone.

04   **Hold on a minute. / Just a minute.**

When asking someone to wait a short time in colloquial conversation, you can use 잠깐만요. It is not a formal expression but is very convenient when you need to take a moment in the middle of a conversation without hurting another person's feelings. You can also use 잠시만요 in the same meaning. However, if you want to use it in a formal situation, you should use 잠깐만(잠시만) 기다려 주세요 instead.

05   **You've called the wrong number.**

When politely explaining that someone has called the wrong number, you can say 전화 잘못 거셨어요. This expression often happens in everyday life, so it will be useful to remember this expression. To make it sound formal, you can say 전화 잘못 거셨습니다 instead.

Conversation 1 Making a call

track 037

유진	여보세요.
마크	여보세요. 저 마크예요.
유진	마크 씨, 안녕하세요.
마크	지금 통화 괜찮아요?
유진	괜찮아요. 말씀하세요.

Yujin	Hello.
Mark	Hello. This is Mark.
Yujin	Hello, Mark.
Mark	Are you available to talk now?
Yujin	Sure. Go ahead.

Conversation 2 Looking for a person on the phone

track 038

마크	여보세요. 폴 씨 계세요?
한국인	지금 안 계신데요. 실례지만, 누구세요?
마크	저는 마크라고 합니다. 메모 좀 전해 주세요.
한국인	잠깐만요.

Mark	Hello. Is Paul there?
Korean	He's not in right now. Excuse me, who's this?
Mark	It's Mark. Could you please give him a message?
Korean	Hold on a minute.

한국인	여보세요. 김수민 씨 좀 바꿔 주세요.
마크	전화 잘못 거셨어요.
한국인	네? 거기 754–8812 아니에요?
마크	아닙니다.
한국인	죄송합니다.

Korean	Hello. Can I talk to Kim Sumin?
Mark	You've called the wrong number.
Korean	What? Isn't this 754-8812?
Mark	No.
Korean	I'm sorry.

Try it Out

In this practice exercise, you will act as Mark, who is having a conversation with Yujin. Mark is speaking with Yujin by phone.

track 040

저, 마크예요.
지금 _____?

_____.

미안해요.
제가 다시 전화할게요.

track **041**

01 네?

02 뭐라고 하셨어요?

03 못 들었어요.

04 다시 한번 말해 주세요.

05 잘 안 들려요.

01 Excuse me? / I'm sorry?

When you can not be sure of what another person has said, you can use 네 with a question mark to ask them to repeat the information. It may sound impolite if you speak it with a strong rising tone. So it is better to say it with a slight rising tone.

02 Pardon me? (lit. What did you say?)

When asking others to repeat something, you can use 뭐라고 하셨어요. Its grammatical form is honorific, but if used for people who are older than you or with higher status, it may sound impolite. So it is better to say it as softly as possible.

03 I couldn't hear you.

When you cannot follow what another person is saying, you can say 못 들었어요. You can express that you could not understand what they said or comprehend their speech for some reason. This expression can be useful when you feel that it is hard to follow Koreans' rapid speech.

04 Please, say it one more time.

When politely asking others to repeat what was said, you can use 다시 한번 말해 주세요. It is a polite and soft expression so you can use it with anybody. When the person was speaking too fast for you to understand, you can also say 천천히 말해 주세요 (Please, speak slowly).

05 I can't hear you well.

When it is hard to hear others because of other noises or because they are using a soft voice, you can use 잘 안 들려요. This expression is often used in telephone conversations. If you want to ask another person to speak more loudly, you can say 크게 말해 주세요 (Please, speak louder).

Conversation 1 — When you couldn't hear what others are saying

유진	진수 씨 전화번호 좀 가르쳐 주세요.
마크	네?
유진	진수 씨 전화번호요.
마크	네, 잠깐만요.

Yujin	Please let me know Jinsu's phone number.
Mark	I'm sorry?
Yujin	Jinsu's phone number.
Mark	All right, hold on a minute.

Conversation 2 — When asking others to repeat what was said

마크	조금 전에 뭐라고 하셨어요?
메이	네?
마크	잘 못 들었어요. 다시 한번 말해 주세요.
메이	네, 알겠어요.

Mark	What did you just say?
Mei	Excuse me?
Mark	I didn't follow that. Please say it one more time.
Mei	OK, I understand.

마크	잘 안 들려요. 좀 크게 말해 주세요.
수잔	*(in a louder voice)* 이제 잘 들려요?
마크	아니요.
수잔	제가 다시 전화할게요.

Mark	I can't hear you well. Please speak loudly.
Susan	*(in a louder voice)* Can you hear me well now?
Mark	No.
Susan	I'll call you back.

Try it Out

In this practice exercise, you will act as Mark, who is having a conversation with a Korean. Mark is asking the person to repeat what was said.

track **045**

저, 다시 한번 _____.

네?

잘 _____.

네, 내일 3시에 오세요.

01 주말 잘 보내세요.

02 안녕히 가세요.

03 내일 봐요.

04 몸조리 잘하세요.

05 연락할게요.

01 **Have a nice weekend.**

Before the weekend, you can use 주말 잘 보내세요 to wish people like your friends or co-workers a good weekend. You can also use this expression on other occasions. For example, if a person is going on vacation, you can replace 주말 (weekend) with 휴가 (vacation, holiday) to say 휴가 잘 보내세요. When responding, you can repeat the expression to return the sentiment to the original speaker.

02 **Goodbye.**

안녕히 가세요 is the most common expression when saying goodbye. There are two slightly different goodbyes in Korean. One is 안녕히 가세요 (lit. Go safely when leaving), and the other is 안녕히 계세요 (lit. Stay safely). To choose the right one, you need to put yourself in the other person's shoes. If the other person is leaving and going to another place, you use 안녕히 가세요. If the other person is staying in the same place, you use 안녕히 계세요. In a close relationship, you can say 잘 가요 instead of 안녕히 가세요 and 잘 있어요 instead of 안녕히 계세요.

03 **See you tomorrow.**

내일 봐요 sounds less formal than 안녕히 가세요, so it can be used between people of a similar age group or between co-workers who share the same status. If you want to use it with people who are older than you or with a higher status in a formal situation, it is better to use the more polite expression 내일 뵙겠습니다.

04 **Take care of yourself.**

When saying goodbye to a person who is experiencing a health problem, you can use 몸조리 잘하세요 with friends and seniors alike. Even though English speakers use "take care of yourself" when saying goodbye, Koreans use this expression only for sick people in order to show their concern and care. When responding, you can say 감사합니다. If you want to tell someone who is suffering to watch out for a specific problem such as the flu, you can say 감기 조심하세요 (Please make sure you don't get the flu. lit. Please be careful of the flu).

05 **I'll contact you.**

When promising that you will contact someone, you can say 연락할게요. This expression can only be used between people in a close relationship. So if you have to say it formally to someone who is older than you or with higher status, it is better to use 연락드리겠습니다 instead.

track **047**

마크	주말 잘 보내세요.
수잔	마크 씨도요.
마크	안녕히 계세요.
수잔	안녕히 가세요.

Mark   Have a nice weekend.

Susan   You too.

Mark   Goodbye. (lit. Stay safely.)

Susan   Goodbye. (lit. Go safely when leaving.)

track **048**

마크	그만 가 볼게요.
유진	잘 가요.
마크	내일 봐요.
유진	내일 봐요.

Mark   I have to go now.

Yujin   Goodbye.

Mark   See you tomorrow.

Yujin   See you tomorrow.

마크	몸조리 잘하세요.	Mark	Take care of yourself.
메이	네, 고마워요.	Mei	I'll. Thank you.
마크	나중에 연락할게요.	Mark	I'll contact you later.
메이	그래요.	Mei	Please do.

Try it Out

In this practice exercise, you will act as Mark, who is having a conversation with Minju. Minju is saying goodbye and wishing Mark a nice vacation. In response, Mark is saying goodbye and wishing Minju a nice vacation.

track **050**

마크 씨, 휴가 잘 보내세요.

민주 씨도 _____.

그럼, 먼저 갈게요.
안녕히 계세요.

_____.

Part 2

24 Scenes in Everyday Life

Chapter **1**
Beginning your journey in Korea

야마다 유키코 (일본)
Yukiko Yamada (Japan)

Chapter 1

Beginning your journey in Korea

좀 천천히 말해 주세요.

Could you please speak slowly?

Yukiko

A Korean bystander

유키코   저……, 몇 번 버스가 명동에 가요?

한국인   잠깐만요. 6001번 버스가 명동에 가요.

유키코   네? 좀 천천히 말해 주세요.

한국인   6001번 버스요.

유키코   버스가 얼마나 자주 있어요?

한국인   20분마다 있어요.

유키코   감사합니다.

Yukiko	Excuse me. Which bus goes to Myeongdong? (lit. What bus number goes to Myeongdong?)
Korean	Hold on. The 6001 bus goes to Myeongdong.
Yukiko	Excuse me? Could you please speak slowly?
Korean	The 6001 bus.
Yukiko	How often does it come by?
Korean	(There's a bus) every 20 minutes.
Yukiko	Thank you.

► New Vocabulary

몇 번 what number, which number

버스 bus

명동 Myeongdong (a place in Seoul)

가다 to go

좀 please, a little

천천히 slowly

말하다 to speak, say, tell

있다 to be

분 minute

마다 every

► New Expressions

저……. Excuse me.

잠깐만요. Hold on.

네? Excuse me?

몇 번 버스가 …에 가요?
Which bus goes to …?
(lit. What bus number goes to…?)

얼마나 자주 …이/가 있어요?
How often (does …. come/is there)…?

► Close-Up

❶ 몇 번
(Asking for numbers)

When asking about specific numbers, you can use the question word 몇 번 (which/what number). For example, 몇 번 can be used to ask about phone numbers, addresses, postal codes, seat numbers in a theater, any kind of number-related question. When asked, you can reply using Sino-Korean numbers (일, 이, 삼, …). If you want someone to repeat the number for confirmation, you can say 몇 번이요? (What number is it?)

Ex. A 전화번호가 몇 번이에요?
　　　What's your phone number?

　　 B 3672-9415예요.
　　　It's 3672-9415.

❷ 얼마나 자주
(Asking for frequency)

When asking about the frequency of a certain action or event, you can use the question word 얼마나 자주 (how often). When asked, there are two ways to reply. One is to give the specific time at which the event reoccurs, for example, 일요일마다 (every Sunday) by adding 마다 to the end of the specific time. The other is to state the specific interval of reoccurrence (for example 일주일에 한 번).

Ex. A 얼마나 자주 모임에 가요?
　　　How often do you go to the meeting?

　　 B 일요일마다 가요.
　　　I go to the meeting every Sunday.
　　　(= 일주일에 한 번 가요.
　　　= I go to the meeting once a week.)

Flashback

• Reading the Sino-Korean Numbers

Let's review the Sino-Korean numbers.

1	2	3	4	5	6	7	8	9	10
일	이	삼	사	오	육	칠	팔	구	십

20	30	40	50	……	100	……	150
이십	삼십	사십	오십	……	백	……	백 오십

(!) Be careful

Let's check the following pronunciation.

11 십일 [시빌]	66 [육씸뉵]
16 십육 [심뉵]	101 [배길]
19 십구 [육씸뉵]	106 [뱅뉵]

Grammar in Focus

–아/어 주세요 Could you please...?

–아/어 주세요 is used with a verb to ask another person to do a specific action for yourself. The verb 하다 is used as 해 주세요. When the stem ends with a vowel ㅏ or ㅗ, –아 주세요 is added to the stem. –어 주세요 is added to the stem for the rest of the vowels. Simply put, first, change the verb expressing the other person's action to the present conjugation –아/어요, then drop 요 and add 주세요 at the end. For example, when asking another person to speak slowly, first change the verb 말하다 to the present conjugation 말해요, then drop 요, and then add 주세요 to complete the sentence.

가르치다	길을 가르쳐 주세요.	Could you please show me which way to go? (lit. Teach me the way.)
말하다	천천히 말해 주세요.	Could you please speak slowly? (lit. Speak slowly.)
오다	여기로 와 주세요.	Could you please come here? (lit. Come here.)
★돕다	도와주세요.	Could you please help me? (lit. Help me.)

When asking another person for an object, use 주세요 after the object. For example, when asking for water, say 물 주세요.

커피 주세요.	Could I please have a coffee? (lit. Give me a coffee.)
영수증 주세요.	Could I please have the receipt? (lit. Give me the receipt.)

좀 means "please" and it is used in order to speak more politely in colloquial conversation. There are two ways it can be used. One is to replace an object marker 을/를. The other is before a verb or an adverb, to emphasize it.

길 좀 가르쳐 주세요.	Can you please show me the way? (lit. Please, teach me the direction.)
좀 천천히 말해 주세요.	Can you please speak slowly? (lit. Please, speak slowly.)

Quiz Yourself !

1~4 Look at the picture and choose the correct answer from the following options.

㉠ 전화번호를 알려 주세요.   ㉡ 사진을 찍어 주세요.

㉢ 천천히 말해 주세요.   ㉣ 도와주세요.

1.

2.

3.

4.

5~7 Complete the conversation by using –아/어 주세요.

Ex. A 약속 시간을 잘 모르겠어요. 저한테 __알려 주세요__. (알리다)

      B 네, 알겠어요.

5. A 길이 많이 막혀요. 조금만 _____. (기다리다)

      B 알겠어요.

6. A 컴퓨터가 고장 났어요. 내일 _____. (고치다)

      B 알겠어요. 내일 7시에 고쳐 드릴게요.

7. A 이 옷이 좀 작아요. 다른 사이즈 옷으로 _____. (바꾸다)

      B 네, 바꿔 드릴게요.

Answer **p.277**

Grammar Rehearsal

(Adverb) 말해 주세요 Understanding the way of speaking

안 들려요. 크게 말해 주세요.
I cannot hear (you). Could you please speak loudly?

너무 빨라요. 천천히 말해 주세요.
(You speak) too fast. Could you please speak slowly?

못 들었어요. 다시 한번 말해 주세요.
I couldn't hear (it). Could you please say it again?

한국어를 몰라요. 영어로 말해 주세요.
I don't know Korean. Could you please speak in English?

(Question) 알려 주세요 Asking for more information

어떻게 가야 해요? 알려 주세요.
How do I get there? Please let me know.

버스비가 얼마예요? 알려 주세요.
How much is the bus fare? Please let me know.

어디에서 표를 사요? 알려 주세요.
Where do I buy the ticket? Please let me know.

시간이 얼마나 걸려요? 알려 주세요.
How long does it take? Please let me know.

Additional Vocabulary

• **Vocabulary related to the bus**
교통 카드 transportation card
충전 recharge
매표소 ticket booth
버스 정류장 bus stop
버스 기사 bus driver
짐 luggage

버스 정류장   짐

Conversation Rehearsal

(time) 에 / (time interval) 마다 있어요   Explaining the bus schedule

몇 시에 버스가 있어요?

➡ 12시에 있어요.

➡ 10분 후에 있어요.

➡ 20분마다 있어요.

➡ 30분마다 있어요.

What time does the bus come by?

➡ (There's a bus) at 12:00.

➡ (There's a bus that arrives) after 10 minutes.

➡ (There's a bus) every 20 minutes.

➡ (There's a bus) every 30 minutes.

(place) 이/가 어디예요   Asking for a location

화장실이 어디예요?

매표소가 어디예요?

버스 정류장이 어디예요?

안내 데스크가 어디예요?

Where is the bathroom?

Where is the ticket sales counter?

Where is the bus station?

Where is the help desk?

Pronunciation Tip

track 054

몇 번 [멷 뻔]

Since the final consonants ㄷ, ㅌ, ㅅ, ㅈ, ㅊ, ㅎ are all pronounced as [ㄷ], 몇 is pronounced as [멷]. The initial sound of the next syllable ㄱ, ㄷ, ㅂ, ㅅ, ㅈ which is followed by the final consonant [ㄱ, ㄷ, ㅂ], is pronounced as [ㄲ, ㄸ, ㅃ, ㅆ, ㅉ]. Therefore, the first sound ㅂ of 번 after [멷] is pronounced as [ㅃ].

예 몇 개 [멷 깨]   몇 잔 [멷 짠]

Coffee Break

How to read bus numbers

Sino-Korean numbers are usually used when reading numbers. So, how should the bus number 602-1 be read? Similar to English, '-' is read as 다시, so 602-1 is read as 육백이 다시 일. If you don't hear the number, ask 네? Using your fingers is also a good idea.

From the airport to your destination

There are three ways to get to your destination by public transportation from Incheon International Airport: airport bus, airport train, or taxi.

First of all, airport buses are cheaper and more comfortable to ride than taxis. Airport buses run from Incheon International Airport via Gimpo Airport to major attractions in Seoul. It takes about 30 minutes from Incheon International Airport to Gimpo Airport and 30 minutes to 1 hour from Gimpo Airport to each area in Seoul. There is a bus ticket office and a bus stop as  soon as you leave the airport. You can check the bus routes by searching for a destination on the touch screen. If you plan to use the airport bus again in the future, it is a good idea to check with the bus driver the location of the bus stop heading to Incheon Airport before you get off the bus. You can also go directly to places like Busan, Gwangju, or Daejeon by bus from Incheon Airport.

 Next, the airport train is the cheapest and fastest way to get to your destination without experiencing any traffic delays. There are direct trains and general trains. The direct train from Incheon International Airport to Seoul Station takes about 30 minutes without stops. General trains take about 60 minutes from Incheon International Airport to Seoul Station. In the case of general trains, transfers can be made at subway stations in Seoul, thereby enabling access to all parts of the metropolitan area. The airport train also has the advantages of clean facilities, low fares, and easy accessibility to stations.

Lastly, taxis are readily available upon leaving the airport, but they are relatively expensive compared to airport buses or airport trains. Still, the advantage of taking a taxi is that you can arrive right in front of your desired destination.

If you are willing to disclose your destination, help can be sought from the information desks found throughout the airport. And if you need translation service, dial 1330 (no area code necessary) to contact translation agents from the Korea Tourism Organization. This free translation service is available 24 hours a day and provides information, in addition to transportation, about restaurants and accommodations.

At a subway station

Asking about subway destinations

반대쪽에서 타세요.

Take the train on the opposite side.

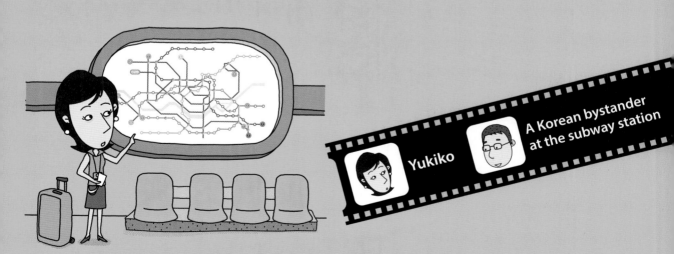

Yukiko

A Korean bystander at the subway station

Conversation

유키코   저……, 이 지하철이 강남역에 가요?

한국인   아니요, 반대쪽에서 타세요.

유키코   반대쪽요?

한국인   네, 저기에서 타세요.

유키코   반대쪽에 어떻게 가요?

한국인   이 계단으로 가세요.

유키코   알겠어요. 감사합니다.

Yukiko	Excuse me, does this train go to Gangnam station?
Korean	No. Take the train on the opposite side.
Yukiko	The opposite side?
Korean	Yes, (you should) get on (the train) over there.
Yukiko	How do I get to the other side?
Korean	(You should) Take these stairs. (lit. go to these stairs.)
Yukiko	I will. (lit. I understand.) Thank you.

▶ New Vocabulary

이 this

지하철 subway

강남역 Gangnam station

에 a marker indicating a destination or the place of a state

반대쪽 the opposite side

에서 a location marker indicating a place in which an action takes place

(으)로 by means of (a marker indicating a method, means, and tool of action)

타다 to get on, get in, ride, take (a vehicle)

저기 over there

어떻게 how

계단 stairs

▶ New Expressions

아니요. No.

반대쪽에서 타세요.
Take… on the opposite side.

반대쪽에 어떻게 가요?
How do I get to the other side?

이 계단으로 가세요.
(You should) Take these stairs.
(lit. Go to these stairs.)

알겠어요. I will.

▶ Close-Up

❶ 이/그/저
(this / that / that)

Like "this and that" in English 이/그/저 are used to indicate specific objects. They should be placed before the noun they refer to. 이 is used when the indicated object is close to the speaker. 그 is used when the indicated object is close to the listener but distant from the speaker. And 그 is also used to indicate an object which is discussed during a conversation but cannot be seen at the moment, 그 is used. 저 is used when the indicated object is distant from the speaker and the listener.

(Ex.) 이 지하철이 명동에 가요?
Does this train go to Myeongdong?

(Ex.) 어제 그 영화가 재미있었어요?
Was that movie yesterday good?

(Ex.) 저 사람 알아요?   Do you know that person?

❷ 에 and 에서
(Indicating a place)

In Korean, the markers 에 and 에서 indicate a place. The marker 에서 is used to indicate the place where action verbs such as 운동하다 or 먹다 occur, and the marker 에 is used with verbs such as 있다 and 없다 to indicate the place of a state.

(Ex.) 보통 저는 집에서 밥을 먹어요.
I usually eat at home.

(Ex.) 지금 집에 있어요.   I'm at home now.

Flashback

• Expressing directions

When indicating a direction in Korean, 쪽 is added. When indicating a direction, use 동쪽 (east), 서쪽 (west), 남쪽 (south), and 북쪽 (north) or use 이쪽 (this way) or 저쪽 (that way) while pointing your hand in the direction.

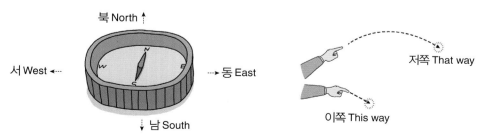

Grammar Chart **p.268**

The imperative –(으)세요 and –지 마세요

–(으)세요 is used when asking, recommending, giving advice, or ordering someone to do something with courtesy in everyday life. –(으)세요 is attached to the stem of a verb. –세요 is used when the verb stem ends in a vowel, and –으세요 is used when it ends in a consonant.

들어오다	들어오세요.	Come in.
앉다	여기 앉으세요.	Sit here.
★ 듣다	아침 뉴스를 들으세요.	Listen to the morning news.

Conversely, add –지 마세요 to the stem of the verb when asking, recommending, advising, or commanding someone not to do something.

피우다	담배를 피우지 마세요.	Don't smoke (cigarettes).
먹다	이 음식을 먹지 마세요.	Don't eat this food.

Most verbs can be made into commands by adding –(으)세요 to the end of the verb stem. However, in a few cases (먹다, 있다, 자다, and 말하다) stems should be changed into special honorific verb forms (드시다, 계시다, 주무시다, and 말씀하시다) respectively when forming instructions or commands.

먹다, 마시다	드시다	Ex. 많이 드세요.	Help yourself. (lit. Eat a lot.)
있다	계시다	Ex. 안녕히 계세요.	Goodbye.
자다	주무시다	Ex. 안녕히 주무세요.	Good night. (lit. Sleep well.)
말하다	말씀하시다	Ex. 좀 크게 말씀하세요.	Please speak a bit louder.

> **! Be careful!**
> There is a difference between –(으)세요 and the –아/어 주세요 learned in Scene 1. –아/어 주세요 is used when you either ask someone to do something for you or ask yourself to something for yourself. On the other hand, –(으)세요 is used when instructing someone to do something that is not used for the speaker. For example, when a female asks a male to buy a bag for her, she uses –아/어 주세요. However, when a female advises a male to buy a bag for him, she uses –(으)세요.

Quiz Yourself !

1~3 Look at the picture and choose the correct answer to complete the sentence.

Ex.

14페이지를 ✔ 펴세요 / ② 펴지 마세요.

1.

의자에 ① 앉으세요 / ② 앉지 마세요.

2.

책을 ① 보세요 / ② 보지 마세요.

3.

영어로 ① 말하세요 / ② 말하지 마세요.

4~6 Choose the correct answer and complete the conversation by using -(으)세요 or -지 마세요.

| 먹다 | 얘기하다 | 피우다 | 건너다 |

Ex. A 한국어를 어떻게 공부해요?

　　　B 한국 사람하고 많이 **얘기하세요** .

4. A 은행에 어떻게 가요?

　　　B 저기 가게 앞에서 길을 ＿＿＿＿＿＿.

5. A 요즘 힘이 없어요.

　　　B 그러면 이 약을 ＿＿＿＿＿＿.

6. A 목이 너무 아파요.

　　　B 담배가 안 좋아요. 담배를 ＿＿＿＿＿＿.

Answer p.277

Grammar Rehearsal

(Adverb indicating direction) 가세요 Showing the way

쭉 가세요.	Go in that direction.
왼쪽으로 가세요.	Go left.
오른쪽으로 가세요.	Go right.
길을 따라 가세요.	Go along the road.

(Action) –지 마세요 Reading signs

뛰지 마세요.	Don't run.
사진을 찍지 마세요.	Don't take any pictures.
음식을 먹지 마세요.	Don't eat any food.
담배를 피우지 마세요.	Don't smoke.

Additional Vocabulary

• **Vocabulary related to the subway**

도착 arrival
출발 departure
출구 exit
입구 entrance
비상구 emergency exit
개찰구 ticket gate

비상구

개찰구

출구, 입구

Conversation Rehearsal

어디에서/어느 역에서 …? Asking for information about a place

어디에서 사요?
➡ 입구에서 사세요.

Where do you buy it?
➡ You can buy it at the entrance.

어디에서 타요?
➡ 반대쪽에서 타세요.

Where do you get on?
➡ Take the train on the opposite side.

어느 역에서 내려요?
➡ 강남역에서 내리세요.

Which station do I get off at?
➡ You can get off at Gangnam station.

어느 역에서 갈아타요?
➡ 시청역에서 갈아타세요.

Which station do I make a transfer at?
➡ Transfer at the City Hall station.

(means, ways) (으)로 가세요 Reporting how to go

어떻게 가야 해요?

How do I get there?

➡ 이쪽으로 가세요.

➡ Please, go this way.

➡ 계단으로 가세요.

➡ Please, go via the stairs.

➡ 엘리베이터로 가세요.

➡ Please, go via the elevator.

➡ 에스컬레이터로 가세요.

➡ Please, go via the escalator.

Pronunciation Tip

track **058**

감사합니다 [감사함니다]

When the final consonant is pronounced as [ㄱ, ㄷ, ㅂ], if the first sound of the last syllable starts with ㄴ, ㅁ, the consonant pronunciation [ㄱ, ㄷ, ㅂ] is pronounced as [ㅇ, ㄴ, ㅁ]. In the example above, the consonant [ㅂ] of 합 is pronounced [ㅁ] because of the ㄴ of the last syllable 니.

예 **죄송합니다** [죄송함니다]   **미안합니다** [미안함니다]

Coffee Break

Directions of subway lines

Line 2 runs in a loop but the other subway lines run in straight routes, so it is important to know the direction in which the subway is heading. If the sign of the subway reads OO 방면, it means that the subway is going in OO direction. For example, if you want to go in the direction of Gimpo Airport on subway line 5, you should look for signs that say 김포 공항 방면 or ask people 이거 김포 공항 방면 지하철 맞아요? (Is this subway heading to Gimpo Airport?)

Seoul's convenient transportation card

Seoul's public transportation system is well laid-out and inexpensive to use. Public transportation can be used with cash and transportation cards. However, it is common to use transportation cards because not only is the transportation card convenient, but cash cannot receive discounts when transferring to other modes of public transportation. Transportation cards can be purchased or refilled at convenience stores. Koreans usually use a credit card with a transportation card function or use a transportation card mobile app.

If you have a transportation card, you can get a discount when transferring to subways and buses in Seoul and Gyeonggi-do. For 1,200 to 2,000 won, you can conveniently travel anywhere from Seoul to the metropolitan area. You can transfer for free to other modes of transportation within 30 minutes. However, if the distance from the first stop to the last stop is 10 km or longer, and the travel time is longer than 1 hour, an additional fee will be charged.

A transportation card is also easy to use. On the subway or bus, you can touch the card to the terminal twice when getting on or off the bus. On the subway, everyone must use a transportation card, but on the bus, several people can pay the bus fare with a single transportation card. To pay for multiple people with one transportation card, when boarding the bus, first, tell the bus driver the number of people, and tap your card on the card reader after the driver instructs accordingly. However, in this case, you must always follow the same exact procedure whenever transferring.

You can also pay for taxi fares with a transportation card. However, be aware that you cannot receive a discount when transferring from either a bus or subway to a taxi.

Inside a subway train

Greeting someone for the first time

외국인이세요?

Are you a foreigner?

Yukiko

A Korean passenger in the subway

Conversation

track 059

유키코	저……, 강남역 멀었어요?
한국인	아직 멀었어요.
유키코	네.
한국인	외국인이세요?
유키코	네, 일본에서 왔어요.
한국인	그런데 한국말을 잘하세요.
유키코	아니에요, 잘 못해요.

Yukiko	Excuse me, are we far from Gangnam station?
Korean	It is still a ways away.
Yukiko	I see.
Korean	Are you a foreigner?
Yukiko	Yes, I came from Japan.
Korean	(But) you speak Korean well.
Yukiko	No, I'm not very good at it.

▶ New Vocabulary

멀다 to be far, distant, remote

아직 still, so far, yet

외국인 foreigner

일본 Japan

그런데 but, however

한국말 Korean (language)

잘하다 to be good at

아니다 not

잘 well

못하다 to not be good at

▶ New Expressions

… 멀었어요?
Are we far from…?

아직 멀었어요.
It is still a ways away.

네. Yes.

한국말을 잘하세요.
You speak Korean well.

아니에요, 잘 못해요.
No, I'm not good at it.

▶ Close-Up

❶ 잘해요 and 못해요
(Doing well or can't do)

When you are good at something that requires a special technique, ability, or skill, such as sports or cooking, you use the verb 잘하다. When you are not good at something that requires a special technique, ability, or skill, you use the verb 못하다. 잘하다 and 못하다 are used together with the marker 을/를, but the marker 을/를 is often dropped in colloquial speech.

(Ex.) 진수 씨는 수영을 잘해요. 그런데 요리를 못해요.
Jinsu is good at swimming. But he can't cook.

❷ 아니요 and 아니에요
(Answering negatively)

아니요 and 아니에요 are both used for negative answers, but they have different uses. 아니요 is the negative answer of 네. On the other hand, 아니에요 has the meaning of 그것이 아니다. In this conversation, 아니에요, 잘 못해요 means "No, I'm not very good at it". Thus, 아니에요 is used and not 아니요.

(Ex.) A 폴 씨, 학생이에요?
Paul, are you a student?

B 아니요, 학생이 아니에요.
No, I am not a student.

Flashback

• Nationality and language

When a country name is followed by 사람 or 인, it means a person of that nationality. Languages of countries are formed by adding 말 or 어 to country names.

	Country	Korea	Japan	China	France	America	Foreign
Nationality	Colloquial Form	한국 사람 Korean person	일본 사람 Japanese person	중국 사람 Chinese person	프랑스 사람 French person	미국 사람 American person	외국 사람 Foreign person
	Literary Form	한국인 Korean	일본인 Japanese	중국인 Chinese	프랑스인 French	미국인 American	외국인 Foreigner
Language	Colloquial Form	한국말 Korean language	일본말 Japanese language	중국말 Chinese language	프랑스말 French language	영어 English	외국말 Foreign language
	Literary Form	한국어 Korean	일본어 Japanese	중국어 Chinese	프랑스어 French	영어 English	외국어 Foreign

(▶ English language is an exception.)

Grammar in Focus

Grammar Chart **p.268**

Honorific -(으)세요

When the subject of the sentence is a person who is older or in a higher position than the speaker, you can convey respect or honor by adding -(으)시- to the predicate of the sentence. You can also use the honorific form when asking a question in a respectful way. When conveying respect, add -(으)세요 to the stem of a verb or an adjective for the present tense, -(으)셨어요 for the past tense, and -(으)실 거 예요 for the future tense. In addition, in order to express respect for the subject of the sentence, 께서 can be used instead of the subject marker 이/가.

Normal	친구가 전화해요.	A friend is calling.
Honorific	아버지께서 전화하세요.	My father is calling.
Normal	친구가 신문을 읽어요.	A friend is reading the newspaper.
Honorific	어머니께서 신문을 읽으세요.	My mother is reading the newspaper.

-(으)세요 is an honorific form used when expressing respect towards the listener. Note that honorifics are used when asking questions to the listener, but not when responding about yourself.

A 어디에 가세요?	Where are you going?
B (제가) 은행에 가요. (O)	I'm going to the bank.
(제가) 은행에 가세요. (X)	

Some verbs mainly used in daily life such as 먹다, 마시다, 있다, 자다, 말하다 are replaced with honorific equivalent verbs 잡수시다, 드시다, 계시다, 주무시다, 말씀하시다 when conveying respect.

> **① Be careful!**
>
> The command form -(으)세요 and the present honorific form -(으)세요 have different meanings but are formed in the same way. However, the negative command form -지 마세요 and the present tense negative honorific form -지 않으세요 are different in both meaning and form. Be careful not to confuse them.
>
> | | The imperative form | The present tense honorific form |
> |---|---|---|
> | Affirmative | 전화하세요. Call me. | 아버지께서 자주 전화하세요. My father calls often. |
> | Negative | 전화하지 마세요. Don't call me. | 아버지께서 자주 전화하지 않으세요. My father doesn't call often. |

Quiz Yourself!

1~5 Yukiko is describing her mother in the following sentences. Complete the sentence by using the given verb.

Ex. 제 어머니는 지금 일본에 __계세요__ . (있다)

1. 여행을 아주 _____ . (좋아하다)

2. 그래서 여행을 자주 _____ . (가다)

3. 어제도 어머니께서 저한테 _____ . (전화하다)

4. 지난달에 어머니가 한국에 _____ . (오다)

5. 그때 한국 음식을 많이 _____ . (먹다)

6~8 Mark is asking questions using the honorific form in the following conversation. Complete the conversation by using the honorific form.

Ex. A 어디에서 __일하세요__ ?
　　 B 우체국에서 일해요.

6. A 자주 텔레비전을 _____ ?
　　 B 네, 자주 봐요.

7. A 어제 어디에 _____ ?
　　 B 집에 있었어요.

8. A 어제 저녁에 무슨 책을 _____ ?
　　 B 한국 문화 책을 읽었어요.

Answer **p.277**

Grammar Rehearsal

(Noun)(이)세요? Verifying the identity of a person with whom you should use honorifics

한국 분이세요?

Are you Korean?

➡ 네, 한국 사람이에요.

➡ Yes, I am Korean.

직장인이세요?

Are you an office worker?

➡ 아니요, 학생이에요.

➡ No, I am a student.

미국 분이세요?

Are you American?

➡ 아니요, 캐나다 사람이에요.

➡ No, I'm Canadian.

언제 -(으)셨어요? Asking a question to a person with whom you should use honorifics

언제 한국에 오셨어요?

When did you come to Korea?

➡ 일주일 전에 왔어요.

➡ I came here a week ago.

언제 처음 서울에 오셨어요?

When did you first come to Seoul?

➡ 이번에 처음 왔어요.

➡ This is my first time.

언제 한국어 공부를 시작하셨어요?

When did you start studying Korean?

➡ 작년에 시작했어요.

➡ I started last year.

Additional Vocabulary

• Vocabulary related to personal information

나라 nation, country

고향 hometown

나이 age

취미 hobby

전공 major (area of study)

연락처 contact information

Conversation Rehearsal

track **061**

(place)에 다녀요/에서 일해요 Talking about what he does

무슨 일 하세요?

➥ 회사에 다녀요.

➥ 학교에 다녀요.

➥ 집에서 일해요.

➥ 학원에서 일해요.

What do you do?

➥ I work at a company.

➥ I go to school.

➥ I work at home.

➥ I work at a private educational institute.

(required time) 걸려요 Talking the required time

여기에서 강남역까지 얼마나 걸려요?

➥ 30분쯤 걸려요.

➥ 1시간쯤 걸려요.

➥ 오래 걸려요.

➥ 얼마 안 걸려요.

How long does it take to get to Gangnam Station from here?

➥ It takes about 30 minutes.

➥ It takes about an hour.

➥ It takes a long time.

➥ It doesn't take long.

Pronunciation Tip

못해요 [모태요]

track **062**

For final consonants, only 7 sounds [ㄱ, ㄴ, ㄷ, ㄹ, ㅁ, ㅂ, ㅇ] can be pronounced. Many other final consonants ㄷ, ㅌ, ㅅ, ㅆ, ㅈ, ㅊ, ㅎ are pronounced as [ㄷ]. For example, 못 is pronounced as [몯]. When one of the final consonants ㄱ, ㄷ, ㅂ, ㅈ is followed by the initial consonant ㅎ in the next syllable, it is pronounced as [ㅋ, ㅌ, ㅍ, ㅊ] respectively. In the above example, the [ㄷ] in [몯] is followed by [ㅎ] in 해요 and is pronounced as [ㅌ]. As such, 못해요 is pronounced as [모태요].

 Coffee Break

Various questions about age

Koreans often ask about age when they first meet because they have to use the proper speech style. To people in your age group, you can ask directly 나이가 어떻게 되세요? (How old are you?). Indirectly, you can ask 몇 년생이세요? (In what year were you born?) or 무슨 띠예요? (Which zodiac sign are you?). When the person is clearly older than you, you can ask 연세가 어떻게 되세요? (How old are you? - honorific)

Korean names

It might seem difficult for foreigners to remember the names of Korean people. This is because many people share the same family name and Korean names often sound similar as they consist of three syllables. There are many people who have the same last name, and with the exception of a few cases, most Korean names sound similar as they consist of three syllables.

There are four dominant family names which comprise 49.6% of the names used by the general population. Of the four family names, 김 (Kim) is the most popular, being used by 21.6% of the population, followed by 이 (Lee) (14.8%), 박 (Park) (8.5%) and 최 (Choi) (4%). Since there are many people with the same last name, in Korea, people are rarely called exclusively by their last name. In the work setting, Koreans attach titles like 사장님 or 부장님 and regard individuals as 김 사장님 or 이 부장님. In private meetings, 씨 is added after a person's full name to convey respect. For example, the name 김진수 is not called 김 씨, but 김진수 씨.

Most Korean names consist of a one-syllable surname and two-syllable given name. Siblings often have a common syllable, which is called 돌림자 (*dollimja*; circling name – a part of name which has been set for each generation). Koreans still keep records of their family trees which are called 족보 (*jokbo*; genealogical tables). If you look into these records, you can see that the order of 돌림자 has already been set for the following generation, and easily understand the family order. For example, if three brothers' names are 박진호, 박영호, 박준호 with 호 as the *dollimja*, their sons in the next generation will have names like 박종원, 박종수 with 종 as the *dollimja*. Because of this *dollimja* system, the names of brothers in Korea sound alike but the names of fathers and sons are never the same as they can be in Western culture. There are no juniors in Korea. Recently, there are cases in which *dollimja* is not used.

One interesting point is that the family name of a Korean woman is not changed after marriage. In Korea, the family bloodline is important, so even if a woman gets married she retains her father's surname. So after marriage, a Korean woman keeps her family name while her husband and children share a family name.

Asking for directions to reach your destination

이쪽으로 쭉 가면 오른쪽에 편의점이 있어요.

If you go straight this way, there is a convenience store on the right.

Yukiko

A Korean bystander

Conversation

유키코	저……, 인사동에 어떻게 가요?
한국인	이쪽으로 쭉 가면 오른쪽에 편의점이 있어요.
유키코	네.
한국인	편의점 앞에서 횡단보도를 건너세요.
유키코	그다음은요?
한국인	조금 더 가면 약국이 보여요. 약국 앞에서 왼쪽으로 가면 인사동이에요.
유키코	고맙습니다.

Yukiko	Excuse me, how do I get to Insadong?
Korean	If you go straight this way there's a convenience store on the right.
Yukiko	I see.
Korean	You should cross the crosswalk in front of the convenience store.
Yukiko	And then?
Korean	If you go a little further, you'll see a pharmacy. From the front of the pharmacy, if you turn to the left and go straight, Insadong is there.
Yukiko	Thank you.

▶ New Vocabulary

인사동 Insadong (a place in Seoul famous for Korean traditional stores and museums)

이쪽 this way, this direction

쭉 straight

오른쪽 the right side

편의점 convenience store

앞 in front of

횡단보도 crosswalk

건너다 to cross, go over

그다음 and then, next

조금 a little

더 more

보이다 to be seen

약국 pharmacy

왼쪽 the left side

▶ New Expressions

⋯에 어떻게 가요? How do I get to...?

그다음은요? And then?

⋯이/가 보여요. You'll see...

고맙습니다. Thank you.

▶ Close-Up

❶ 그다음은요?

(Asking for the next instruction)

In colloquial speech, repetitions are often omitted. When the same question is repeated, the repeated part is omitted, and 요 is added to express respect. In this conversation, repeated questions are omitted and 요 is added.

> (Ex.) A 어떻게 지내요?
>   How are you?
>
>   B 저는 잘 지내요. 진수 씨는요? (= 진수 씨는 어떻게 지내요?)
>   I'm good. What about you? (= How are you, Jinsu?)
>
>   A 저도 잘 지내요.
>   I'm good too.

❷ The marker (으)로

(Asking for the address of a place)

In Korean, when expressing a direction with a motion verb like 가다 or 오다, the marker indicating direction is followed by the marker (으)로. For example, people point their hand and say, "이쪽으로 가세요". On the other hand, when expressing the position of an object with the stative verb 있다, the marker 에 is added after the word indicating the location. For example, say, "화장실이 이쪽에 있어요".

Flashback

• Expressions for locations

책상 위
on the desk

책상 옆
next to the desk

책상 아래
under the desk

컵하고 시계 사이
between the cup and the clock

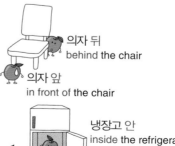

의자 뒤
behind the chair

의자 앞
in front of the chair

냉장고 안
inside the refrigerator

냉장고 밖
outside of the refrigerator

Grammar Chart **p.269**

-(으)면 If...

-(으)면 indicates a conditional clause in a sentence. In Korean, a conditional clause always comes first and the main clause for stating a fact or situation follows. In the below example, the conditional clause, 오른쪽으로 쭉 가면 (If you go straight to the right), comes first and the main clause 인사동이에요 (Insadong is there) follows. -(으)면 is combined with a verb stem or an adjective stem. If the verb stem or adjective stem ends in a vowel, -면 is used, and if it ends in a consonant, -으면 is used.

-(으)면 is also used when expressing an assumption that is different from reality. For example, write the conditional clause 돈이 있으면 if you don't have money right now, but are imagining you have money. Then you can add the main clause 세계 여행을 갈 거예요 (I would travel around the world).

| 가다 | 왼쪽으로 가면 약국이 있어요.
If you turn to the left and go straight, the pharmacy is there. |

| 오다 | 내일 비가 안 오면 등산하러 갈 거예요.
If it doesn't rain tomorrow, I will go hiking. |

| 좋다 | 날씨가 좋으면 같이 산책해요!
If the weather is good, let's go for a walk together! |

| ★ 듣다 | 한국 음악을 많이 들으면 듣기를 잘할 거예요.
If I listen to Korean music a lot, my listening will improve. |

| ★ 춥다 | 날씨가 추우면 다음에 만나요.
If the weather is cold, let's meet later. |

> **ⓘ Be careful!**
> When the stem ends with ㄹ, such as the verb 살다 (to live) or the adjective 멀다 (to be far), -면 is used instead of -으면 since 으 cannot come after the stem consonant ㄹ.
> 살다 → 살면 (O)　　(Ex.) 한국에서 살면 한국어를 빨리 배울 거예요.
> 　　　　살으면 (X)　　　　If I live in Korea, I'll learn Korean quickly.
> 멀다 → 멀면 (O)　　(Ex.) 집이 학교에서 멀면 피곤할 거예요.
> 　　　　멀으면 (X)　　　　If your home is far from school, you'll be tired.

Quiz Yourself !

1~4 Connect the condition with the result.

1. 오른쪽으로 가면 •

2. 날씨가 좋으면 •

3. 한국 친구가 있으면 •

4. 옷이 너무 비싸면 •

• ㉠ 그 옷을 안 살 거예요.

• ㉡ 산책할 거예요.

• ㉢ 병원이 보여요.

• ㉣ 한국어를 빨리 배울 거예요.

5~7 Complete the conversation by looking at the map below.

5. A 실례합니다. 영화관이 어디에 있어요?

　 B 이쪽으로 쭉 가면 약국이 보여요. 횡단보도를 건너면 ＿＿＿＿＿이/가 있어요. 약국에서 ＿＿＿＿＿으로 가면 오른쪽에 있어요.

6. A 실례합니다. 공원이 어디에 있어요?

　 B 이쪽으로 쭉 가면 ＿＿＿＿＿이/가 있어요. 길을 건너면 ＿＿＿＿＿이/가 있어요. 우체국에서 ＿＿＿＿＿으로 가면 공원이 오른쪽에 있어요.

7. A 실례합니다. 주차장이 어디에 있어요?

　 B 이쪽으로 ＿＿＿＿＿가면 사거리가 보여요. 사거리를 지나서 가면 ＿＿＿＿＿에 있어요. 카페 ＿＿＿＿＿에 있어요.

Answer p.277

Grammar Rehearsal

-(으)면 (place)이/가 있어요/보여요 Explaining the way

박물관에 어떻게 가요? | How do I get to the museum?
➡ 왼쪽으로 가면 박물관이 있어요. | ➡ If you go left, you'll see the museum.

지하철역에 어떻게 가요? | How do I get to the subway station?
➡ 오른쪽으로 가면 지하철역이 보여요. | ➡ If you go right, you'll see the subway station.

식당에 어떻게 가요? | How do I get to the restaurant?
➡ 저 건물을 지나면 식당이 보여요. | ➡ If you pass that building, you'll see the restaurant.

-(으)면 -(으)세요 Making a request

횡단보도를 보면 건너세요. | If you see the crosswalk, cross the street.

약국이 보이면 오른쪽으로 가세요. | If you see the pharmacy, go right.

질문이 있으면 언제든지 물어보세요. | If you have a question, ask me anytime.

Additional Vocabulary

• Vocabulary related to the street

사거리 intersection, four-way stop
횡단보도 crosswalk
신호등 traffic light
간판 sign, billboard
골목 alley
쓰레기통 garbage can

Conversation Rehearsal

이 근처에 (place)이/가 있어요? Asking for information from a nearby place

이 근처에 화장실이 있어요?
➡ 네, 2층에 있어요.

이 근처에 편의점이 있어요?
➡ 네, 저기에 있어요.

이 근처에 영화관이 있어요?
➡ 네, 저 건물 뒤에 있어요.

Is there a bathroom nearby?
➡ Yes, it is on the second floor.

Is there a convenience store nearby?
➡ Yes, it is over there.

Is there a movie theater nearby?
➡ Yes, it's behind that building.

얼마나 멀리/오래/많이/자주 …? Asking how much

얼마나 멀리 가야 해요?
➡ 500m쯤 가면 돼요.

얼마나 오래 가야 해요?
➡ 10분쯤 가면 돼요.

사람이 얼마나 많이 있어요?
➡ 100명쯤 있어요.

How far do I have to go?
➡ You have to go about 500 m.

How long do I have to go?
➡ You have to go for around ten minutes.

How many people are there?
➡ About 100 people.

Pronunciation Tip

track **066**

앞 [압] / 앞에서 [아페서]

When a syllable ends with a final consonant, as in the first example above, the final consonant ㄱ, ㅋ is pronounced as [ㄱ], ㄷ, ㅅ, ㅌ, ㅈ, ㅊ, ㅎ is pronounced as [ㄷ], and ㅂ, ㅍ is pronounced as [ㅂ] respectively. However, in the case of vowels, the final consonant of the syllable is pronounced in the initial consonant of the following syllable. As in the second example above, the consonant ㅍ is pronounced as [ㅍ] in [아페서].

Coffee Break

Asking for directions

Seoul has a 600-year history. Since the road was built in the past, there are many places where the road is not straight. The street names on the map are officially used in addresses, but they are different from the local names that people often use. That's why sometimes you can't find your way even with a map app. When navigating, it's a good idea to check for large buildings or famous landmarks near your destination. You can ask, 그 근처에 큰 빌딩 뭐가 있어요? (Is there a big building nearby?).

How Koreans show courtesy and intimacy

Koreans value hierarchy according to age and position. Likewise, the way they show manners and treat others changes accordingly. Thus, when dealing with someone who is older or of higher status, Koreans give a formal bow upon greeting and use both hands when shaking hands or handing something over. Even when shaking hands, which is a Western-style greeting, the  right hand to shake hands is held in a position as if it is supported by the left hand. Even when drinking with an older person, Koreans often turn their body to avoid showing the drinking gesture to a more senior person in order to show respect.

However, just bowing your head or using both hands is not enough to consider someone polite. Eye contact is something Westerners consider important when communicating with other people, but it is burdensome for Koreans to make eye contact with elders. In Korea, when listening to senior people or being scolded, it is considered disrespectful to raise their heads and look directly into the eyes of the senior person. Instead, it is considered more polite if you bow your head slightly while listening to the senior person. Westerners may regard this behavior of not making eye contact as disrespectful, but Koreans consider it polite to avoid making eye contact with seniors. These cultural differences may lead to minor misunderstandings.

Some older Koreans pat the head or cheek of an unknown child they met on the street, and this behavior is also one of the ways to show intimacy. Some even give snacks like candy or chocolate to unfamiliar children. Westerners may think that it is strange, but Koreans think that it is a considerate gesture towards children.

Koreans value showing intimacy with peers as important as showing courtesy to seniors. For example, on the streets of Korea, you can often see young high school girls and college girls

holding hands or walking around with arms linked. It is common for Korean men to put their arms around each other's shoulders. For Koreans, same-sex physical contact does not indicate one's sexual orientation. It's just a way to show intimacy. There are differences from person to person, but it can be generally said that Koreans are more affectionate in their relationships compared to Westerners.

Chapter 2

Preparing the necessary items for living in Korea

마크 로빈슨 (미국)
Mark Robinson (USA)

Chapter 2

Preparing the necessary items for living in Korea

At the immigration office

Applying for a foreigner registration card

외국인 등록증을 신청하고 싶어요.

I want to apply for a foreigner registration card.

Mark

An Immigration officer

Conversation

마크	외국인 등록증을 신청하고 싶어요.
직원	신청서를 주세요.
마크	여기 있어요.
직원	여권하고 사진 주세요.
마크	여기요. 외국인 등록증이 언제 나와요?
직원	2주 후에 나와요.
마크	우편으로 받고 싶어요.
직원	알겠습니다. 여기에 주소를 써 주세요.

Mark	I'd like to apply for a foreigner registration card.
Officer	Please, pass me your application form.
Mark	Here it is.
Officer	Please, give me your passport and a photo (of yourself).
Mark	Here you go. When will the foreigner registration card be issued?
Officer	It'll be issued in two weeks.
Mark	I would like to receive it by mail.
Officer	I see. Please, write your address here.

▶ New Vocabulary

외국인 foreigner

등록증 registration card

신청하다 to apply

신청서 application form

여기 here

여권 passport

하고 and

사진 photo

주다 to give

언제 when

나오다 to be issued, come out

주 week

후 after, later

우편 mail

받다 to receive, get

주소 mailing address

쓰다 to write

▶ New Expressions

…을/를 주세요. Please, give me…

여기 있어요. Here it is.

여기요. Here you go.

▶ Close-Up

❶ The marker 하고
(Adding multiple nouns)

The marker 하고 is written after a noun to indicate that the preceding noun is added to the noun that follows. Whether the preceding noun ends in a vowel or a consonant, 하고 is added. Instead of 하고, you can use the 와/과 or (이)랑. 와/과 is mainly used in formal or written forms and (이)랑 is used in the colloquial. The marker 하고 can be used in both formal and colloquial forms.

Ex. 사과하고 포도를 먹어요.(= 사과와 포도, 사과랑 포도)
I eat apples and grapes.

Ex. 책하고 가방을 샀어요.(= 책과 가방, 책이랑 가방)
I bought a book and a bag.

❷ The marker (으)로
(Indicating the means by which something is done)

(으)로 is a marker used to convey a means of or way. If the preceding noun ends in a vowel or ends in a consonant ㄹ, 로 is combined, and if the preceding noun ends in a consonant, 으로 is combined.

Ex. 매일 버스로 집에 가요.
I go home by bus every day.

Ex. 청구서는 이메일로 보내 주세요.
Please, send the bill by e-mail.

Ex. 검은색 펜으로 이름을 써요.
Write your name with a black pen.

Flashback

• Expressing time based on the present

Let's review the expressions for indicating specific points in time based on the present. Note that days, weeks, and years are read with Sino-Korean numbers (일, 이, 삼), and the month is read with native Korean numbers (하나, 둘, 셋).

그저께 the day before yesterday	어제 yesterday	현재 오늘 today	내일 tomorrow	모레 the day after tomorrow
지지난 주 the week before last week	지난주 last week	이번 주 this week	다음 주 next week	다다음 주 the week after next week
지지난달 the month before last month	지난달 last month	이번 달 this month	다음 달 next month	다다음 달 the month after next month
재작년 the year before last year	작년 last year	올해 this year	내년 next year	후년 the year after next year

Grammar in Focus

Grammar Chart **p.269**

-고 싶다 want to...

-고 싶다 is used to express your desire to do something. Simply add -고 싶다 to the verb stem, regardless of whether the verb stem ends in a vowel or a consonant. The subject of the sentence -고 싶다 can be used only in the first person form when it is a declarative sentence, and only in the second person when it is an interrogative sentence. However, it is worthwhile noting that Koreans often omit the first person subject 저는 in colloquial speech.

하다	한국어를 잘하고 싶어요.	I want to speak Korean well.
마시다	커피를 마시고 싶어요.	I want to drink some coffee.
먹다	한국 음식을 먹고 싶어요.	I want to eat Korean food.
보다	재미있는 한국 영화를 보고 싶어요.	I want to see a good Korean movie.
살다	A 어디에서 살고 싶어요?	Where do you want to live?
	B 서울에서 살고 싶어요.	I want to live in Seoul.

To express the speaker's past desires, combine the past tense marker -았/었- with 싶다 as -고 싶었다.

| 받다 | 생일 때 선물로 화장품을 받고 싶었어요. |
| | I wanted to receive makeup as a gift for my birthday. |

지난달에 제주도에 여행 가고 싶었어요. 그런데 시간이 없었어요.
Last month, I wanted to go on a trip to Jeju Island. But I had no time.

> ! **Be careful!**
> In a declarative sentence, the third person subject cannot be used with -고 싶다, but can be used with -고 싶어 하다.
> (Ex.) 마크 씨가 한국어를 잘하고 싶어요. (X)
> 마크 씨가 한국어를 잘하고 싶어 해요. (O) Mark wants to speak Korean well.

Quiz Yourself !

1~3 Look at the picture and complete the sentence by using –고 싶다.

Ex. 좀 추워요. 커피를 <u>마시고 싶어요</u> .

1. 배가 고파요.
   샌드위치를 _____ .

2. 다음 주에 휴가가 시작해요.
   휴가 때 제주도에 _____ .

3. 이번 주말에 시간이 있어요.
   친구하고 영화를 _____ .

4~8 Connect the question and answer. Complete the sentence by using –고 싶다.

Ex. 언제 여행 가고 싶어요? •

4. 누구를 만나고 싶어요? •

5. 뭐 먹고 싶어요? •

6. 무슨 운동을 배우고 싶어요? •

7. 어디에서 일하고 싶어요? •

8. 누구하고 영화를 보고 싶어요? •

• ㉠ 불고기를 _____ .

• ㉡ 친구하고 영화를 _____ .

• ㉢ 부모님을 _____ .

• ㉣ 은행에서 _____ .

• ㉤ 여름에 <u>여행 가고 싶어요</u> .

• ㉥ 태권도를 _____ .

Answer **p.277**

Grammar Rehearsal

-고 싶은데요
Initiating a conversation by stating the purpose of your visit

비자를 바꾸고 싶은데요. I want to change my visa.

비자를 연장하고 싶은데요. I want to extend my visa.

외국인 등록증을 신청하고 싶은데요. I want to apply for a foreigner registration card.

비자를 신청하고 싶은데요. I want to apply for a visa.

-고 싶어요
Answering questions about the purpose of your visit

무엇을 도와드릴까요? How can I help you?

➡ 예약하고 싶어요. ➡ I want to make a reservation.

➡ 예약을 취소하고 싶어요. ➡ I want to cancel the reservation.

➡ 예약을 목요일로 바꾸고 싶어요. ➡ I want to change the reservation to Thursday.

➡ 예약을 다음 주로 연기하고 싶어요. ➡ I want to postpone the reservation to next week.

Additional Vocabulary

• **Vocabulary related to documents**

성 family name
이름 first name
성별 gender
생년월일 date of birth
주소 address
국적 country of citizenship

Conversation Rehearsal

(Noun) 주세요   Asking for something

여권 주세요.	Passport, please.
신분증 주세요.	ID, please.
사진 주세요.	Photo, please
증명서 주세요.	Certificate, please.

-(으)러 왔어요   Talking about the specific purpose of your visit

왜 한국에 오셨어요?   Why did you come to Korea?

➡ 일하러 왔어요.   ➡ I'm here to work.

➡ 여행하러 왔어요.   ➡ I came to travel.

➡ 가족을 만나러 왔어요.   ➡ I'm here to see my family.

➡ 한국어를 공부하러 왔어요.   ➡ I came to study Korean

Pronunciation Tip

등록증 [등녹쯩]   track 070

When a final consonant ㅇ or ㅁ is followed by an initial consonant ㄹ in the next syllable, this ㄹ is pronounced as [ㄴ]. In the above example, because the final consonant ㅇ in 등 is followed by the initial consonant ㄹ in 록, this ㄹ is pronounced as [ㄴ]. So 등록 is pronounced as [등녹]. And, consonants like ㄱ, ㄷ, ㅂ, ㅅ, ㅈ that follow the final consonant [ㄱ, ㄷ, ㅂ] are pronounced as [ㄲ, ㄸ, ㅃ, ㅆ, ㅉ]. Therefore, 등록증 is pronounced as [등녹쯩].

Coffee Break

Useful vocabulary to know before visiting the immigration office

It is not easy for a foreigner who is not familiar with Korean to apply independently for documentation at the immigration office. If there is no Korean to ask for help, it is a good idea to familiarize yourself with basic terms before visiting. Terms such as 신청, 연장 or 변경 for a visa or 신청 or 재발급 for an alien registration card are notable examples.

Taboos in Korean life

In old buildings in Korea, you can see an F written on the elevator instead of the fourth floor. Even in buildings that were built earlier, there are cases where unit 403 is followed by 405 without 404. This is because the pronunciation of the number 4 by Koreans is the same as the pronunciation of the Sino-Korean number 사 meaning death. Despite these superstitions, buildings these days mark the 4th floor and unit 404, but Koreans still avoid 4 because they think it is related to death.

Similarly, there is a reluctance to write names in red. Occasionally, a foreigner writes his or her name or someone else's name with a red pen. At that time, most Koreans will be surprised and recommend that you write your name in a different color. In Korea, only the names of the deceased are written in red. In other words, it would be rude to write the name of a living person in red.

Do not stick spoons or chopsticks up-front in a meal even when eating. This is because positioning a spoon or chopsticks in the up-front position is an act of setting up food for a deceased ancestor and offering a meal to a ghost. If you ever get a chance to dine with Koreans, you can see that Koreans never leave their spoons and chopsticks upfront in their food.

If you ever have a chance to learn the traditional Korean greeting method, 절, remember that the number of times you bow is important. Even now, Koreans bow when they want to convey a heartfelt greeting. For example, when a man visits the bride's parents for marriage permission, he usually greets them with a bow. However, at this time, you must bow to the living person only once. This is because Koreans bow twice only to the dead. Therefore, Koreans only bow twice to the deceased at a funeral or when performing ancestral rites or rites.

Koreans dislike those who sit on a chair and shake their legs. Since ancient times, Korean adults have warned children who shake their legs by saying, "If you shake your legs, good fortune will run away." If you meet an elderly person in Korea, you should not shake your legs. If you are invited to a Korean house, be careful not to step on the doorsill. Koreans believe that if you step on the doorsill, good fortune will "run away". In addition, in Korea, it is still taboo to cut your nails or whistle at night and to sleep with your head facing north.

At the real estate agency

Finding a house

지금 이 집을 볼 수 있어요?

Can I view this house now?

Mark

A Real Estate agent

Conversation

마크	부동산 앱에서 집을 봤어요.
중개인	그래요? 저한테 보여 주세요.
마크	*(Pointing at the phone)* 이 집이에요. 지금 이 집을 볼 수 있어요?
중개인	네, 볼 수 있어요.
마크	언제 이사할 수 있어요?
중개인	계약하면 바로 이사할 수 있어요.
마크	그럼, 지금 집을 보고 싶어요.
중개인	알겠어요. 지금 갑시다.

Mark	I saw a house (that I am interested in) on a real estate app.
Agent	Really? Please, show it to me.
Mark	*(Pointing at the phone)* This is the house. Can I view this house now?
Agent	Yes, you can view it.
Mark	When can I move in?
Agent	You can move in immediately after signing a contract.
Mark	Then, I would like to view the house now.
Agent	Alright. Let's go (together to view it).

부동산 real estate

앱 app (application)

집 house

보다 more than

저 that

한테 to

보여 주다 to show, display

지금 now

이사하다 to move

계약하다 to make a contract

바로 immediately

그럼 then

그래요? Really?

저한테 보여 주세요.
Please, show it to me.

이 집이에요. This is the house.

지금 집을 보고 싶어요.
I would like to view the house now.

지금 갑시다. Let's go now.

❶ The marker 한테

(Referring to an objective or affiliation)

The marker 한테 is used with verbs such as 주다, 보내다 to indicate giving or sending something to someone. The marker 한테 has the same meaning as 에게. The marker 한테 is mainly used in colloquial and informal forms, and 에게 is mainly used in written and formal forms.

Ex. 제가 친구한테 문자를 보내요.
I'm texting my friend. (= 친구에게)

Ex. 어머니가 이웃한테 도움을 주고 있어요.
My mother is helping a neighbor. (= 이웃에게)

❷ -(으)ㅂ시다

(Expressing what is going to be done)

-(으)ㅂ시다 proposes an action in the formal form. It is usually used when discussing something and finally reaching a conclusion about how to do something. It is better to use -(으)ㅂ시다 towards the end of the discussion, because it can give off a conclusive, demanding tone. -(으)ㅂ시다 is combined with a verb. If the stem of the verb ends in a vowel, -ㅂ시다 is used. If the stem ends in a consonant, -읍시다 is used.

Ex. 밥 먹으러 갑시다. Let's go eat.

Flashback

• Names for rooms in a Korean house

현관 entrance

부엌 (주방) kitchen

화장실 toilet

욕실 shower room

거실 living room

방 (침실) bedroom

다용도실 multi-purpose room

Grammar in Focus

Grammar Chart **p.270**

-(으)ㄹ 수 있다 can

-(으)ㄹ 수 있다 is used with verbs and adjectives to express that something is possible or that someone is able to do something. When a verb stem or an adjective stem ends in a vowel, -ㄹ 수 있다 is used, and if a verb stem or an adjective stem ends in a consonant, -을 수 있다 is used.

하다	폴 씨는 중국어를 할 수 있어요.	Paul can speak Chinese.
읽다	저는 한자를 읽을 수 있어요.	I can read Sino-Korean characters.
받다	30분 후에 전화를 받을 수 있어요.	I can speak in 30 minutes (lit. I can receive your phone call in 30 minutes.)
★만들다	저는 한국 음식을 만들 수 있어요.	I can make Korean food.
★덥다	오늘 이 옷이 더울 수 있어요.	These clothes may be too hot for today.

Use -(으)ㄹ 수 없다 to express an impossibility of a certain situation or incapability to carry out an action.

치다	새라 씨는 피아노를 칠 수 없어요. (= 못 쳐요)	Sarah cannot play piano.
먹다	A 유키코 씨는 매운 음식을 먹을 수 있어요? Yukiko, can you eat spicy food? B 아니요, 저는 매운 음식을 먹을 수 없어요. (= 못 먹어요) No. I cannot eat spicy food.	
★듣다	시끄러워서 여기에서 음악을 들을 수 없어요. (= 못 들어요) It is noisy so I cannot hear the music here.	

When indicating that an action could have been performed or the possibility of a certain situation in the past, the past tense marker -았/었- is combined with 있다 and used in the form of -(으)ㄹ 수 있었다.

| 만나다 | 어제 저는 친구를 만날 수 없었어요.
I was unable to meet my friend yesterday. |
| 타다 | 전에 커피를 가지고 버스에 탈 수 있었어요.
In the past, I was able to get on the bus with coffee. |

Quiz Yourself !

1~5 Look at the picture and choose the correct answer.

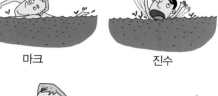

마크   진수

Ex. 마크는 수영을   ✓ 할 수 있어요.
                 ② 할 수 없어요.

1. 진수는 수영을   ① 할 수 있어요.
                 ② 할 수 없어요.

마크   진수

2. 마크는 생선을   ① 먹을 수 있어요.
                 ② 먹을 수 없어요.

3. 진수는 생선을   ① 먹을 수 있어요.
                 ② 먹을 수 없어요.

마크   진수

4. 마크는 한국 음식을   ① 만들 수 있어요.
                     ② 만들 수 없어요.

5. 진수는 한국 음식을   ① 만들 수 있어요.
                     ② 만들 수 없어요.

6~8 Complete the conversation by using -(으)ㄹ 수 있다 or -(으)ㄹ 수 없다.

Ex.   A   영어를 할 수 있어요?
       B   네, **할 수 있어요**.

7.   A   이번 주말에 만날 수 있어요?
       B   네, _____.

6.   A   한자를 읽을 수 있어요?
       B   아니요, _____.

8.   A   혼자 한복을 입을 수 있어요?
       B   아니요, _____.

Answer **p.277**

Grammar Rehearsal

지금 -(으)ㄹ 수 있어요? — Asking if it is possible

지금 만날 수 있어요?	Can we meet now?
지금 얘기할 수 있어요?	Can we talk now?
지금 출발할 수 있어요?	Can we leave now?
지금 계약할 수 있어요?	Can I sign a contract now?

-(으)면 바로 -(으)ㄹ 수 있어요 — Talking about possible conditions

준비되면 바로 출발할 수 있어요.	When you're ready, you can leave right away.
전화하면 바로 예약할 수 있어요.	You can make a reservation right away by calling.
신청하면 바로 시작할 수 있어요.	Once you apply, you can start right away.
문제가 생기면 바로 취소할 수 있어요.	If something goes wrong, you can cancel it right away.

Additional Vocabulary

• **Vocabulary related to the house**

보증금 security deposit
월세 monthly rent
관리비 maintenance fees
계약금 down payment
중개인 broker
집주인 landlord

Conversation Rehearsal

track 073

track 073

(description of the house) 집을 찾고 있어요   Specifically describing the house you are looking for

어떤 집을 찾고 있어요?

➡ 새 집을 찾고 있어요.

➡ 싼 집을 찾고 있어요.

➡ 조용한 집을 찾고 있어요.

➡ 지하철역 근처 집을 찾고 있어요.

What house are you looking for?

➡ I'm looking for **a new** house.

➡ I'm looking for **an affordable** house.

➡ I'm looking for **a quiet** house.

➡ I'm looking for a house **near a subway station.**

-(으)면 좋겠어요   Saying the price you want to pay

한 달에 50만 원 정도면 좋겠어요.

한 달에 60만 원 정도면 좋겠어요.

보증금 1,000만 원에 월세 50만 원 정도면 좋겠어요.

보증금 없고 월세 60만 원 정도면 좋겠어요.

I hope it is around 500,000 won per month.

I hope it is around 600,000 won per month.

It would be nice if the deposit is 10 million won and the monthly rent is 500,000 won.

It would be nice if there is no deposit and the monthly rent is around 600,000 won.

Pronunciation Tip

볼 수 있어요 [볼 쑤 이써요]

track 074

The initial sound ㄱ ㄷ, ㅂ, ㅅ, ㅈ which is followed by the noun modifier -(으)ㄹ is pronounced as [ㄲ, ㄸ, ㅃ, ㅆ, ㅉ]. In the above example, the ㅅ of 수 follows after 볼 and is pronounced as [ㅆ]. Therefore, 볼 수 is pronounced as [볼 쑤]. Also, in the above example, the ㅆ of 있어요 is pronounced as [이써요] as the ㅆ in 있 moves to become the initial consonant of the next syllable. Thus, 볼 수 있어요 is pronounced as [볼 쑤 이써요].

☕ Coffee Break

Paying rent in Korea: 월세, 전세, 연세

When taking on a lease of a house, it is common to put down about 2-3 months' payment of rent and a security deposit. But when renting a house in Korea, there is a unique system called 전세 in addition to monthly rent. When looking for a house, you can ask for a 전세 or monthly rent according to your circumstances. In addition, on Jeju Island, there are cases when the cumulative annual monthly rent is added to the yearly rent.

Apartment culture in Korea

As Korea is regarded as a 'republic of apartments', apartment buildings are the iconic housing type. In particular, in densely populated urban areas such as Seoul, apartments are an efficient form of housing. However, if you think that apartments are a way of living for ordinary people, you are mistaken. Apartments in Seoul are a representative residential culture of the middle class, and even in the wealthy neighborhoods of Seoul, there are apartments boasting high housing prices.

Why do Koreans like apartments? First of all, apartments have the advantage of being easy to manage. Since apartments have a management office, the management office is responsible for managing mini parks and playgrounds in the apartment and managing waste separation and collection. In addition, the management office is responsible for managing various problems such as parking issues and noise between floors that may occur in an apartment complex.

The apartment is also effective for preventing crime. There are many security cameras (CCTV) installed in the apartment, so you can think of it as good for crime prevention. But above all else, there is an element of anonymity as all the suites in the apartment look the same from the outside. No matter how fancy the interior of an apartment house is, the front door and apartment window seen from the outside are the same, so any house appears the same from the outside. This feature fits the characteristics of Koreans who prefer not to stand out.

Moreover, Koreans prefer apartments because they can expect a rise in real estate prices while enjoying the convenience of living. Since apartments are preferred, an apartment has better cash flow than a single-family house. When looking at the trend of real estate prices in Korea, apartment price trends reveal how apartments are the representative housing type in Korea.

However, these days, people who yearn for a different life in the city are starting to try various housing methods other than apartments.

At a phone store

Opening a cell phone account

얼마 동안 돈을 내야 돼요?

For how long do I have to pay?

Mark

An Employee at the phone store

Conversation

직원	어서 오세요.
마크	핸드폰을 보고 싶어요.
직원	여기 핸드폰이 많이 있어요. 천천히 보세요.
마크	이거 얼마예요?
직원	잠시만요, 핸드폰 가격하고 요금이 한 달에 6만 원이에요.
마크	얼마 동안 돈을 내야 돼요?
직원	2년 동안 돈을 내야 돼요.
마크	그래요? 이거 좀 볼 수 있어요?
직원	그럼요.

Employee	Welcome.
Mark	I would like to see some cell phones.
Employee	There are a lot of cell phones here. Please, take your time.
Mark	How much is this?
Employee	One moment. The price of the cell phone, inclusive of charges, is 60,000 won per month.
Mark	For how long do I have to pay?
Employee	You have to pay for two years.
Mark	Really? Can I look at this one?
Employee	Sure.

▶ New Vocabulary

핸드폰 cell phone

많이 a lot

천천히 slowly, leisurely

이거 this one

얼마 how much

가격 price

요금 charge, fee

달 month

얼마 동안 how long

돈 money

돈을 내다 to pay

년 year

▶ New Expressions

어서 오세요. Welcome.

천천히 보세요. Please, take your time.

이거 얼마예요? How much is this?

잠시만요. One moment.

한 달에 6만 원이에요.
60,000 won per month.

이거 좀 볼 수 있어요?
Can I look at this one?

그럼요. Of course.

▶ Close-Up

❶ 이거
(Defining a subject or an object)

이거 is used colloquially with the same meaning as 이 것. In colloquial speech, the subject marker 이/가 and the object marker 을/를 tend to be omitted, so 이거 is used both as a subject and as an object in conversations. In this conversation, the first 이거 is used as the subject with the same meaning as 이것이, and the second 이거 is used as an object with the same meaning as 이것을.

(Ex.) 이거 맛있어요. (= 이것이)
This is tasty.

(Ex.) 어제 저는 이거 샀어요. (= 이것을)
Yesterday, I bought this.

❷ The marker 에
(Indicating a limited range)

The marker 에 is not only used to indicate a place but is also used to indicate scope or range. In this conversation, 한 달에 highlights the limit of 한 달. However, remember that, unlike in English, a range or group is written first, followed by a specific quantity such as the numerical frequency or cost.

(Ex.) 하루에 2번 커피를 마셔요.
I drink coffee twice a day.

(Ex.) 사과 8개에 만 원이에요.
It costs 10,000 won for 8 apples.

Flashback

• Reading prices

Sino-Korean numbers are used when reading Korean money.

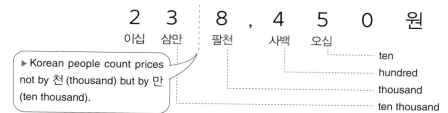

However, only when the monetary amount starts with 1, the first digit is read without 일.

(Ex.) 160원   백육십 원(일백 육십 원 X)   15,000원   만 오천 원(일만 오천 원 X)

1,800원   천 팔백 원(일천 팔백 원 X)   ▶ Exception   100,000,000원   일억 원

Grammar in Focus

–아/어야 되다 have to, must...

–아/어야 되다 is used when a certain condition is necessary or there is a prerequisite. –아/어야 되다 is combined with verbs and adjectives. The verb 하다 (for example 일 하다, 공부하다, etc.) or the adjective 하다 (for example 유명하다, 피곤하다, etc.) are used as 해야 되다. When the stem ends with a vowel ㅏ or ㅗ, –아야 되다 is attached to the stem. In all other cases, –어야 되다 is attached to the stem. –아/어야 되다 can be used interchangeably with –아/어야 하다 without any difference in meaning.

공부하다	학생이 열심히 공부해야 돼요.	Students must study hard.
친절하다	직원이 손님에게 친절해야 돼요.	The staff must be kind to customers.
기다리다	얼마나 기다려야 돼요?	How long do I have to wait?
오다	직원은 10시까지 와야 돼요.	Employees have to arrive by 10 o'clock.
먹다	아이들은 과일을 많이 먹어야 돼요.	Children have to eat a lot of fruit.
좋다	이번 일요일에 날씨가 좋아야 돼요.	The weather has to be good this Sunday.
★ 크다	농구 선수가 되려면 키가 커야 돼요.	To be a basketball player, you must be tall.
★ 부르다	한 사람씩 노래를 불러야 돼요.	You must sing one by one.

There is a passive meaning to 되다 in –아/어야 되다, so it can be used softly compared to –아/어야 하다. –아/어야 되다 is mainly used in informal or colloquial forms, and –아/어야 하다 is mainly used in formal or written forms.

마시다	물을 많이 마셔야 돼요.	You have to drink a lot of water.
하다	운전할 때에는 운전에 집중해야 합니다.	When driving, you have to stay focused.

> ! **Be careful!**
> When something doesn't need to be done, add –지 않아도 되다 to the end of the stem.
> Ex) 여러 가지 신경 쓰지 않아도 돼요.
> You don't need to care for so many things.
> Ex) 배부르면 끝까지 다 먹지 않아도 돼요.
> You don't need to eat it all.

Quiz Yourself !

1~4 Choose the correct answer to complete the sentence.

Ex. 많이 아파요. 그러면 ① 공원에 가야 돼요.
                          ✔ 병원에 가야 돼요.

1. 배가 고파요. 그러면 ① 음식을 먹어야 돼요.
                          ② 음식을 안 먹어야 돼요.

2. 한국어를 잘하고 싶어요. 그러면 ① 한국어를 공부해야 돼요.
                                    ② 일본어를 공부해야 돼요.

3. 극장에서 영화를 보고 싶어요. 그러면 ① 돈을 사야 돼요.
                                    ② 표를 사야 돼요.

4. 아이들이 자요. 그러면 ① 조용해야 돼요.
                        ② 시끄러워야 돼요.

5~7 Complete the sentences by using –아/어야 되다.

몸이 안 좋아요.
어떻게 해야
해요?

Ex. 먼저, 매일 30분씩 <u>**운동해야 돼요**</u>.
                        (운동하다)

5. 그리고 채소를 많이 _____.
                        (먹다)

6. 또 물을 많이 _____.
                (마시다)

7. 마지막으로, 스트레스가 _____.
                      (없다)

Answer p.278

Grammar Rehearsal

얼마 동안 –아/어야 돼요? Asking about the amount of time needed

얼마 동안 기다려야 돼요?   For how long do I have to wait?

얼마 동안 돈을 내야 돼요?   For how long do I have to pay?

얼마 동안 병원에 다녀야 돼요?   For how long do I have to go to the hospital?

얼마 동안 아르바이트해야 돼요?   For how long do I have to work part-time?

–까지 –아/어야 돼요 Talking about conditions

오늘까지 신청해야 돼요.   You must apply by today.

내일까지 가입해야 돼요.   You must sign up by tomorrow.

다음 주까지 준비해야 돼요.   You must be ready by next week.

이번 달까지 기다려야 돼요.   You must wait until this month.

Additional Vocabulary

• **Vocabulary related to phones**
전원을 켜다 to turn on the power
전원을 끄다 to turn off the power
충전하다 to charge, recharge
비밀번호 password
문자 메시지 text message
음성 메시지 voice message

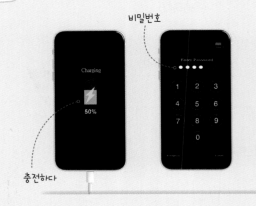

비밀번호

충전하다

음성 메시지

문자 메시지

Conversation Rehearsal

track 077

-아/어 봐도 돼요? Asking permission from a worker

이거 만져 봐도 돼요?	Can I touch this?
이거 먹어 봐도 돼요?	Can I try this? (lit. Can I eat this?)
이거 입어 봐도 돼요?	Can I wear this?
이거 신어 봐도 돼요?	Can I try this on?

-(으)ㄴ/는 게 뭐예요? Asking a worker

요즘 인기가 많은 게 뭐예요?	What's popular these days?
요즘 평이 좋은 게 뭐예요?	What's favorably received these days?
요즘 많이 팔리는 게 뭐예요?	What sells well these days?
요즘 많이 세일하는 게 뭐예요?	What's on sale these days?

Pronunciation Tip

track 078

육만 원 [융마 뉀]

When the sound of the final consonant [ㄱ, ㄷ, ㅂ] position is followed by the initial consonant ㄴ, ㅁ in the next syllable, [ㄱ] is pronounced as [ㅇ], [ㄷ] is pronounced as [ㄴ], and [ㅂ] is pronounced as [ㅁ]. The consonant ㄴ in 만 moves to the first sound of the next syllable, 원, which begins with a vowel, and is pronounced as [마 뉀]. Therefore, 육만 원 is pronounced as [융마 뉀].

Coffee Break

Another way to read phone numbers

Sino-Korean numbers are used when reading phone numbers. However, even for Koreans, 1 (일) and 2 (이) sound similar. In order to clearly distinguish the two numbers, 1 is oftentimes read as 하나 (native Korean number) and 2 is read as 이 (Sino-Korean number). For example, if you read the number 3123, you'd say 삼-하나-이-삼. When there are many zeros like 5000 or 7000, it is sometimes read as 오천 번 or 칠천 번.

The figures on Korean banknotes

"Won" is the official currency of South Korea. The current design of Korean banknotes was decided for 1,000 won, 5,000 won, and 10,000 won in the 1980s, and 50,000 won was added in the 2000s. What is unusual is that all the characters of the current four types of Korean banknotes are from the Joseon Dynasty. In recent years, the use of cash has significantly decreased due to credit cards or mobile phones, but you can still think about the value of a country by looking at the banknotes of that country.

First, the person found on the 1,000 won bill is 퇴계 이황 (1501–1570), an iconic Confucian scholar in the mid-Joseon period. Next to 퇴계 이황 are the plum blossoms he liked (a flower that symbolizes the scholastic spirit) and Sungkyunkwan Myeongnyundang (International Student School) where he studied and trained junior scholars. 퇴계 이황, a master of Neo-Confucianism, thought it was important to put effort into learning. This sentiment is encapsulated in the bill itself.

Next, the person engraved on the 5,000 won bill is 율곡 이이 (1536–1584), another iconic Confucian scholar in the mid-Joseon Dynasty. 율곡 이이 along with 퇴계 이황 is considered the best Confucian scholars of the Joseon Dynasty. However, unlike 퇴계 이황, 율곡 이이 interests centered on social reform. He focused on living an upright life and emphasized the practice of learning. On the banknote, next to 율곡 이이 is Ojukheon, the place of his birth.

The figure engraved on the 10,000 won banknote is the fourth king of the Joseon Dynasty, 세종대왕 이도 (1397–1450). As King Sejong the Great is well known for inventing and promulgating Hangeul, 용비어천가 (the first book written in Korean) and 일월오봉도 (the symbol of the king) are drawn next to King Sejong on the banknotes. King Sejong, who prayed for the people to live comfortably and prosperously, achieved numerous scientific achievements such as the advent of Hangeul, clocks, and other astronomic observational instruments.

Lastly, the person found on the 50,000 won bill is 신사임당 (1504–1551), a female artist of the Joseon Dynasty. She is the only woman on Korean banknotes and the mother of 율곡 이이. Although women were excluded from social roles in the Joseon Dynasty, 신사임당 flourished in the arts while cultivating scholarship. 신사임당's representative works, 묵포도도 (a picture of grapes) and 초충도수병 are depicted next to her on the banknote.

At a restaurant

Ordering food at a restaurant

제가 매운 음식을 못 먹어요.

I can't eat spicy food.

Mark

A Restaurant employee

Conversation

직원	어서 오세요. 여기 앉으세요.
마크	영어 메뉴 있어요?
직원	죄송합니다. 영어 메뉴가 없어요.
마크	제가 매운 음식을 못 먹어요. 안 매운 음식이 있어요?
직원	*(Pointing at the menu)* 이 음식이 안 매워요.
마크	이거 뭘로 만들어요?
직원	돼지고기하고 두부로 만들어요.
마크	그럼, 이거 하나 주세요.

Employee	Welcome. Please take a seat over here.
Mark	Do you have an English menu?
Employee	Sorry. We do not have an English menu.
Mark	I can't eat spicy food. Do you have any non-spicy food?
Employee	*(Pointing at the menu)* This dish is not spicy.
Mark	What is this made of?
Employee	It is made with pork and tofu.
Mark	Then, give me this one, please.

앉다 to sit

영어 English

메뉴 menu

제가 I

맵다 to be spicy

음식 food

못 cannot

안 not

뭘로 by means of what

만들다 to make, create

돼지고기 pork

두부 tofu

(으)로 by means of

▶ **New Expressions**

여기 앉으세요.
Please take a seat over here.

죄송합니다. Sorry.

안 매운 음식이 있어요?
Do you have any non-spicy food?

이거 뭘로 만들어요?
What is this made of?

이거 하나 주세요. Give me this one, please.

▶ **Close-Up**

❶ 안 and 못
(Expressing negation)

Whereas 안 is used for negation (do not), 못 expresses the impossibility of a certain action. The place to use 안 and 못 is the same. 안 is used before verbs or adjectives, and 못 is used before verbs. However, in the case of the verb 하다, 안 and 못 are used between the noun and 하다.

(Ex.) 저는 게임 안 해요.
I don't play games.

(Ex.) 요즘 잘 못 자요.
I can't sleep these days.

❷ The marker (으)로
(Representing the material something is made of)

The marker (으)로 is also used with material or food ingredients. The marker (으)로 is used after a noun that pinpoints material or food ingredient. If the noun ends in a vowel or consonant ㄹ, 로 is combined, and if it ends in a consonant, 으로 is used.

(Ex.) 이 음식은 김치로 만들었어요.
This food is made with kimchi.

(Ex.) 이 찌개는 생선으로 만들었어요.
This stew is made with fish.

Flashback

• **Adjectives for describing tastes**

맵다	"매워요."	매운 음식	
to be spicy	"It is spicy."	spicy food	
달다	"달아요."	단 음식	
to be sweet	"It is sweet."	sweet food	
짜다	"짜요."	짠 음식	
to be salty	"It is salty."	salty food	
싱겁다	"싱거워요."	싱거운 음식	
to be bland	"It's bland."	bland food	
기름기가 많다	"기름기가 많아요."	기름기가 많은 음식	
to be greasy	"It is greasy."	greasy food	

Grammar in Focus

Grammar Chart **p.270**

-(으)ㄴ The noun modifier

-(으)ㄴ is placed before a noun to modify the noun. -(으)ㄴ is also combined with adjective stems. When an adjective stem ends in a vowel, -ㄴ is added and, when it ends in a consonant, -은 is added. For example, when describing a large bag, add ㄴ after the stem 크 in the adjective 크다 as 큰 가방. When describing a small bag, add 은 after the stem 작 in the adjective 작다 as 작은 가방. If the adjective is OO있다/없다 (for example 맛있다, 재미없다), -는 is used between the adjective stems (for example 맛있는, 재미없는).

크다 → 크+-ㄴ	큰 가방이 비싸요.	Big bags are expensive.
작다 → 작+-은	어제 작은 우산을 샀어요.	I bought a small umbrella yesterday.
맛있다 → 맛있+-는	맛있는 음식을 먹고 싶어요.	I want to eat delicious food.

When the stem of an adjective ends with ㄹ, such as 길다 (to be long), 멀다 (to be far), ㄹ is dropped, and -ㄴ is used as in 긴, 먼.

★ 길다 → 기+ㄹ+-ㄴ	긴 머리가 불편해요.	Having long hair is uncomfortable.

When the stem of an adjective ends with ㅂ, such as 맵다 (to be spicy), 춥다 (to be cold), ㅂ is changed to 우 and 은 is used as in 매운, 추운.

★ 맵다 → 매+우+-ㄴ	매운 음식을 잘 못 먹어요.	I cannot eat spicy food.
★ 춥다 → 추+우+-ㄴ	추운 날씨 때문에 감기에 걸렸어요.	I caught the flu because of the cold weather.

Quiz Yourself !

1~4 Look at the picture and choose the correct answer.

1.

① 큰 가방　② 작은 가방

2.

① 긴 머리　② 짧은 머리

3.

① 맛있는 음식　② 맛없는 음식

4.

① 더운 날씨　② 추운 날씨

5~7 Complete the conversation by using -(으)ㄴ.

Ex.　A　어떤 음악을 좋아해요?

　　　B　**조용한** 음악을 좋아해요.
　　　　　(조용하다)

5.　A　왜 옷을 안 사요?

　　　B　지금 돈이 없어서 _____ 옷을 살 수 없어요.
　　　　　　　　　　　　　　(비싸다)

6.　A　어떤 영화를 보고 싶어요?

　　　B　_____ 영화를 보고 싶어요.
　　　　　(재미있다)

7.　A　한국 음식이 어때요?

　　　B　맛있어요. 저는 _____ 음식을 좋아해요.
　　　　　　　　　　　　　(맵다)

Answer **p.278**

Grammar Rehearsal

-(으)ㄴ 것을 별로 안 좋아해요
Talking about something you don't like

매운 것을 별로 안 좋아해요.	I don't like **spicy** things very much.
뜨거운 것을 별로 안 좋아해요.	I don't like **hot** stuff very much.
불편한 것을 별로 안 좋아해요.	I don't like **uncomfortable** things very much.
시끄러운 것을 별로 안 좋아해요.	I don't like **noisy** things very much.

-(으)ㄴ 것 있어요?
Asking an employee

같은 것 있어요?	Do you have **the same** thing?
다른 것 있어요?	Do you have anything else?
안 매운 것 있어요?	Do you have anything **non-spicy**?
안 비싼 것 있어요?	Do you have anything **that isn't expensive**?

Additional Vocabulary

• Vocabulary related to meals

밥 rice
국 soup
찌개 stew
반찬 side dish
숟가락 spoon
젓가락 chopsticks
개인 접시 (= 앞접시) individual plate

Conversation Rehearsal

track 081

이 집에서 뭐가 제일 …? Asking for something specific

이 집에서 뭐가 제일 **매워요**?
What's the **spiciest** at this restaurant?

이 집에서 뭐가 제일 **비싸요**?
What's the most **expensive dish** at this restaurant?

이 집에서 뭐가 제일 **맛있어요**?
What's the **tastiest dish** at this restaurant?

이 집에서 뭐가 제일 **인기가 많아요**?
What's the most **popular dish** at this restaurant?

(Noun) 빼고 주세요 Requesting for something to be removed

버섯 빼고 주세요.
Please, remove **the mushrooms.**

오이 빼고 주세요.
Please, remove **the cucumber.**

양파 빼고 주세요.
Please, remove **the onion.**

마늘 빼고 주세요.
Please, remove **the garlic.**

Pronunciation Tip

못 먹어요 [몬 머거요]

track 082

못 is pronounced as [몯]. However, when the sound of the final consonant [ㄱ, ㄷ, ㅂ] is followed by the initial consonant ㄴ, ㅁ in the next syllable, it should be pronounced as [ㅇ, ㄴ, ㅁ] respectively. In the above example, when the final consonant [ㄷ] in [몯] is followed by the initial consonant [ㅁ] in the next syllable 먹, 못 [몯] is pronounced as [몬]. When the final consonant ㄱ in 먹 is followed by an initial syllable that is a vowel, it is pronounced as [머거요]. So 못 in 못 먹어요 is pronounced as [몬머거요].

예 **못 마셔요** [몬 마셔요]   **못 만나요** [몬 만나요]

Coffee Break

Counting quantities of food

When counting quantities of food, it is important to use the proper words for quantities and units as in 한 개, 두 개. However, in real life, you can omit the unit and simply use the native Korean number. For example, if you want to order one bibimbap, you can say 비빔밥 하나 주세요. On the other hand, when ordering meat dishes like galbi or bulgogi, Sino-Korean numbers are used with the counting word 인분 (meaning the "amount that a person can eat"). For example, you can say 갈비 2(이)인분 주세요. (Please, serve two portions of ribs).

Korean food culture: alone and together

Koreans seldom go out to eat alone during lunch at school or work. In Korean restaurants, many people come in pairs. If you go in to eat alone, you may feel embarrassed. In Korea, the dining culture is not just for eating, but for making friends. Of course, eating together anywhere in the world means that you can spend more time with the other person, but in Korea, dining is an act of community building – it strengthens everyday human relationships. Therefore, there are many people who dine out or have a get-together at lunchtime in a group such as at work or school.

Of course, there are quite a few people who 혼식 (eating alone) due to the increasing number of single-person households these days. It is not uncommon for a restaurant to install a partition on the dining table for those who dine alone so that they can eat without worrying about the people next to them. Ironically, however, this partition installation more clearly reveals the psychology of Koreans who are uncomfortable eating alone.

Because of the eating culture of Korean people, you can discover some interesting facts when you go to a Korean restaurant. First, if you go to a Korean restaurant, there are side dishes that are provided free of charge. Traditionally, Korean food consists of rice and soup with side dishes around the main dish such as stew or broth. In fact, most Korean restaurant menus only list the main dishes. Moreover, even if you order additional side dishes from the owner after eating all the side dishes during a meal, most restaurants do not charge for refills.

In addition on the menu of Korean restaurants, meats such as bulgogi, ribs, and pork belly, or stews such as hotpot, are often sold in portions that can be eaten with other people, not for one person. In many cases, rather than a single portion, the amount of food is written on the menu of a restaurant as 대 (large), 중 (medium), 소 (small). If you are not familiar with Korean food, it is also a good idea to check how many servings there are when ordering at a Korean restaurant.

Chapter 3

Making appointments with friends in Korea

샘 브라운 (영국)
Sam Brown (United Kingdom)

Chapter 3

Making appointments with friends in Korea

Over the telephone

Making an appointment by phone

우리 같이 영화 볼까요?

Do you want to see a movie together?

Sam

Yujin

샘	여보세요. 유진 씨, 저 샘이에요.	Sam	Hello. Yujin, this is Sam.
유진	안녕하세요.	Yujin	Hi.
샘	내일 시간 있어요?	Sam	Do you have time tomorrow?
유진	네, 있어요. 왜요?	Yujin	Yes, I have time. Why?
샘	우리 같이 영화 볼까요?	Sam	Do you want to see a movie together?
유진	좋아요. 같이 영화 봐요! 몇 시요?	Yujin	Sounds good. Let's watch a movie together! What time?
샘	3시쯤 어때요?	Sam	How about 3 o'clock?
유진	그래요. 그럼 내일 봐요.	Yujin	OK. See you tomorrow, then.
샘	내일 만나요.	Sam	See you tomorrow.

▶ New Vocabulary

씨 Mr., Mrs., Ms., Miss

내일 tomorrow

시간 time

왜 why

우리 we, our, us

같이 together

영화 movie

좋다 to be good, fine

몇 시 what time

쯤 around

만나다 to meet

여보세요. Hello

▶ New Expressions

좋아요. Sounds good.

3시쯤 어때요? How about 3 o'clock?

그래요. OK.

내일 봐요. See you tomorrow.

내일 만나요. See you tomorrow.
(lit. I'll meet you tomorrow.)

▶ Close-Up

❶ 저 (이름)예요/이에요
(Identifying yourself by phone)

When you meet someone in person and introduce yourself, you say, 저는 (이름)예요/이에요. However, when the caller identifies himself, he does not say 저는 and omits the 는, so he only refers to himself as 저 and says his name. It is natural to speak in such a way.

(Ex.) A 여보세요. Hello?

B 안녕하세요. 저 민수예요. Hello. I am Minsoo.

❷ 우리 같이 -아/어요! and 어때요?
(Suggesting a plan to do it together)

우리 같이 is a commonly used expression in daily life. For example, when Koreans propose to eat together, they say, 우리 같이 밥 먹어요 (Let's have a meal together). Alternatively, you can say 어때요 (How about…) to ask the other person. When the suggestion is a noun, write 어때요 after the noun, and when it is a verb, add –는 게 어때요 to the stem of the verb.

(Ex.) A 우리 같이 점심 먹어요! Let's have lunch together!

B 그래요. 비빔밥 어때요? Sure. How about bibimbap?

(Ex.) A 좋아요. 우리 집에서 먹는 게 어때요? Sounds good. How about eating at my house?

B 네, 좋아요. Yes. Sounds good.

Flashback

• Reading the time

When reading the time in Korean, hours are read using native Korean numbers, while minutes are read using Sino-Korean numbers.

3시	10분
세	십
native Korean number	Sino-Korean number

2시
두

6시
여섯

10시
열

1시 10분
한　십

4시 45분
네 사십오

7시 30분
일곱 삼십

= 반 (half hour)

Grammar in Focus

Grammar Chart **p.271**

-(으)ㄹ까요? Shall we...?

-(으)ㄹ까요 is used with a verb to suggest doing something together with someone. If the verb stem ends in a vowel, -ㄹ까요 is used, and if the verb stem ends in a consonant, -을까요 is used. It is often used with the adverb 같이 (together). Since there is a question mark, raise the intonation slightly at end of the sentence when saying -(으)ㄹ까요. Let's check the following examples to see how you can answer such propositions.

보다	A 같이 영화 볼까요?	Shall we go see a movie together?
	B 좋아요. 같이 영화 봐요.	OK. Let's see a movie together.
	미안해요. 시간이 없어요.	I'm sorry. I don't have time.

먹다	A 같이 점심 먹을까요?	Shall we have lunch together?
	B 좋아요. 같이 점심 먹어요.	OK. Let's have lunch.
	미안해요. 다른 약속이 있어요.	I'm sorry, I have another appointment.

You can use -(으)ㄹ까요 and 어때요 to suggest and coordinate alternative opinions as follows.

만나다	A 몇 시에 만날까요?	What time shall we meet?
	B 3시 어때요?	How's 3 o'clock?
	A 좋아요. 3시에 만나요.	Sounds good, let's meet at 3 o'clock.

★ 걷다	A 좀 걸을까요?	Shall we walk?
	B 좋아요. 공원에 갈까요?	Sounds good. Shall we go to the park?
	A 그럽시다.	Let's do that.

Quiz Yourself !

1~3 Complete the conversation by using –(으)ㄹ까요.

Ex. A 내일 같이 <u>식사할까요</u> ?

　　B 좋아요. 같이 식사해요.

1.　A 주말에 같이 영화를 _____?

　　B 좋아요. 같이 영화를 봐요.

2.　A 이따가 같이 커피를 _____?

　　B 미안해요. 오늘 일이 많아요.

　　　그래서 같이 커피를 마실 수 없어요.

3.　A 일요일에 같이 점심을 _____?

　　B 미안해요. 다른 약속이 있어요.

　　　그래서 같이 점심을 먹을 수 없어요.

4　Rearrange the conversation sentences.

ㄱ 어디에서 볼까요?

ㄴ 네, 시간 괜찮아요.

ㄷ 지하철역에서 만나요.

ㄹ 좋아요. 같이 식사해요.

ㅁ 이번 주 토요일 12시에 시간 있어요?

ㅂ 네, 좋아요. 그럼, 그때 만나요.

ㅅ 그럼, 같이 식사할까요?

ㅁ → □ → □ → □ → □ → □ → □

Answer **p.278**

Grammar Rehearsal

track 084

우리 같이 -(으)ㄹ까요?   Making a proposal to another person

우리 같이 산책할까요?   Shall we **take a walk** together?

➡ 좋아요. 같이 산책해요!   ➡ Sounds good. Let's go for a walk together!

우리 같이 밥 먹을까요?   Shall we **eat** together?

➡ 그래요. 같이 밥 먹어요!   ➡ OK. Let's eat together!

우리 같이 커피 마실까요?   Shall we **drink coffee** together?

➡ 그래요. 같이 커피 마셔요!   ➡ OK. Let's drink coffee together!

제가 -(으)ㄹ까요?   Asking another person's opinion

제가 밥을 살까요?   Shall I buy the meal?

제가 먼저 말할까요?   Shall I tell you first?

제가 표를 예매할까요?   Shall I book a ticket?

제가 친구들한테 연락할까요?   Shall I contact my friends?

Additional Vocabulary

• **Vocabulary related to appointments**

날짜 date

시간 time

장소 place

약속하다 to make an appointment, promise

취소하다 to cancel

예약하다 to make a reservation

예매하다 to buy a ticket in advance

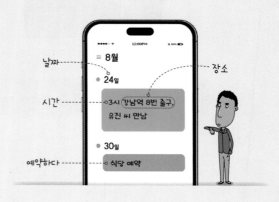

Conversation Rehearsal

track 085

(Noun) 괜찮아요? Asking another person's opinion

3시 괜찮아요?	Are you all right with 3 o'clock?
토요일 괜찮아요?	Are you all right with Saturday?
한국 음식 괜찮아요?	Are you all right with Korean food?
액션 영화 괜찮아요?	Are you all right with an action movie?

A 말고 B은/는 어때요? Presenting something else to another person

3시 말고 4시는 어때요?	How about 4 o'clock instead of 3 o'clock?
토요일 말고 일요일은 어때요?	How about Sunday instead of Saturday?
한국 음식 말고 중국 음식은 어때요?	How about Chinese food instead of Korean food?
액션 영화 말고 코미디 영화는 어때요?	How about a comedy movie instead of an action movie?

Pronunciation Tip

track 086

같이 [가치]

When the final consonant ㄷ, ㅌ is followed by the vowel ㅣ, the sound of ㄷ, ㅌ is changed to [ㅈ, ㅊ] respectively and moves to become the initial consonant of the next syllable. In the above example, the ㅌ of 같 is changed to [ㅊ] before 이 and is pronounced as [가치] since it becomes the initial consonant of the next syllable.

예 해돋이 [해도지] 밭이 [바치]

Coffee Break

Confirming an appointment

When making an appointment over the phone, you often need to confirm the time, location, and related numbers. At this time, say what you want to double-check by asking 맞아요?. Or, say 확인할게요 (I'll just confirm that) to indicate that you want to check first and then repeat the information to the listener. These phrases will reduce misunderstandings when making appointments.

Korean popular culture

Korean popular culture such as K-pop, K-dramas, and K-movies in Korea is loved by many people around the world. The Korean wave, which started in Asia in the early 2000s, has spread internationally.

First, K-pop has emerged as the most loved field in the world. BTS, a representative Korean singer group, even reached number one on the US Billboard Singles Chart. What is even more fascinating is that the K-pop songs sung by people around the world are Korean. K-pop is so popular that even foreigners who do not know Korean sing along to the lyrics in Korean. What is the enduring appeal of K-pop? Above all, Korean agencies play a big role in forming the best team to produce good music, making songs, and systematically training singers. In addition, the perfect group dance choreography and dynamic dancing skills of Korean idol singers, which can be said to be the trademarks of Korean K-pop, can be cited. This is possible because teenage boys and girls selected as trainees through fierce competition at a Korean agency devote their childhood practicing dance and song. It can be said that the fandom was formed thanks to their passion, persistence, and ability to pursue their dreams.

The Korean wave has blossomed from K-dramas and K-movies. Korean dramas, the protagonists of the Korean Wave in the early 2000s, are so popular that they dominate the top 10 list on Netflix Asia's charts, accounting for 60–70% of popularity. Korean dramas have secured a diverse fan base as the subject matter of Korean dramas has expanded  with various themes and the popularity of dramas has increased the recognition of Korean actors. Recently, dramas adapted from popular webtoons are gaining popularity. In addition, Korean films are attracting attention as the director directly participates in the screenplay, directs the work in his own colors, and unfolds a distinct world of his/her own. Director Park Chan-wook, famous for <올드보이>, director Hong Sang-soo adored by the Cannes Film Festival, director Lee Chang-dong renowned for his literary films, and director Bong Joon-ho for <기생충>, which won Best Picture, Screenplay, and Best Film at the 2020 Academy Awards, are notable examples. Korean films that create their own unique cinematography are loved by many.

On a video call

Inviting a friend

내일 친구들하고 영화를 보려고 해요.

I'm going to see a movie with my friends tomorrow.

Sam

Mei

Conversation

메이	여보세요.
샘	안녕하세요. 메이 씨, 지금 통화할 수 있어요?
메이	네, 괜찮아요.
샘	내일 친구들하고 영화를 보려고 해요. 같이 영화 봐요!
메이	좋아요. 그런데 무슨 영화를 볼 거예요?
샘	아직 안 정했어요.
메이	알겠어요. 내일 얘기해요!
샘	그럼, 내일 만나요. 끊을게요.

Mei	Hello.
Sam	Hello. Mei, are you available to talk now?
Mei	Yes, I'm good.
Sam	I'm going to see a movie with my friends tomorrow. Let's watch a movie together!
Mei	Sounds good. But which kind of movie are you going to watch?
Sam	We haven't decided yet.
Mei	Alright. Let's talk about it tomorrow!
Sam	See you tomorrow, then. Bye. (lit. I'm hanging up.)

통화하다 to talk over the telephone

괜찮다 okay, alright, good

친구 friend

들 plural marker

그런데 but, however

무슨 which

정하다 to decide, determine

얘기하다 to say, tell, speak

끊다 to hang up

New Expressions

지금 통화할 수 있어요?
Are you available to talk now?

괜찮아요.
I'm good.

아직 안 정했어요.
We haven't decided yet.

내일 얘기해요!
Let's talk about it tomorrow!

끊을게요.
Bye. (lit. I'm hanging up.)

Close-Up

❶ The marker 하고
(Expressing company)

The particle marker 하고 indicates doing something together with someone. Although the form is the same, the 하고 (with) learned in this Scene has a different meaning from the 하고 (and) learned in Scene 5. Add 하고 to the end of a noun that indicates something is with you. 하고 is used whether the noun ends in a vowel or a consonant. 하고 can be used interchangeably with the 와/과 used in written and formal forms, and (이)랑 in colloquial and informal forms.

Ex. 매일 친구하고 밥을 먹어요.
I eat with my friends every day.

Ex. 다음 주에 가족하고 여행할 거예요.
I'm going to travel with my family next week.

❷ 무슨
(Asking which one?)

무슨 is used before a noun to ask about the noun it modifies. It is mainly used for questions about the type of noun. In this conversation, to ask about the genre of the movie (comedy, action, romance, etc.), 무슨 영화 is asked. If you use the interrogative word 어느 to ask 어느 영화, it can imply choosing one of two or more movies.

Ex. A 무슨 음식을 좋아해요? Which food do you like?

B 저는 한국 음식을 좋아해요. I like Korean food.

Ex. A 어느 음식을 드시겠어요?
Which food would you like to eat?

B 저는 비빔밥을 먹을게요. I will eat bibimbap.

Flashback

• Vocabulary related to places

OO관 refers to a large building	OO장 refers to a type of place	OO실 refers to a type of room
영화관 movie theater	운동장 sports grounds	교실 classroom
미술관 art gallery	수영장 the pool	사무실 office
박물관 museum	행사장 event hall	휴게실 lounge

Grammar Chart **p.271**

-(으)려고 하다 be going to...

-(으)려고 하다 is used with a verb to indicate that the subject of a sentence intends to or has a will to do something. It is mainly used when describing the plan of one's will or the speaker's intention. Add -려고 하다 to the end of the verb stems ending in a vowel and -으려고 하다 to the end of a verb stem that ends in a consonant.

| 쉬다 | 이번 주말에 저는 집에서 쉬려고 해요. | This weekend I intend to rest at home. |

| 찾다 | 유진 씨는 졸업 후 일을 찾으려고 해요. | Yujin intends to find work after graduating. |

| 시작하다 | A 마크 씨, 한국어 공부가 끝나면 뭐 하려고 해요? |
Mark, what do you plan to do after you complete studying Korean?
B 저는 한국에서 일을 시작하려고 해요. I intend to start working in Korea.

| 피우다 | 이제부터 담배를 피우지 않으려고 해요. | I intend to stop smoking from now on. |

| ★ 걷다 | 건강을 위해서 매일 30분씩 걸으려고 해요.
I intend to walk for 30 minutes every day for my health.

| ★ 살다 | 저는 이 집에서 계속 살려고 해요. | I intend to continue living in this house. |

In order to express an intention of the past, the past tense marker -았/었- is combined with the 하다 of -(으)려고 하다 as -(으)려고 했다.

| 말하다 | 어제 말하려고 했어요. 그런데 말 못 했어요.
I was going to tell you yesterday. But I couldn't speak.

| 배우다 | 전에 수잔 씨가 한국 요리를 배우려고 했어요. 그런데 시간이 없어서 못 했어요.
Before, Susan intended to learn Korean cooking. But she couldn't because she didn't have time.

> **! Be careful!**
>
> While -(으)ㄹ 거예요 describes the subject's schedule objectively, -(으)려고 하다 describes the plan according to the subject's intent. If the subject of the sentence is not a person, -(으)ㄹ 거예요 is interpreted as a description of the schedule. However, in the case of -(으)려고 하다, it cannot be interpreted as the subject's intent and is interpreted instead as something that is going to occur.
>
> (Ex) 저는 이번 주말에 여행 갈 거예요. I am going on a trip this weekend.
> 저는 이번 주말에 여행 가려고 해요. I intend to go on a trip this weekend.
>
> (Ex) 곧 졸업식이 시작할 거예요. The graduation ceremony will start soon.
> 곧 졸업식이 시작하려고 해요. The graduation ceremony is going to start soon.

Quiz Yourself !

1~5 Complete the sentence by choosing the correct answer.

1. 이번 달에 돈을 너무 많이 썼어요. 그래서 앞으로 돈을 많이 ① 쓰려고 해요.

    ② 쓰지 않으려고 해요.

2. 매일 늦게 일어나서 늦어요. 내일부터 일찍 자고 일찍 ① 일어나려고 해요.

    ② 일어나지 않으려고 해요.

3. 담배를 피워서 건강이 나빠졌어요. 이제부터 담배를 ① 피우려고 해요.

    ② 피우지 않으려고 해요.

4. 이제부터 책을 ① 읽으려고 해요. 그래서 오늘 서점에서 책을 많이 샀어요.

    ② 읽지 않으려고 해요.

5. 어제 한국 음식을 ① 만들려고 해요. 그런데 시간이 없어서 못 만들었어요.

    ② 만들려고 했어요.

6~9 Complete the conversation by using -(으)려고 하다.

6. A 수업 후에 뭐 할 거예요?
    B 친구하고 밥을 _____.
    　　　　　　　　(먹다)

7. A 휴가 때 뭐 할 거예요?
    B 혼자 제주도에 여행 _____.
    　　　　　　　　　　(가다)

8. A 이번 주말에 뭐 하려고 해요?
    B 그냥 집에 _____.
    　　　　　　(있다)

9. A 앞으로 어떻게 말하기를 연습하려고 해요?
    B 한국 친구를 _____.
    　　　　　　　(찾다)

Answer p.278

Grammar Rehearsal

(time)부터 -(으)려고 해요   Talking about your plans

오늘부터 다이어트하려고 해요. I'm going to start dieting from today.

오늘부터 게임을 안 하려고 해요. I'm not going to play games starting from today.

내일부터 운동을 시작하려고 해요. I'm going to start exercising from tomorrow.

내일부터 영어로 말하지 않으려고 해요. I'm going to try not speak English from tomorrow.

-(으)ㄹ 거예요?   Asking about another person's plans

어떻게 집에 갈 거예요? How are you going home?

이번 주말에 뭐 할 거예요? What are you going to do this weekend?

어디에서 친구를 만날 거예요? Where will you meet your friends?

언제 한국어 공부를 시작할 거예요? When will you start studying Korean?

Additional Vocabulary

• **Vocabulary related to calling on the phone**

전화를 걸다 to make a call

전화를 받다 to pick up (the phone)

통화하다 to talk over the telephone

전화를 끊다 to hang up (the phone)

문자 메시지를 보내다 to send a text (message)

문자 메시지를 받다 to receive a text (message)

영상 통화하다 to make a video call

영상 통화하다

전화를 걸다

Conversation Rehearsal

-(으)면 어때요? Making a proposal to another person

좀 걸으면 어때요?

How about a walk?

같이 식사하면 어때요?

How about eating together?

내일 일찍 만나면 어때요?

How about meeting early tomorrow?

다른 친구도 부르면 어때요?

How about calling another friend too?

-아/어 줘서 고마워요 Expressing thanks

전화해 줘서 고마워요.

Thanks for your call.

걱정해 줘서 고마워요.

Thanks for your concern.

얘기 들어 줘서 고마워요.

Thanks for listening to me.

그렇게 말해 줘서 고마워요.

Thanks for saying that.

Pronunciation Tip

괜찮아요 [괜차나요]

track 090

When an ending that starts with a vowel comes after the double consonant ㄶ or ㅀ, the sound of the second final consonant ㅎ of ㄶ, ㅀ is dropped. Thus, the first consonant ㄴ, ㄹ of the double final consonant ㄶ or ㅀ moves to the initial consonant of the next syllable and is pronounced respectively. In the above example, 괜찮아요, the ㅎ of ㄶ in 찮 is dropped and the ㄴ moves to the initial sound of the last syllable in the next syllable and is pronounced as [괜차나요].

예 끊어요 [끄너요] 앓아요 [아라요]

Coffee Break

How to say goodbye when ending a phone call

Say 안녕히 계세요 when you hang up on the phone with someone of the same age who you are in a more formal relationship with (for example, a business partner). When you hang up the phone with someone who is of similar age or someone you have a close relationship with (for example, a school friend), say 끊을게요 or 끊어요 to give a sense of closeness and friendliness. If you hang up the phone with the person you need to talk to (for example, a boss, friend's parents, etc.) in the most polite way possible, say 들어가세요.

Special foods on special occasions

There are traditional foods to eat during the Korean holidays. Rice cake soup is consumed on New Year's Day and *songpyeon* on *Chuseok*. In addition to these holiday foods, there are foods that come to mind at specific moments of our daily life.

Seaweed soup on birthdays

In Korea, you always eat seaweed soup on your birthday. Older adults often ask young people on their birthdays, "Have you eaten seaweed soup?". Seaweed soup is rich in nutrients and eaten by mothers after childbirth. This custom is said to have originated in the past when seaweed soup was placed on the table to pray for a baby.

Korean taffy or sticky rice cake before an examination

Koreans give taffy or sticky rice cakes with a strong "sticky" feeling to those who hope to "pass" an exam. Eating taffy or sticky rice cake is like giving a present of good luck. It's easy to find taffy and sticky rice cakes sold here and there in the city ahead of Korea's national university entrance exam in mid-November. It is worth noting that Koreans do not eat seaweed soup before a major test. The "slippery" feeling of seaweed soup is reminiscent of slipping and failing to pass a test.

Pajeon and *makgeolli* on a rainy day

Many Koreans think of makgeolli and pajeon on a rainy day. Some explain that high-calorie foods raise the body temperature on a rainy day, while others say that it is because hearing rain reminds them of the sound of frying *pajeon* in oil. For whatever reason, there are many restaurants that sell *pajeon* on rainy days. *Makgeolli* is an alcoholic rice drink that goes well with *pajeon*. Of course, you can drink beer or soju with *pajeon*, but on a rainy day, the tradition of eating *pajeon* with *makgeolli* is iconic.

At the meeting place

Changing the meeting place

사람이 많아서 유진 씨가 안 보여요.

I can't see you, Yujin, because there are too many people here.

Sam

Yujin

샘	여보세요. 유진 씨, 지금 어디에 있어요?
유진	저는 홍대입구역에 있어요.
샘	몇 번 출구에 있어요?
유진	9번 출구에 있어요.
샘	그런데 여기에 사람이 많아서 유진 씨가 안 보여요.
유진	그래요? 그럼, 역 근처 공원 알아요?
샘	네, 알아요.
유진	그럼, 거기에서 봐요.
샘	알겠어요. 지금 갈게요.

Sam	Hello. Yujin, where are you now?
Yujin	I'm at Hongik University Station.
Sam	Which number exit are you at?
Yujin	I am at exit number 9.
Sam	I can't see you, Yujin, because there are too many people here.
Yujin	Really? Then do you know the park near the station?
Sam	Yes, I know it.
Yujin	Then let's meet there.
Sam	OK, I'll go there now.

▶ New Vocabulary

어디에   where

홍대입구역   Hongik University Station

출구   exit

사람   people

많다   to be a lot

역   station

근처   near (in the vicinity of)

공원   park

알다   to know

거기   there

▶ New Expressions

지금 어디에 있어요?
Where are you now?

몇 번 출구에 있어요?
Which number exit are you at?

… 알아요? Do you know…?

거기에서 봐요.
Let's meet there.

지금 갈게요.
I'll go there now.

▶ Close-Up

❶ 여기/거기/저기
(Here/there/over there)

여기 refers to a place close to the speaker, and 저기 refers to a place away from both the speaker and the listener. 거기 refers to a place far from the speaker but close to the listener. Also, 거기 refers to a place referred to in the conversation which cannot be seen at the moment from the view of the person you are conversing with.

(Ex.) 여기에 핸드폰이 있어요. There is a phone here.

(Ex.) 부산에 갔어요. 거기 날씨가 좋았어요.
I went to Busan. The weather there was nice.

(Ex.) 시계가 저기에 있어요.   There is a watch over there.

❷ 역 근처 공원
(From large units to small units)

Unlike in English, in Korean, when referring to a specific place or time, units are written from large to small units. In this conversation, 역 근처 공원 refers to a large area near the station, specifically the park in the middle. In fact, even when writing addresses in Korea, they are written from large to small units. Time is also described from large to small units. For example, when making an appointment, say the date first, like "the 10th at 3 pm", then the time zone and the specific time.

(Ex.) 다음 주 화요일 오후 6시에 학교 근처 카페에서 만나요.
See you next Tuesday at 6 pm at the cafe near the school.

Flashback

• Frequently used conjunctions

그리고 And	날씨가 좋아요. 그리고 사람들이 친절해요 The weather is nice. And the people are friendly.
그런데, 하지만 But	한국어 공부가 재미있어요. 그런데 좀 어려워요. Studying Korean is fun. But it's a little difficult.
그래도 Even so	많이 먹었어요. 그래도 배가 고파요. I ate a lot. Even so, I'm still hungry.
그래서 So, therefore	배가 아파요. 그래서 병원에 가요. My stomach hurts. So, therefore I'm going to the hospital.
그러니까 So, therefore	비가 와요. 그러니까 우산을 가지고 가세요. It's raining. So bring an umbrella.
그러면 (= 그럼) Then	한국어를 잘하고 싶어요? 그러면 한국 친구하고 많이 얘기하세요. Do you want to speak Korean well? Then speak a lot with your Korean friends.
왜냐하면 Because	오후에 시간이 없어요. 왜냐하면 오후에 아르바이트해요. I don't have time in the afternoon. Because I work part-time in the afternoon.

Grammar in Focus

Grammar Chart **p.271**

–아/어서 because

–아/어서 is used to indicate the cause or reason for something. –아/어서 is a grammar form that connects two sentences indicating cause/reason and effect into one sentence with the connecting adverb 그래서. In Korean, unlike in English, the clause indicating the reason for the combination of –아/어서 is always written before the result. –아/어서 is combined with verbs and adjectives. The verb 하다 is used as 해서. –아서 is used when the stem ends with a vowel ㅏ or ㅗ and –어서 is used with all other stem endings.

| 유명하다 | 김치가 유명해서 김치를 살 거예요. Since kimchi is famous, I will buy kimchi. |

유명하다　김치가 유명해서 김치를 살 거예요. Since kimchi is famous, I will buy kimchi.

바쁘다　요즘 일이 바빠서 시간이 없어요.
I don't have time because I'm busy at work nowadays.

있다　한국 친구가 있어서 한국어를 배워요.
I am learning the Korean language because I have a Korean friend.

가다　다음 주에 여행 가서 여행 가방을 사요.
I'm buying a travel bag because I'm traveling next week.

만나다　친구를 만나서 기분이 너무 좋아요.
I'm in a good mood because I'm going to meet my friend.

★덥다　날씨가 더워서 힘이 없어요. Because of the hot weather, I'm exhausted.

Even though the cause or reason lies in the past, verbs or adjectives in the past tense cannot be used with –아/어서. The present tense verb or adjective form should be used with –아/어서 regardless of whether the sentence is in the past tense or the present tense.

아프다　어제 아파서 친구를 만날 수 없었어요. (O)
Yesterday I was sick and could not see my friend.

　　　　　어제 아팠어서 친구를 만날 수 없었어요. (X)

> (!) **Be careful!**
> –아/어서 cannot be used when making a command with –(으)세요 and when proposing an action with –(으)ㅂ시다. Therefore, when talking about the reasons for the command and the proposition, use –(으)니까 instead of –아/어서.
> (Ex) 날씨가 좋아서 산책합시다. (X)
> 날씨가 좋으니까 산책합시다. (O) The weather is nice, so let's go for a walk.

Quiz Yourself !

1~4 Connect the first half and second half of the sentence with –아/어서.

Ex. 친구가 <u>바빠요</u>. 그래서 시간이 없어요.

→ **바빠서**

1. 한국 사람이 <u>친절해요</u>. 그래서 저를 많이 도와줬어요.

→

2. 한국어를 잘 <u>몰라요</u>. 그래서 길을 잃어버렸어요.

→

3. 어제 배가 <u>아팠어요</u>. 그래서 병원에 갔어요.

→

4. 아까 많이 <u>먹었어요</u>. 그래서 지금 배가 불러요.

→

5~7 Complete the conversation by using –아/어서.

Ex. A 왜 피곤해요?

B **일이 많아서** 피곤해요.
(일이 많다)

5. A 왜 일찍 자요?

B _____ 일찍 자요.
(내일 아침에 약속이 있다)

6. A 왜 한국어를 공부해요?

B _____ 공부해요.
(한국 사람하고 말하고 싶다)

7. A 왜 어제 전화를 안 받았어요?

B _____ 전화 못 받았어요.
(핸드폰이 고장 나다)

Answer **p.278**

Grammar Rehearsal

track **092**

-아/어서 -(으)ㄹ 수 없어요   Making excuses

바빠서 만날 수 없어요.	I can't meet you because I'm busy.
피곤해서 운동할 수 없어요.	I can't exercise because I'm tired.
시간이 없어서 만날 수 없어요.	I can't meet you because I don't have time.
돈이 없어서 옷을 살 수 없어요.	I can't buy clothes because I don't have money.

-아/어서 안 돼요   Making a negative comment

비싸서 안 돼요.	I can't buy it because it's expensive.
머리가 아파서 안 돼요.	I can't because my head hurts.
시간이 없어서 안 돼요.	I can't meet you because I don't have time.
날씨가 나빠서 안 돼요.	I can't go because the weather is bad.

Additional Vocabulary

• **Work as an excuse**
바빠요. I am busy.
일이 많아요. I have a lot of work.
시간이 없어요. I don't have time.

• **Health as an excuse**
머리가 아파요. I have a headache.
몸이 안 좋아요. I'm not feeling well.
감기에 걸렸어요. I caught a cold.

• **Transportation as an excuse**
길이 막혀요. The road is blocked.
교통이 복잡해요. There is heavy traffic.
길에 차가 많아요. There are many vehicles on the road.

Conversation Rehearsal

track 093

(place) 어디에 … ? Asking for a specific location

학교 어디에 있어요?

➡ 학교 정문 앞에 있어요.

Where at school are you?

➡ I'm at the main entrance of the school.

지하철역 어디에 있어요?

➡ 지하철역 2번 출구에 있어요.

Where at the subway station are you?

➡ I'm at exit 2 of the subway station.

서울 어디에 살아요?

➡ 서울 강남에 살아요.

Where in Seoul do you live?

➡ I live in Gangnam, Seoul.

(situation) 제가 다시 전화할게요 Hanging up the phone

다른 전화가 와요. 제가 다시 전화할게요.

There is another incoming call. I'll call you back.

배터리가 다 됐어요. 제가 다시 전화할게요.

The battery is about to die. I'll call you back.

소리가 잘 안 들려요. 제가 다시 전화할게요.

I can't hear well. I'll call you back.

이제 끊어야겠어요. 제가 다시 전화할게요.

I have to hang up now. I'll call you back.

Pronunciation Tip

track 094

영화 [영화]

When consonants ㄴ, ㅇ, ㄹ, ㅁ are connected with ㅎ, the ㅎ is pronounced weakly. In the above example, the ㅎ following the consonant ㅇ of 영 is weakened and pronounced as [영화], but it is actually heard as [영와] because ㅎ is weakened to the extent that it is hardly audible.

예 전화 [전화]　운동화 [운동화]

☕ Coffee Break

When you can't hear well on the phone

If you can't hear the other person well while talking on the phone, say 잘 안 들려요. The other person will speak in a louder voice. Of course, you can also directly ask the other person to speak more loudly by saying 더 크게 말해 주세요. Alternatively, you can simply say 네? as an indirect way of asking the other person to repeat themself.

Street food in Korea

Foreigners are shocked when they come to Seoul as the prices of goods are higher than they thought. In particular, the price of coffee, which is higher than the price of rice at a restaurant is a notable example. However, Korean food is not limited to expensive Korean cuisine, so-called *hanjeongsik*, which provides pleasure to both the tastebuds and visuals, but also a variety of street food stalls.

Tteokbokki

Tteokbokki is one of Korea's representative street foods as it is a food people enjoy casually at street food stalls and cheap eateries. It is a dish made by boiling red pepper paste in water, cutting rice cakes into easy-to-bite pieces, and simmering them with various vegetables. It is also very easy to make. *Tteokbokki* is a popular dish enjoyed for its spicy taste among students in the 10s-20s range, young women, and young people alike. What is interesting is that *tteokbokki*, the common food for anyone, was once considered a royal food that was listed on the King's royal table in the past. It is said that in the past, royal *tteokbokki* used soy sauce instead of red pepper paste, so the color of the food was not red, and the ingredients were not in the form of rice cakes and vegetables, but in the form of a hotpot with finely chopped meat and mushrooms.

Bungeoppang

Bungeoppang is a snack that can be easily seen on the street when the cold wind starts to blow. It is made by kneading flour thinly, putting the batter in a mold with the same shape on both sides, and placing red bean paste in the middle and baking it. People call it *bungeoppang* because the baking frame is shaped like and looks like a carp when it finishes baking.

baking. Koreans enjoy eating *bungeoppang* in cold weather because it is crispy on the outside and hot red beans are found inside. Because the frame of *bungeoppang* is made with the same frame on the left and right, Koreans sometimes refer to "father-son" who resemble each other as "*bungeoppang*".

At a café

Ordering coffee

죄송합니다.
지금 빵이 없습니다.

Sorry. There is no bread right now.

Café

Sam

a café employee

Conversation

직원	어서 오세요.
샘	아이스 커피 한 잔하고 딸기 주스 두 잔 주세요.
직원	알겠습니다. 또 필요한 거 없으세요?
샘	그리고 빵도 세 개 주세요.
직원	죄송합니다. 지금 빵이 없습니다.
샘	그래요? 그럼, 커피하고 주스만 주세요.
직원	네, 전부 15,000원입니다.
샘	여기 있어요.

Employee	Come in.
Sam	I would like one ice coffee and two strawberry juices, please.
Employee	Alright. Is there anything else you need?
Sam	Three slices of bread too, please.
Employee	Sorry. There is no bread right now.
Sam	Really? Then, just the coffee and juice, please.
Employee	Alright, the total is 15,000 won.
Sam	Here you go.

▶ New Vocabulary

커피 coffee

아이스 커피 ice coffee

잔 cup

딸기 strawberry

주스 juice

또 as well, too, also

필요하다 to be needed, necessary

거 thing

그리고 also, and

빵 bread

도 also, too

개 counter word for general things

만 only

전부 all

원 won

▶ New Expressions

또 필요한 거 없으세요?
Is there anything else you need?

그리고 빵도 세 개 주세요.
Three slices of bread too, please.

커피하고 주스만 주세요.
Just the coffee and juice, please.

전부 15,000원입니다.
The total is 15,000 won.

▶ Close-Up

❶ 하고 and 그리고
(Adding)

Both 하고 and 그리고 have meanings that correspond to the English "and", but the conjugation conditions of 하고 and 그리고 differ. When connecting more than two nouns, add 하고 to the end of the first noun. When connecting sentences, add 그리고 to the end of the first sentence after the punctuation mark.

> (Ex.) 저는 불고기하고 김치를 좋아해요.
> I like bulgogi and kimchi.

> (Ex.) 비빔밥이 싸요. 그리고 맛있어요.
> Bibimbap is cheap. And, it's delicious.

❷ Markers 도 and 만
(Expressing "more" and "only")

The markers 만 and 도 add special meaning and emphasis to the noun. The marker 도 means "also, too". The marker 만 means "only, just". When the markers 도 and 만 are combined with subject marker 이/가 or the object marker 을/를, the subject marker and object marker are omitted and only the marker 도 and 만 are used. However, when 도 and 만 are combined with markers that are not the subject and object markers, the other markers are neither dropped nor omitted.

> (Ex.) 아침을 안 먹었어요. 점심도 안 먹었어요.
> I didn't eat breakfast. I didn't even eat lunch.

> (Ex.) 제가 고기하고 채소를 좋아해요. 그런데 생선만 안 좋아해요.
> I like meat and vegetables. But I only don't like fish.

Flashback

• Counting words

When counting things, native Korean numbers are used with a special counting word. The counting word changes depending on the noun that is being counted. Unlike English, you put the noun first, then a native Korean number, followed by an appropriate counting word. For example, 모자 한 개 (for one hat) and 사람 두 명 (for two people).

one	한 개	한 명	한 분	한 잔	한 권	한 장
two	두 개	두 명	두 분	두 잔	두 권	두 장
three	세 개	세 명	세 분	세 잔	세 권	세 장
many	여러 개	여러 명	여러 분	여러 잔	여러 권	여러 장

Grammar in Focus

Grammar Chart **p.272**

The formal form -(스)ㅂ니다

In Korean, changing the nuance of a sentence and showing the appropriate formality is done by changing the sentence endings. The ending form -(스)ㅂ니다 has a formal and official sound to it, but it is used to treat others more formally. For example, it is often used when dealing with a person in a business relationship, when speaking to your boss at work, or when public speaking. You've probably heard of -(스)ㅂ니다 from employees in uniforms at the department store or flight attendants during a flight. The formal form -(스)ㅂ니다 is different from the ending form -아/어요. -아/어요 is mostly used in casual or friendly situations like conversations with juniors or seniors at school or local shopkeepers. The formal form -(스)ㅂ니다 is used with verbs and adjectives. When the stem of a verb or an adjective ends in a vowel, -ㅂ니다 is used, and when the stem of an adjective ends in a consonant, -습니다 is used.

하다	이제 회의가 시작합니다.	The meeting will begin now.
춥다	요즘 날씨가 춥습니다.	The weather is cold nowadays.
이다	저는 미국 사람입니다.	I'm American.

To make the past tense pattern, combine -았/었- with -(스)ㅂ니다 to the end of a verb or adjective stem.

일하다	어제 아침부터 일했습니다.	I've been working since yesterday morning.
찾다	조금 전에 동료가 서류를 찾았습니다.	

A colleague found the documents a little while ago.

When asking a question using the formal form, add -(스)ㅂ니까 to the end of a verb or adjective stem instead of -(스)ㅂ니다.

어떻다	A 회사 생활이 어떻습니까?	How is your work life?
재미있다	B 재미있습니다.	It is enjoyable.
끝나다	A 회의가 언제 끝났습니까?	When did the meeting end?
	B 조금 전에 끝났습니다.	It ended a little while ago.

Quiz Yourself!

1~5 Change the underlined part into the formal form –(스)ㅂ니다, as shown in the example.

Ex. 저는 한국 영화를 정말 <u>좋아해요</u>. → **좋아합니다**

1. 그래서 주말에 친구하고 영화를 <u>봐요</u>. →

2. 영화가 끝나면 같이 점심을 <u>먹어요</u>. →

3. 가끔 커피도 <u>마셔요</u>. →

4. 지난주에도 영화를 <u>봤어요</u>. →

5. 정말 <u>재미있었어요</u>. →

6~8 Complete the conversation by using –(스)ㅂ니다.

Ex. A 이름이 무엇입니까?
B 저는 <u>**마크입니다**</u>.

6. A 어느 나라에서 왔습니까?
B 미국에서 _____.

7. A 지금 무슨 일을 합니까?
B 은행에서 _____.

8. A 언제 일을 시작하셨습니까?
B 6개월 전에 _____.

Answer p.278

Grammar Rehearsal

하나도 (negative expression) Using negative expressions

빵이 하나도 없습니다.	There isn't a single piece of bread.
돈이 하나도 없습니다.	I don't have any money.
모자가 한 개도 없습니다.	There isn't a single hat.
학생이 한 명도 없습니다.	There isn't a single student.

뭐든지/누구든지/언제든지/어디든지 Speaking with emphasis

뭐든지 다 있습니다.	We have everything.
누구든지 올 수 있습니다.	Anyone can come.
언제든지 살 수 있습니다.	You can buy it anytime.
어디든지 갈 수 있습니다.	You can go anywhere.

Additional Vocabulary

• **Vocabulary related to stores**

문을 열다 to open the store
문을 닫다 to close the store
주문하다 to order
계산하다 to pay
줄을 서다 to line up
영수증 receipt

줄을 서다

계산하다

문을 열다

OPEN

문을 닫다

CLOSED

Conversation Rehearsal

(Noun) 드릴까요? Asking about the other person's intentions

영수증 드릴까요?

➡ 아니요, 괜찮아요.

뭐 드릴까요?

➡ 샌드위치 주세요.

몇 개 드릴까요?

➡ 두 개 주세요.

Would you like a receipt?

➡ No, I'm fine.

What would you like?

➡ A sandwich, please.

How many would you like?

➡ Please, give me two.

따로 (-아/어) 주세요 Requesting something additional to a worker

얼음을 따로 주세요.

설탕을 따로 주세요.

따로 계산해 주세요.

따로 포장해 주세요.

Please, set aside the ice.

Please, set aside the sugar.

Please, pay it separately.

Please, pack it separately.

Pronunciation Tip

없어요 [업써요]

When the double final consonant is followed by a vowel, only the second part of the double final consonant is moved to be the initial consonant of the next syllable. However, when the double final consonant that begins with [ㄱ, ㄷ, ㅂ] is followed by ㄱ, ㄷ, ㅂ, ㅅ, ㅈ the double final consonant is pronounced as [ㄲ, ㄸ, ㅃ, ㅆ, ㅉ]. In the above example, the second consonant ㅅ in 없 is moved to become the initial consonant of the next syllable and is pronounced as [ㅆ] because the first part of the double consonant in 없 is [ㅂ]. Therefore, 없어요 is pronounced as [업써요].

 Coffee Break

Some expressions to say to store employees

When you want to take out a drink or food item from a store, you can say 가져갈 거예요 or 테이크아웃 (take-out)할 거예요. If you eat some of the food and there are leftovers, you can tell an employee 싸 주세요 or 포장해 주세요.

Scenery from a Korean cafe

If you go to cafes in Korea, you can see people drinking coffee and chatting with others, but it is also common to see people studying or typing away on their laptops. Coffee in Korea is not cheap, but even college students often use cafes instead of libraries to read or study. Some people say that cafes are better than libraries when it comes to focusing, while others prefer a pleasant cafe instead of their home.

Foreigners are surprised how Koreans leave their laptops on the table while using the café toilet. Some Koreans even leave their expensive laptops and cell phones on their seats for more than 30 minutes without asking others to look after their devices. What is even more surprising to foreigners is that no one steals an unoccupied laptop or cell phone. Koreans think that if there is a laptop, cell phone, outerwear, or bag on the table in a café, someone is using it. Thus, no one touches it or cares about it.

Some suggest that Koreans are accustomed to crime prevention due to Korea's world-class security. While others suggest that most café customers, who are from the young generation, have grown up with the attention of their parents from a young age, so they do not care about other people's belongings. At any rate, an important thing to note is that you don't have to carry your belongings to the toilet when you go to a café in Korea.

Chapter 4

Adapting to life in Korea

수잔 피터스 (호주)
Susan Peters (Australia)

Chapter 4

Adapting to life in Korea

At an electronics store

Comparing electronics

더 싼 거 있어요?

Is there anything cheaper?

Susan

An Employee at a store

수잔	선풍기 좀 보여 주세요.
직원	이거 어때요?
수잔	다른 디자인 없어요?
직원	그럼, 이거 어때요? 이 디자인이 인기가 많아요.
수잔	좀 비싸요. 더 싼 거 있어요?
직원	여기 있어요. 이게 제일 싼 거예요.
수잔	그래요? 좀 더 보고 올게요.

Susan	Could you show me some fans?
Employee	How about this one?
Susan	Is there a different design?
Employee	Then what about this one? This design is very popular.
Susan	It's a little expensive. Is there anything cheaper?
Employee	Here you go. This is the cheapest.
Susan	Really? I'll go look around a bit more.

▶ New Vocabulary

선풍기 fan

다르다 to be different

디자인 design

인기가 많다 to be popular

비싸다 to be expensive

더 more

좀 a bit, a little

싸다 to be cheap

제일 (the) most

오다 to come

▶ New Expressions

… 좀 보여 주세요. Could you show me…

이거 어때요? How about this one?

다른 디자인 없어요?
Is there a different design?

이 디자인이 인기가 많아요.
This design is very popular.

좀 비싸요. It's a little expensive.

더 싼 거 있어요?
Is there anything cheaper?

이게 제일 싼 거예요. This is the cheapest.

좀 더 보고 올게요.
I'll go look around a bit more.

▶ Close-Up

❶ 좀
(Please and a little)

좀 has two meanings. One meaning of 좀 expresses politeness. In this conversation, the 좀 in "선풍기 좀 보여 주세요" corresponds to this. The other is an abbreviated form of 조금 which is often used in colloquial conversations. In this conversation, the 좀 of "좀 비싸요" and "좀 더 보고 올게요" corresponds to this.

Ex. 바지가 좀 커요. 작은 바지 좀 보여 주세요.
The pants are a little big. Please show me the small-sized pants.

❷ The pronoun 거
(The pronoun "one")

거 is mainly used in colloquial conversations when indicating a previously referred to noun. In the conversation, 싼 거 is used in place of 싼 선풍기. The original form of 거 is 것, but it is changed into 거 to make pronunciation easy in colloquial conversations.

Ex. 가방이 너무 커요. 작은 거 (= 가방) 있어요?
The bag is too big. Do you have a smaller one?

Flashback

• Adjectives with opposite meanings

5,000원   2,000,000원

싸다 ↔ 비싸다
to be cheap   to be expensive

많다 ↔ 적다
to be many to be few

크다 ↔ 작다
to be big   to be small

키가 크다 ↔ 키가 작다
to be tall   to be short

같다 ↔ 다르다
to be same   to be different

재미있다 ↔ 재미없다
to be fun   to be not fun

쉽다 ↔ 어렵다
to be easy   to be difficult

춥다 ↔ 덥다
to be cold   to be hot

편하다 to be comfortable ↔ 불편하다 to be uncomfortable

가볍다 to be light ↔ 무겁다 to be heavy

좋다 to be good ↔ 나쁘다 to be bad

깨끗하다 to be clean ↔ 더럽다 to be dirty

Grammar in Focus

Grammar Chart **p.272**

The Comparative 보다 더 and the superlative 제일, 가장

In Korean, unlike in English, when comparing objects, markers and adverbs are used. Comparatives are expressed by adding the marker 보다 to the object being compared and using the adverb 더. For example, if you want to say that Busan is hotter than Seoul in the summer, make the subject 부산 first and add 보다 to the end of the object of comparison, 서울. Then, add 더 in front of the adjective 더워요 to complete the sentence. Even if the adverb 더 is omitted, the meaning of the comparative can be conveyed.

여름에 부산이 서울보다 더 더워요.
Busan is hotter than Seoul in summer.

비빔밥이 불고기보다 (더) 맛있어요.
Bibimbap is more delicious than bulgogi.

The superlative is expressed using the adverbs 제일 or 가장. For example, if you want to express which city is the hottest in summer among Seoul, Incheon, and Busan, select 부산 as the subject and add the adverb 제일 or 가장 in front of the adjective 더워요.

월요일이 제일 바빠요.
Mondays are the busiest.

축구가 가장 재미있어요.
Soccer is the most fun (sport).

When limiting the choices in comparing objects, 중에서 is used. For example, you can express a limited range by using 중에서 or you can specify the comparison by saying A하고 B 중에서.

A 봄하고 가을 중에서 뭐를 더 좋아해요?
Which do you like more, spring or autumn?

B 봄을 더 좋아해요.
I like spring more.

A 스포츠 중에서 뭐가 제일 재미있어요?
What sport do you enjoy the most?

B 수영이 제일 재미있어요.
Swimming is the most fun.

> ! **Be careful!**
> Be careful with the vowel pronunciation 더. Different pronunciations have totally different meanings.
>
> (Ex) 더 (more): 커피가 주스보다 더 싸요.
> Coffee is cheaper than juice.
> (Ex) 다 (both, all): 고기하고 생선 다 좋아해요.
> I like both meat and fish.
> (Ex) 도 (also): 야채가 싸요. 그리고 물도 싸요.
> Vegetables are cheap, and water is cheap, too.

Quiz Yourself!

1~3 Look at the picture and complete the sentence.

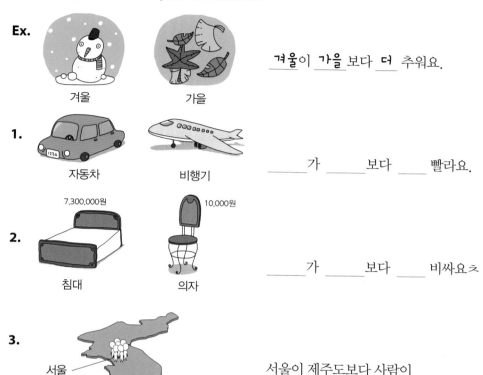

Ex.

겨울   가을

_겨울_이 _가을_ 보다 _더_ 추워요.

1.

자동차   비행기

_____가 _____보다 _____ 빨라요.

2.

7,300,000원   10,000원

침대   의자

_____가 _____보다 _____ 비싸요ᄎ

3.

서울
제주도

서울이 제주도보다 사람이 _____.

4~7 Complete the conversation by choosing the correct answer.

4. A 여름하고 겨울 중에서 뭐가 (① 더 / ② 제일) 좋아요?
   B 여름이 좋아요.

5. A 진수하고 마크 중에서 누가 (① 더 / ② 제일) 키가 커요?
   B 마크가 키가 커요.

6. A 영화하고 음악하고 그림 중에서 뭐를 (① 더 / ② 제일) 좋아해요?
   B 영화를 가장 좋아해요.

7. A 봄, 여름, 가을, 겨울 중에서 어떤 계절을 (① 더 / ② 제일) 좋아해요?
   B 가을을 가장 좋아해요.

Answer p.278

Grammar Rehearsal

track **100**

더 -(으)ㄴ 거 있어요? — Requesting for something

너무 비싸요. 더 싼 거 있어요? — (It's) too expensive. Do you have anything cheaper?

너무 커요. 더 작은 거 있어요? — (It's) too big. Do you have **a smaller** one?

너무 무거워요. 더 가벼운 거 있어요? — (It's) too heavy. Do you have something lighter?

너무 어두워요. 더 밝은 거 있어요? — (It's) too dark. Do you have something brighter?

이 중에서 뭐가 제일 …? — Asking for specific information

이 중에서 뭐가 제일 **싸요?** — Which one is the cheapest?

이 중에서 뭐가 제일 **튼튼해요?** — Which one is the strongest?

이 중에서 뭐가 제일 **인기가 많아요?** — Which one is the most popular?

이 중에서 뭐가 제일 **후기가 좋아요?** — Which one has the best review?

Additional Vocabulary

• **Vocabulary related to products**

세일하다 to have a sale
할인하다 to give a discount
포장하다 to pack, wrap
배달하다 to deliver
보증서 guarantee, warranty
보증 기간 the terms of the guarantee, the warranty period
서비스 센터 service center

Conversation Rehearsal

track 101

다른 (Noun) 없어요? Requesting for something

이거 어때요?

➡ 다른 거 없어요?

➡ 다른 색 없어요?

➡ 다른 모델 없어요?

➡ 다른 디자인 없어요?

How about this?

➡ Is there anything else?

➡ Is there any other color?

➡ Is there any other model?

➡ Is there any other design?

(service) 돼요? Asking for service availability

카드 돼요?

➡ 네, 됩니다.

포장 돼요?

➡ 네, 됩니다.

배달 돼요?

➡ 죄송합니다. 안 됩니다.

Do you accept credit cards?

➡ Yes, we do.

Can I take out it?

➡ Yes, you can.

Do you deliver?

➡ Sorry. We don't.

Pronunciation Tip

track 102

많아요 [마나요] / 많고 [만코]

When a double consonant ㄶ or ㅀ in the final consonant precedes immediately a vowel in the next syllable, the second consonant ㅎ of the double consonant ㄶ or ㅀ is omitted and not pronounced, and the first consonant ㄴ, ㄹ is used as the initial sound of the next syllable. In the example above, ㅎ is omitted as a vowel is followed by the second consonant ㅎ in the double consonant ㄶ of 많. The first consonant ㄴ of 많 moves to the initial sound 아 in the next syllable and is pronounced as [마나요]. On the other hand, in the second example, if ㄱ, ㄷ, ㅈ is combined after the double consonant ㄶ of 많, ㅎ is combined with the sounds of ㄱ, ㄷ, ㅈ and is pronounced as [ㅋ, ㅌ, ㅊ]. Thus, 많고 is pronounced as [만코].

☕ Coffee Break

Useful expressions for shopping

There are times when you go into a store to buy something, and there are times when you just look and don't buy. If you only go to take a quick look, the first time you enter the store, say 그냥 구경 좀 할게요. You can freely browse items under the guidance of friendly staff. If you come across an item you want to take a closer look at, say to the staff, OO 좀 보여 주세요. As in the conversation above, when you come out without buying anything, you can say 좀 더 보고 올게요 or 다음에 올게요.

Korean pronunciation of English words

There are many words of foreign origin in Korean that derive from English. However, some foreigners can't understand these English words because Koreans' English pronunciation is so different. Looking at the Korean method of pronouncing English words will help foreigners to communicate with Koreans.

First, Korean syllables consist of vowels connected with consonants. So when pronouncing a word, consonants alone cannot be pronounced and vowels must be added. For words that end in a consonant like "d" and "s" (such as "salad" or "Christmas"), Korean people have to add a weak vowel sound such as ㅡ to the end of the consonant when pronouncing it. So when pronouncing "salad" and "Christmas" each syllable is divided based on consonant-vowel blends (such as 드 or 스). Likewise, "salad" is broken down as sal-la-d and becomes 샐러드, and "Christmas" is broken down as ch-ri-s-ma-s and becomes 크리스마스.

Second, Korean doesn't have distinct sounds for f/p, b/v, or r/l. So, "f" and "p" are both pronounced ㅍ, "b" and "v" are both pronounced ㅂ, and ㄹ is used for both "r" and "l". So while having completely different pronunciations in English, "fan" and "pan" are pronounced as 팬 in Korean. Likewise, "wifi" becomes 와이파이 and "pie" becomes 파이; thereby, sharing the same ㅍ sound. Similarly, since there is no distinction between "b" and "v", "box" and "vox" make use of the same ㅂ sound as 박스. And, since there is no distinction between "r" and "l", "reader" and "leader" is pronounced with the same ㄹ as 리더.

Third, in English, there are stresses when pronouncing a word, so the strength and weakness are clear, but in Korean, there is no special stress, so all syllables are pronounced with the same length and speed. For example, "Macdonald's" is pronounced 맥도날드 by dividing it into syllables as mac-do-nal-d and then these syllables are pronounced evenly with the same length and speed without any stress. Starbucks

is also pronounced "Starbucks" by dividing it into syllables as s-tar-buck-s and pronouncing it without stress. If you take a taxi in Korea and say your destination and the taxi driver can't understand English words, make sure you are dividing your words into syllables and pronouncing each syllable with an even length and tone.

In addition, there are cases where English words were created by Koreans and settled as Korean English (Konglish). For example, the Korean word used for Warranty Service is "After service" Also, in Korean, a signature is 사인 (sign), a cell phone is 핸드폰 (hand-phone), and the meaning of drinking an alcoholic drink bottom up is 원샷 (one shot).

Getting used to Korean words of foreign origin means getting used to Korean pronunciation. Let's have fun studying while reading the signboards on the streets in Korea.

너무 짧지 않게 잘라 주세요.

Please cut it so that it is not too short.

Susan   A Hairdresser

직원	어서 오세요. 여기 앉으세요.
수잔	감사합니다.
직원	머리를 어떻게 할까요?
수잔	너무 짧지 않게 잘라 주세요.
직원	어느 정도로 잘라 드릴까요?
수잔	*(Showing the length of hair with her fingers)* 이 정도요.
직원	네, 앞머리는 어떻게 할까요?
수잔	앞머리는 자르지 마세요.
직원	알겠습니다.

Employee	Come in. Please, take a seat here.
Susan	Thank you.
Employee	How would you like your hair to be done?
Susan	Please cut it so that it is not too short.
Employee	How short would you like it (to be cut)?
Susan	*(Showing the length of hair with her fingers)* This much.
Employee	Okay. How would you like your bangs?
Susan	Do not cut my bangs, please.
Employee	All right.

▶ New Vocabulary

머리 hair

너무 too

짧다 to be short

않다 to be not, do not

자르다 to cut

어느 which

정도 how much

앞머리 bangs (lit. front hair)

▶ New Expressions

머리를 어떻게 할까요?
How would you like your hair to be done?

잘라 주세요. Please, cut/trim it.

어느 정도로 잘라 드릴까요?
How short would you like it (to be cut)?

이 정도요. This much.

앞머리는 어떻게 할까요?
How would you like your bangs?

자르지 마세요. Do not cut it, please.

▶ Close-Up

① -(으)ㄹ까요?
(Gently asking another person's intention)

-(으)ㄹ까요? is used to politely ask about the other person's intentions in a soft manner. Although you can semantically convey politeness without this specific pattern, -(으)ㄹ까요? comes across as a cautious means. In this conversation, "머리를 어떻게 할까요?" has the same meaning as "머리를 어떻게 해요?", but the hairdresser uses -(으)ㄹ까요? to carefully ask the customer's intention or preference.

> Ex. A 앞머리를 자를까요?   Should I cut your bangs?
>
> B 네, 조금 잘라 주세요.   Yes, please cut it a little.

② 이 정도
(Using the hand to indicate the approximate quantity or the level)

이 정도 is used when indicating a certain amount or measuring by using your thumb and index finger. In this conversation, 이 정도 (this much) is used with a finger gesture to describe the length of hair to be cut. Simply use 이 정도 when you want to explain a rough amount or length of an object in an easy-to-understand way.

Flashback

• Irregular verbs I: 으 and 르

1. The omission of 으

When a stem ending with a vowel (for example -아요 or -어요) is combined between a verb stem or an adjective stem ending in ㅡ, the ㅡ at the end syllable of the stem is always dropped.

- 모으다 (to collect/gather): 모으 + -아요 → 모 + -아요 → 모아요
  > Ex. 저는 우표를 모아요. I collect stamps.
- 슬프다 (to be sad): 슬프 + -어요 → 슬ㅍ + -어요 → 슬퍼요
  > Ex. 친구하고 헤어져서 슬퍼요. I am sad because I parted ways with my friend.

2. The irregular 르

If a stem ending with a vowel -아/어 (for example -아/어요, -았었어요) is combined between a verb stem or an adjective stem ending in 르 the ㅡ is omitted and ㄹ is added.

- 다르다 (to be different): 다르 + -아요 → 다ㄹ + -아요 → 달ㄹ + -아요 → 달라요
  > Ex. 한국어는 영어하고 너무 달라요. Korean is very different from English.
- 부르다 (to call): 부르 + -었어요 → 부ㄹ + -었어요 → 불ㄹ + -었어요 → 불렀어요
  > Ex. 어제 친구하고 한국 노래를 불렀어요. Yesterday, I sang a Korean song with my friend.

Grammar in Focus

–게 Changing an adjective into an adverb

Add –게 to the end of the adjective stem to make an adverb regardless of whether the stem ends in a vowel or a consonant. –게 is used to modify an action or condition. For example, to make 비싸게, add –게 to the stem of the adjective 비싸다.

크다	크게 말해 주세요.	Please speak loudly.
슬프다	여자가 슬프게 울었어요.	The woman cried sadly.
반갑다	저는 친구하고 반갑게 인사했어요.	I warmly greeted my friend.
깨끗하다	어제 방을 깨끗하게 청소했어요.	I cleaned the room neatly yesterday.
쉽다	쉽게 문제를 해결했어요.	I solved the problem easily.

You can emphasize the adverb's meaning by using 아주, 정말, 너무 before the adverb.

남자가 아주 거만하게 말했어요.	The man spoke very arrogantly.
친구하고 정말 맛있게 음식을 먹었어요.	I really enjoyed the food with my friend.
여자 친구하고 너무 쉽게 헤어졌어요.	He broke up with his girlfriend so easily.

When using two or more adverbs, connect the adverbs with –고 and use it as follows.

시골에 가서 여름 방학을 재미있고 알차게 보냈어요.

I went to the countryside and had a fun and fulfilling summer vacation.

(!) Be careful!

Some adjectives don't use –게 when making adverbs. The following are examples of the most common exceptions.

많다 → 많이: 점심을 너무 많이 먹었어요.	I ate too much for lunch.
빠르다 → 빨리: 지금 빨리 가야 돼요.	Now I have to go quickly.
멀다 → 멀리: 회사에서 멀리 살아요.	I live far from the office.

Quiz Yourself !

1~4 Match the picture with the appropriate sentence.

> ㉠ 조용하게 말해 주세요.   ㉡ 맵게 만들어 주세요.
>
> ㉢ 건강하게 잘 지내세요.   ㉣ 다른 의자에 편하게 앉으세요.

1.

2.

3.

4.

5~8 Complete the sentences by using –게.

Ex. 수잔이 **예쁘게** 화장했어요.
       (예쁘다)

5. 수잔이 매일 _____ 일해요.
           (바쁘다)

6. 수잔이 케이크를 _____ 만들었어요.
             (크다)

7. 수잔이 머리를 _____ 자르고 싶어요.
            (짧다)

8. 수잔이 문제를 _____ 해결했어요.
            (쉽다)

Answer **p.278**

Grammar Rehearsal

track **104**

-게 -아/어 주세요 Specifically requesting something to be done

크게 말해 주세요.   Please, speak **out** loudly.

맵게 만들어 주세요.   Please, make **it** spicy.

따뜻하게 **빵을** 데워 주세요.   Please, heat up **the bread** so that it is **warm**.

시원하게 **에어컨을** 틀어 주세요.   Please, turn on **the air conditioner** so that it is **cool**.

너무 -지 않게 잘라 주세요 Specifically requesting something not to be done

너무 **짧지** 않게 잘라 주세요.   Please, **cut it** so that it is not too **short**.

너무 **크지** 않게 잘라 주세요.   Please, **cut it** so that it is not too **big**.

너무 **길지** 않게 잘라 주세요.   Please, **cut it** so that it is not too **long**.

너무 **두껍지** 않게 잘라 주세요.   Please, **cut it** so that it is not too **thick**.

Additional Vocabulary

- **Vocabulary related to the hair salon**

  자르다 to cut

  다듬다 to trim

  파마하다 to perm

  염색하다 to dye

  기본 요금 basic fee

  추가 요금 additional fee

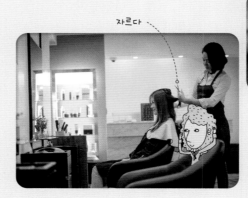

자르다

파마하다

Conversation Rehearsal

track 105

(interrogative pronoun) –(으)ㄹ까요? Carefully asking another person's opinion

몇 시에 연락할까요?
➥ 저녁 6시에 연락해 주세요.

이 물건을 어디에 놓을까요?
➥ 여기에 놓아 주세요.

이 음식을 어떻게 할까요?
➥ 냉장고에 넣어 주세요.

What time should I contact you?
➥ Please call me at 6 pm.

Where would you like me to place this stuff?
➥ Please place it here.

What should I do with this food?
➥ Please put it in the refrigerator.

이게 … 뭐예요? Asking the meaning of something

이게 영어로 뭐예요?

이게 한국어로 뭐예요?

이게 무슨 의미예요?

이게 무슨 뜻이에요?

What is this in English?

What is this in Korean?

What does this signify?

What does this mean?

Pronunciation Tip

track 106

어떻게 [어떠케]

When the consonant ㅎ is followed by ㄱ, ㄷ, ㅈ and ㄱ, ㄷ, ㅈ are combined to be pronounced as [ㅋ, ㅌ, ㅊ]. In the above example, ㅎ of 떻 in 어떻게 is pronounced as [ㅋ] as ㄱ proceeds 떻. Therefore, 어떻게 is pronounced as [어떠케].

예 이렇다 [이러타]　그렇죠 [그러쵸]

Coffee Break

Expressions for styling hair

When you go to a Korean hair salon, you may find it difficult to describe the details of styling your hair in Korean. If so, ask them to show you a photo or magazine with different hairstyles so you can see and choose for yourself. Or, find a picture of the hairstyle you want, show it to the hairdresser, and say, 이렇게 해 주세요. When expressing the length, you can use your hands to say 이 정도, and when expressing the shape, you can use your hands to say 이렇게.

K - beauty

All women care about their skin, but Korean women especially pay special attention to skincare to maintain healthy skin. Moreover, in Korea, people prefer pale skin like white jade rather than sun-tanned skin, so they do not neglect their efforts to maintain fair skin. In midsummer, when the sun is shining brightly, sunscreen is essential, and it is to see young women on the street using parasols to protect their skin from strong UV rays. It is not easy to tell the age of a woman based on her appearance alone in Korea as 동안(젊어 보이는 얼굴) (young-looking face) is the spectacle of the public eye.

Korean cosmetics, well known as "K-beauty", is an iconic example that reveals how much Koreans care about their appearance. Korean cosmetics emphasize translucent skin that shines rather than emphasizing flashy colors, and various products focus on skin color correction and flaw reduction. In addition, the price range is also diverse to accommodate teenagers who lack pocket money to career women in their 30s and 40s. These days, there are cosmetics for young men who care about their skin, and even cosmetics stores sell cosmetics for soldiers in the military. The protective color applied to the face inconspicuously during military training is a cosmetic made with high-quality ingredients.

In Korea, skin care and plastic surgery are common. Gangnam, a wealthy town in Seoul, is crowded with dermatology and plastic surgery clinics for people who invest in their appearance. There are many people who want to follow or resemble Korean celebrities who are active in the movie, drama, and singing sectors. Recently,

the number of foreigners who visit Korean dermatology and plastic surgery clinics is increasing. Who doesn't want to look younger and prettier? In Korean society, K-beauty can be understood as a desire of people who want to flaunt their beauty.

At a gym

Asking for information

토요일에 하지만 일요일에 쉽니다.

We are open on Saturdays but closed on Sundays.

Susan

An Employee at the gym

수잔	다음 달부터 운동하려고 해요. 한 달에 얼마예요?	Susan	I'd like to exercise starting next month. How much is it for a month?
직원	한 달에 10만 원입니다.	Employee	It's 100,000 won per month.
수잔	몇 시부터 몇 시까지 해요?	Susan	From what time to what time are you open?
직원	아침 6시부터 밤 10시까지 합니다.	Employee	From 6 am to 10 pm.
수잔	토요일에도 하죠?	Susan	You are open on Saturdays too, right?
직원	네, 토요일에 하지만 일요일에 쉽니다.	Employee	Yes, we are open on Saturdays but closed on Sundays.
수잔	안을 볼 수 있어요?	Susan	Can I look around inside?
직원	그럼요. 이쪽으로 오세요.	Employee	Of course. Come this way, please.

▶ New Vocabulary

다음 달 next month

부터 from (time), starting

운동하다 to exercise

하다 to do, to have

아침 morning (am)

밤 night (pm)

토요일 Saturday

일요일 Sunday

쉬다 to rest (not work)

안 inside

▶ New Expressions

한 달에 얼마예요?
How much is it for a month?

몇 시부터 몇 시까지 해요?
From what time to what time are you open?

토요일에도 하죠?
You are open on Saturdays too, right?

안을 볼 수 있어요?
Can I look around inside?

이쪽으로 오세요.
Come this way, please.

▶ Close-Up

❶ Markers 부터 and 까지
(Expressing beginning and end times)

부터 indicates the beginning of time, and 까지 indicates the end of time. In this conversation, when asking about the operating hours of the gym, 아침 6시부터 밤 10시까지 express that it opens at 6 am and closes at 10 pm. Unlike the range of time, the markers 에서 and 까지 are used with distances to indicate the start and end points.

(Ex.) 월요일부터 금요일까지 아르바이트해요.
I work part-time from Monday to Friday.

(Ex.) 서울에서 부산까지 기차로 가요.
I go from Seoul to Busan by train.

❷ 죠?
(Checking information)

In colloquial conversation, 죠? is used to confirm that the listener already knows what the speaker is saying. 죠? is combined with verbs and adjectives regardless of whether the stem ends in a vowel or a consonant. Its original form is 지요?, but it is shortened and used as 죠? in practice.

(Ex.) A 거기 마크 씨 집이죠?   That's Mark's house over there, isn't it?

     B 네, 맞아요.   Yes, that's right.

Flashback

• Days of the week

The following terms describe the days of the week.

◄――――――― 주중 Weekdays ―――――――►◄					주말 Weekend ―――►	
월요일	**화**요일	**수**요일	**목**요일	**금**요일	**토**요일	**일**요일
Monday	Tuesday	Wednesday	Thursday	Friday	Saturday	Sunday

휴일 (Holidays) rest days, days–off 평일 (Weekday) ordinary days, neither a weekend nor a holiday.

첫째 주: the first week

둘째 주: the second week

셋째 주: the third week

넷째 주: the fourth week

다섯째 주: the fifth week

지난주: last week

이번 주: this week

다음 주: next week

Grammar in Focus

Grammar Chart **p.272**

–지만 but

–지만 is used when you want to indicate a contrast between what is said before and after. –지만 is a grammar pattern that connects two sentences that are opposite to each other with the connecting adverb 그렇지만 or 하지만 into one sentence. –지만 is used with verbs and adjectives. Simply add –지만 to the end of the verb or adjective stem regardless of whether it ends in a vowel or a consonant.

비싸다	이 식당은 비싸지만 맛이 없어요.

This restaurant is expensive, but not very tasty.

좋다	오늘 날씨가 좋지만 어제 날씨가 안 좋았어요.

The weather today is good, but the weather yesterday was bad.

하다	토요일에는 하지만 일요일에는 하지 않아요.

It opens on Saturday, but closes on Sunday.

있다	한국 친구가 있지만 자주 만날 수 없어요.

I have a Korean friend, but we can't meet often.

먹다	저는 생선을 먹지만 고기를 안 먹어요.

I eat fish, but I don't eat meat.

보고 싶다	그 영화를 보고 싶지만 시간이 없어요.

I want to see that movie, but I have no time.

To make contrasts involving the past, –았/었지만 is used adding –았/었– to –지만 to indicate the past tense.

작다	어렸을 때 키가 작았지만 지금은 키가 커요.

I was short when I was young, but now I am tall.

보다	영화를 봤지만 제목이 생각 안 나요.

I saw the movie, but I can't remember the title.

먹다	아까 점심을 먹었지만 배가 고파요.

I ate lunch a while ago, but I'm still hungry.

Quiz Yourself !

1~4 Complete the sentence by choosing the correct answer.

1. 시간이 있지만 ① 돈이 있어요.
　　　　　　　　　② 돈이 없어요.

2. 한국 음식을 좋아하지만 ① 김치를 먹을 수 있어요.
　　　　　　　　　　　　② 김치를 먹을 수 없어요.

3. 어제 친구를 기다렸지만 ① 친구가 왔어요.
　　　　　　　　　　　　② 친구가 안 왔어요.

4. 부산에 안 갔지만 ① 제주도에는 갔어요.
　　　　　　　　　② 제주도에는 안 갔어요.

5~9 Complete the sentence by using –지만.

5. 이 구두가 정말 <u>멋있어요</u>. <u>하지만</u> 너무 비싸요.
　　　→

6. 한국어를 많이 공부하고 <u>싶어요</u>. <u>하지만</u> 시간이 없어요.
　　　　→

7. 비빔밥이 <u>매워요</u>. <u>하지만</u> 맛있어요.
　　→

8. 어제 숙제를 <u>했어요</u>. <u>하지만</u> 안 가져 왔어요.
　　→

9. <u>약을 먹었어요</u>. <u>하지만</u> 효과가 없어요.
　　→

Answer p.278

Grammar Rehearsal

track 108

-지만 Saying the opposite

2층에 남자 화장실이 없지만
여자 화장실이 있어요.

There's no men's restroom on the 2nd floor,
but there's a women's restroom.

주말에 사람이 많지만
주중에 사람이 많지 않아요.

There are a lot of people on the weekends,
but there are not many people on the
weekdays.

평일에 일찍 일어나지만
주말에 늦게 일어나요.

I get up early on weekdays,
but late on weekends.

-았/었지만 Saying something opposite from your expectations

운동했지만 살이 안 빠져요.

I've been working out, but I'm not losing
weight.

밥을 먹었지만 아직도 배고파요.

I ate, but I'm still hungry.

커피를 마셨지만 자고 싶어요.

I drank coffee, but I want to sleep.

한국어를 공부했지만 아직 어려워요.

I studied Korean, but it is still difficult.

Additional Vocabulary

• **Vocabulary related to exercise**

탈의실 changing room
샤워실 shower room
사물함 (로커) private locker
운동복 gym suit
운동화 gym shoes, running shoes
수건 towel, washcloth

수건   운동복

샤워실

탈의실

Conversation Rehearsal

(time)부터 (time)까지 Talking about a term

언제부터 언제까지 휴가예요?

➡ 수요일부터 금요일까지 휴가예요.

며칠부터 며칠까지 여행 가요?

➡ 23일부터 26일까지 여행 가요.

몇 시부터 몇 시까지 가게를 해요?

➡ 아침 9시부터 저녁 8시까지 해요.

From when to when are you on vacation?

➡ I'm on vacation from Wednesday to Friday.

From what day to what day are you traveling?

➡ I'm going on a trip from the 23rd to the 26th.

From what time to what time do you open the shop?

➡ From 9 am to 8 pm.

죠? Verifying something

주말에 사람이 많죠?

➡ 네, 주말에 사람이 많아요.

사물함이 있죠?

➡ 네, 사물함이 있어요.

휴일에 문을 닫죠?

➡ 네, 휴일에 문을 닫아요.

There are many people on the weekend, right?

➡ Yes, there are a lot of people on the weekends.

Do you have lockers, don't you?

➡ Yes, there are lockers.

Are you closed on holidays, right?

➡ Yes, we are closed on holidays.

Pronunciation Tip

몇 시 [멷 씨]

Since the consonants ㄷ, ㅌ, ㅅ, ㅈ, ㅊ, ㅎ are all pronounced as [ㄷ], 몇 is pronounced as [멷]. The initial sound of the next syllable ㄱ, ㄷ, ㅂ, ㅅ, ㅈ which is followed by the final consonant [ㄱ, ㄷ, ㅂ], is pronounced as [ㄲ, ㄸ, ㅃ, ㅆ, ㅉ]. Therefore, the first sound ㅅ of 시 after [멷] is pronounced as [씨].

예 **몇 분** [멷 뿐] **몇 장** [멷 짱]

Coffee Break

Expressions for periods

In Scene 7, we learned how the marker 에 is used to group ranges. In the previous conversation, the amount corresponding to a period of one month was expressed as 한 달에 10만 원이에요. If you pay the same amount 매달, you can say 매달 10만 원이에요. It is useful to know words like 매일 (every day), 매주 (every week), 매달 (every month), 매년 (every year).

Holidays in Korea

Korean holidays are based on the date. Except for a few cases, there are no additional holidays even when weekends and nationally recognized holidays overlap. So, when the calendar comes out, Koreans check the holidays marked in red every year. Let's find out about Korean holidays.

Korean holidays are celebrated according to the lunar calendar and include 설날 (Korean New Year's Day, the first day of the first month of the lunar calendar) and 추석 (Korean Thanksgiving Day, the 15th day of the 8th month of the lunar calendar). 설날 and 추석 In the case of these holidays, one day before and after both 추석 and 설날 are also considered legal holidays.

There are also public holidays that commemorate specific historical or religious days. The chronological order of public holidays in Korea is as follows.

- 양력설 (January 1st of the solar calendar): The Gregorian calendar New Year
- 삼일절 (March 1st of the solar calendar): A day of remembrance for the 1919 movement for Korean independence from Japanese colonization
- 석가탄신일 (April 8th of the lunar calendar): The birthday of Buddha
- 어린이날 (May 5th of the solar calendar): A day when families spend time with their children
- 현충일 (June 6th of the solar calendar): A day to honor those who lost their lives for their country
- 광복절 (August 15th of the solar calendar): A day to commemorate when Korea became an independent nation overcoming Japanese colonization after the end of the Second World War in 1945
- 개천절 (October 3rd of the solar calendar): A day to commemorate the founding of Korea's founding father, 단군, about 5,000 years ago
- 한글날 (October 9th of the solar calender): A day to commemorate the promulgation of Hangeul by King Sejong of the Joseon Dynasty (1946)
- 성탄절 (December 25th of the solar calendar): The day that Jesus Christ was born

비행기로 보내시겠어요?

Would you like to send it by plane?

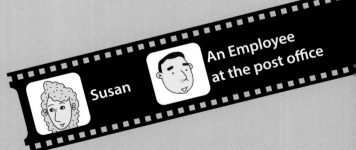

Susan

An Employee at the post office

수잔	택배를 보내고 싶어요.
직원	어디로 보내실 거예요?
수잔	호주로 보낼 거예요.
직원	택배를 비행기로 보내시겠어요? 배로 보내시겠어요?
수잔	시간이 얼마나 걸려요?
직원	비행기는 3~4일, 배는 1~2달쯤 걸려요.
수잔	그럼, 비행기로 보낼게요.
직원	알겠습니다.

Susan	I would like to send a parcel.
Employee	Where would you like to send it?
Susan	I'd like to send this to Australia.
Employee	Would you like to send it by airmail or by ship?
Susan	How long would it take?
Employee	By airmail, it would take 3-4 days, and by ship, it would take about 1-2 months.
Susan	Then, I'll use airmail.
Employee	Alright.

▶ New Vocabulary

택배 parcel

보내다 to send

호주 Australia

비행기 airplane

배 boat, ship

걸리다 to take (time)

은/는 the marker for comparison

일 day

▶ New Expressions

어디로 보내실 거예요?
Where would you like to send it?

비행기로 보내시겠어요?
Would you like to send it by airmail?

배로 보내시겠어요?
Would you like to send it by ship?

시간이 얼마나 걸려요?
How long would it take?

비행기로 보낼게요.
I'll use airmail.

▶ Close-Up

❶ The marker 은/는
(Emphasizing a comparison)

When comparing two or more objects, you can add 은/는 to the end of the objects to emphasize the comparison. When a noun ends in a vowel, 는 is used, and when a noun ends in a consonant, 은 is combined. In this conversation, to contrast the plane and the ship, the marker 은/는 was used. Using this marker is like pointing to each object with your finger and raising your tone slightly as you compare them.

Ex. 한국 사람은 매운 음식을 잘 먹는데 제 한국 친구는 매운 음식을 잘 못 먹어요.
Koreans eat spicy food well, but my Korean friend does not eat spicy food well.

❷ How to read a period
(Reading periods of 3-4 days or 1-2 months)

When reading a period, the number written before 일 (date), 주 (week), 년 (year) is read as a Sino-Korean number, and the number before 달 (month) is read as a native Korean number. As in the conversation, 3-4일 is read 삼 사 일 and 1-2달 is read 한두 달. If it is not a continuous number, include the marker 에서 as in 3-7일 (three to seven days) (삼 일에서 칠 일) and 2-5달 (two to five months) (두 달에서 다섯 달).

Ex. 일주일에 2-3번 (두세 번) 운동해요.
I exercise 2 to 3 times a week.

Ex. 배로 3-5달 (세 달에서 다섯 달)쯤 걸려요.
It takes about 3 to 5 months by ship.

Flashback

• Reading dates

When reading dates in Korean, Sino-Korean numbers are used. However, unlike in English, when reading dates in Korean, units are read from largest to smallest such as 년/월/일 (year/month/date).

Year	Month	Day
2021년	10월	10일
이천이십일 년	시 월	십 일

월 month

1월	2월	3월	4월
5월	▶6월	7월	8월
9월	▶10월	11월	12월

▶ Exception
▶ 6월(유월) ▶ 10월(시월)

! **Be careful!**
Unlike in English, when reading the year in Korean, the years are not read in a series of two digits.
Ex. 1973년: "19" "73" (x) → 천구백칠십삼 년 (O)

! **Be careful!**
Note the following pronunciations.
6(육)년 [융년]   8(팔)년 [팔련]   10(십)년 [심년]

Grammar in Focus

Grammar Chart **p.273**

Expressing intent: −겠− and −(으)ㄹ게요

−겠− is used to express the intention or will of the speaker. −겠− is combined with a verb, regardless of whether the stem ends in a vowel or a consonant. Since the subject of −겠− in declarative sentences is always the first person, the subject of −겠− in the sentence where the subject is omitted is I (저는 or 제가).

시작하다	오늘부터 운동을 시작하겠어요.	I want to start exercising today.
읽다	앞으로 매일 30분씩 책을 읽겠습니다.	I will read a book for 30 minutes every day from now on.

−겠− expresses the intention of the speaker in a declarative sentence and expresses the intention of the listener in the interrogative sentence. When asking about the intentions of someone who is older or of higher status than you (for example, when a store employee speaks with customers) the meaning of respect −(으)시− is combined with −겠− and written −(으)시겠어요. When a verb stem ends in a vowel use −시겠어요 and when it ends in a consonant use −으시겠어요. Since there is a question mark for −(으)시겠어요, say it while raising your tone at the end of the sentence. When answering a question, use −겠−. In everyday life, −(으)ㄹ게요 is often used instead of −겠−. When a verb stem ends in a vowel, it is combined with −ㄹ게요, and when it ends with a consonant, −을게요 is combined.

보다	A 어떤 영화를 보시겠어요?	What movie would you like to see?
	B 저는 코미디 영화를 보겠어요. (= 볼게요)	I want to watch (= I'll see) a comedy movie.
앉다	A 소파에 앉으시겠어요?	Would you like to sit on the sofa?
	B 아니요, 저는 의자에 앉겠어요. (= 앉을게요)	No, I'll sit (= I'll sit down) on the chair.

Some verbs (먹다, 마시다, 있다, 자다, 말하다) are used with −(으)시− to convey respect.

먹다	A 어떤 걸로 드시겠어요?	What would you like to eat?
	B 저는 불고기를 먹겠어요. (= 먹을게요.)	I'd like to eat bulgogi. (= I'll eat.)

> **⚠ Be careful!**
> −(으)ㄹ게요 and the future tense −(으)ㄹ 거예요 look similar, but they have different meanings. −(으)ㄹ 거예요 is used to describe what will happen in the future or when talking about a plan or schedule. −(으)ㄹ게요 also is used to indicate the speaker's intention or will, and expresses the speaker's determination or willingness to make a promise to another person.
>
> (Ex) 제가 커피를 살게요.　　　　I'll buy the coffee.
> (Ex) 내일 저는 친구한테 커피를 살 거예요.　　Tomorrow I'm going to buy coffee for my friend.

Quiz Yourself !

1~4 Complete the sentences by using -겠- or -(으)ㄹ게요.

Ex. 저는 이제부터 한국어를 열심히 <u>**공부하겠습니다/공부할게요**</u>.
(공부하다)

1. 저는 매일 아침에 일찍 _____.
(일어나다)

2. 앞으로 채소를 많이 _____.
(먹다)

3. 이제부터 열심히 책을 _____.
(읽다)

4. 한국 사람하고 영어로 _____.
(말하지 않다)

5~8 Look at the picture and complete the conversation by using -(으)시겠어요.

5.

A 어떤 색 가방을 _____?
B 저는 빨간색 가방을 살게요.

6.

A 어떤 옷을 _____?
B 양복을 입을게요.

7.

A 어떤 영화를 _____?
B 저는 이 영화를 볼게요.

8.

A 뭐 _____?
B 저는 커피를 마실게요.

Answer p.278

Grammar Rehearsal

track 112

-(으)시겠어요?, -(으)ㄹ게요 — Asking and answering about intentions

무슨 커피를 드시겠어요?　　　　　　What coffee would you like?

➥ 따뜻한 커피를 마실게요.　　　　　➥ I'll drink hot coffee.

무슨 영화를 보시겠어요?　　　　　　What movie would you like to see?

➥ 코미디 영화를 볼게요.　　　　　　➥ I'd like to watch a comedy movie.

무슨 음악을 들으시겠어요?　　　　　What music would you like to listen to?

➥ 한국 음악을 들을게요.　　　　　　➥ I'll listen to Korean music.

다음에 -(으)ㄹ게요 — Making a promise to another person

감사합니다. 다음에 제가 밥을 살게요.　　Thank you. Next time I'll buy the meal.

감사합니다. 다음에 제가 집에 초대할게요.　Thank you. I'll invite you to my house next time.

미안합니다. 다음에 늦지 않을게요.　　I'm sorry. I won't be late next time.

반갑습니다. 다음에 꼭 연락할게요.　　Nice to meet you. I'll be sure to contact you next time.

Additional Vocabulary

- **Vocabulary related to the post office**

택배　parcel
편지　letter
엽서　postcard
등기　registered mail
보내는 사람　sender (from)
받는 사람　recipient (to)

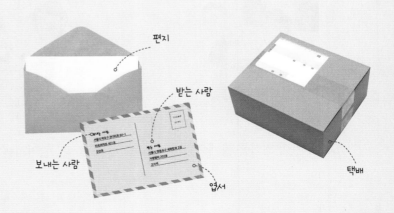

편지
받는 사람
보내는 사람
엽서
택배

Conversation Rehearsal

track 113

(Noun) 에 따라 달라요 Speaking about variables

값이 얼마예요?   How much does it cost?

➡ 무게에 따라 달라요.   ➡ It depends on **the weight**.

시간이 얼마나 걸려요?   How long does it take?

➡ 가격에 따라 달라요.   ➡ It depends on **the price**.

김치 맛이 어때요?   How does kimchi taste?

➡ 지역에 따라 달라요.   ➡ It depends on **the region**.

(Noun) 말고 다른 거 있어요? Requesting something else

비행기 말고 다른 거 있어요?   Is there something other than **airplanes**?

커피 말고 다른 거 있어요?   Is there something other than **coffee**?

이거 말고 다른 거 있어요?   Is there something other than **this**?

저거 말고 다른 거 있어요?   Is there something other than **that**?

Pronunciation Tip

track 114

걸려요 [걸려요]

The consonant ㄹ is pronounced differently depending on the situation. When ㄹ comes in the first sound of a syllable, it is pronounced close to [r], and when ㄹ is the final consonant, it is pronounced close to [l]. However, when ㄹ comes as the first sound after the consonant ㄹ, the first sound becomes [l] and is pronounced as [ll].

예 **골라요** [골라요]   **이걸로** [이걸로]

☕ Coffee Break

Registered mail: 등기

If you are concerned about the loss of mail, try using 등기, which allows you to track mail. At the post office, say 등기로 해 주세요 (I'd like to send it by registered mail, please.) and pay the 등기 수수료 (registered mail fee). However, it is advisable to check the registered value first, as the cost varies depending on the weight and time taken for the registered mail.

Korea's fast delivery service culture

Koreans like to do things quickly as they have a 빨리빨리 (quickly quickly) culture. In a densely populated city life, fast delivery service is a very important virtue. For example, even when it comes to the shipping of online products, companies boast of fast delivery which is often referred to as 총알 배송 (bullet delivery). Terms like 당일 배송, which is delivered on the same day of order, and 새벽 배송, where items ordered in the evening are delivered at dawn the next day have been in use for quite some time. Shipping 2-3 days after an order is considered a slow delivery service in Korea. Some believe that the reason why there was no daily necessity crisis in Korea during the COVID-19 pandemic in 2020 is that fast delivery service was commercialized.

Food delivery also boasts fast and accurate service in Korea. Even if you deliver food from a park, home, or workplace that does not have an exact address, you can receive food delivered quickly and accurately. It's amazing how they deliver food accurately and quickly to the person who ordered it from among many people in the expansive Han River Park.

Services such as internet installation are also fast. In Korea, it is rare that the driver does not come to install the Internet cable on the same day that you apply for the Internet. Installation completion on the day of application is taken for granted in Korea. Korea's fast delivery service culture is deemed essential for Koreans who live a busy life and 빠름 (quickness) is revered as a virtue in an era where everything is fast.

Chapter 5
Working out problems

장 메이 (중국)
Mei Chang (China)

Chapter 5

Working out problems

At a hospital

Explaining symptoms

열도 있고 콧물도 나요.

I have a fever and a runny nose.

Mei

A Doctor

Conversation

의사	어떻게 오셨어요?
메이	목이 아파서 왔어요.
의사	다른 데는 괜찮아요?
메이	열도 있고 콧물도 나요.
의사	언제부터 그랬어요?
메이	3일 전부터요.
의사	(*After the examination*) 좀 쉬어야 돼요. 약을 먹고 3일 후에 다시 오세요.

Doctor	What brings you here?
Mei	I came because my throat hurts.
Doctor	Is everything else all right?
Mei	I have a fever and a runny nose.
Doctor	Since when have you had these symptoms?
Mei	Since 3 days ago.
Doctor	(*After the examination*) You need to take a rest. Please, take the medicine and come back again in 3 days.

▶ New Vocabulary

목 throat

아프다 to be hurt, sick

데 part, place, spot

열 fever

콧물 runny nose

나다 to get (a medical disease),
have (a symptom)

언제부터 since when

전 before

약 medicine

약을 먹다 to take medicine

다시 again

▶ New Expressions

어떻게 오셨어요?
What brings you here?

다른 데는 괜찮아요?
Is everything else all right?

열도 있고 콧물도 나요.
I have a fever and a runny nose.

언제부터 그랬어요?
Since when have you had these
symptoms?

3일 전부터요. Since 3 days ago.

다시 오세요. Please, come back again.

▶ Close-Up

❶ 어떻게 오셨어요?
(Asking about the purpose of the visit)

어떻게 오셨어요? can be interpreted in two ways. One asks what kind of transportation you used to get to a destination, and the other asks about the purpose of your visit. In this conversation, the second meaning was used as the doctor asks what brought the patient to the hospital. The question 어떻게 오셨어요? is mainly used as a question to ask the purpose of the visit to someone who visits a public institution.

Ex. A 어떻게 오셨어요?   What brings you here?

B <u>소화가 안돼서</u> 왔어요. I came <u>because of digestion trouble.</u>

❷ The marker 은/는
(Emphasizing)

The marker 은/는 is used to emphasize a specific noun. In the conversation, a patient who comes to the hospital with a sore throat is asked by the doctor if she is okay and emphasis is given to 다른 데 (another part) other than the neck. When the marker 은/는 is used with the subject marker 이/가 or the object marker 을/를, the subject or object marker is omitted and only the marker 은/는 is used. However, if markers other than the subject marker or object marker (for example 에, 에서, etc) are used with 은/는 the initial marker is not dropped and instead used together with 은/는 (for example 에는, 에서는, etc).

Ex. A 머리가 너무 아파요.   My head hurts a lot.

B 그래요? 약은 먹었어요? Really? Did you take any medicine?

Flashback

• Words for parts of the body

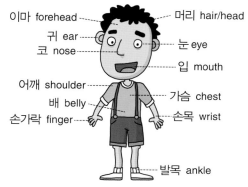

이마 forehead
귀 ear
코 nose
어깨 shoulder
배 belly
손가락 finger
머리 hair/head
눈 eye
입 mouth
가슴 chest
손목 wrist
발목 ankle

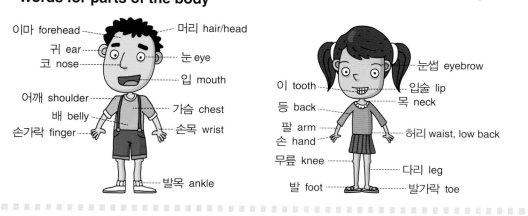

이 tooth
등 back
팔 arm
손 hand
무릎 knee
발 foot
눈썹 eyebrow
입술 lip
목 neck
허리 waist, low back
다리 leg
발가락 toe

Grammar in Focus

Grammar Chart **p.273**

-고 and

-고 is used to list an event, action, condition, or fact. -고 connects two sentences listed with the connecting adverb 그리고 into one sentence. -고 is used with verbs, and adjectives, regardless of whether a verb stem or adjective stem ends in a vowel or a consonant. The marker 도 is sometimes used to emphasize repetition when listing something.

좋아하다	사과도 좋아하고 배도 좋아해요.	I like apples and I like pears.

재미있다   한국어 공부도 재미있고 한국 생활도 재미있어요.
Learning Korean is fun and living in Korea is also fun.

오다	비도 오고 바람도 불어요.	It's raining and the wind is also blowing.
있다	열도 있고 콧물도 나요.	I have a fever and a runny nose.

-고 is also used to connect consecutive actions. When linking past continuous actions, the past tense marker -았/었- is not combined with -고. Therefore, even if the tense is different, the conjugation of -고 is the same.

현재	보통 밥을 먹고 산책해요.	I usually eat and go for a walk.
과거	어제 밥을 먹고 산책했어요.	Yesterday I ate and went for a walk.
미래	내일 밥을 먹고 산책할 거예요.	I'm going for a walk tomorrow after eating.

Quiz Yourself !

1~3 Look at the picture and complete the sentence by using -고.

Ex.

싸다   +   맛있다

→ 이 음식은 <u>싸고</u> 맛있어요.

1.

운동하다   +   쉬다

→ 메이는 보통 _____ 10분 쉬어요.

2.

춥다   +   머리가 아프다

→ 메이는 _____ 머리가 아파요.

3.

먹다   +   마시다

→ 메이는 어제 저녁을 _____ 녹차를 마셨어요.

4~8 Complete the sentence by using -고.

Ex. 친구하고 같이 <u>식사해요</u>. 그리고 <u>얘기해요</u>.   → **식사하고**

4. 보통 오후에 커피를 <u>마셔요</u>. 그리고 일을 시작해요.   →

5. 주말에 영화를 <u>봐요</u>. 그리고 저녁을 먹어요.   →

6. 어제 일이 <u>끝났어요</u>. 그리고 친구를 만났어요.   →

7. 지난주에 편지를 <u>썼어요</u>. 그리고 우체국에서 편지를 보냈어요. →

8. 한국어를 <u>배울 거예요</u>. 그리고 한국에서 일할 거예요. →

Answer p.279

Grammar Rehearsal

track 116

(Noun) 도 -고 (Noun) 도 ··· Listing

몸이 어때요?

➥ 머리도 아프고 목도 아파요.

여행이 어때요?

➥ 날씨도 좋고 음식도 맛있어요.

보통 주말에 뭐 해요?

➥ 운동도 하고 친구도 만나요.

How are you feeling?

➥ My head hurts and my neck hurts.

How is your trip?

➥ The weather is nice and the food is delicious.

What do you usually do on the weekends?

➥ I exercise and meet friends.

-고 -(으)세요 Advising another person

약을 먹고 푹 쉬세요.

30분씩 운동하고 채소를 자주 드세요.

책을 읽고 사람들하고 얘기해 보세요.

회원 가입하고 인터넷으로 예약하세요.

Take the medicine and make sure you rest well.

Exercise for 30 minutes and eat vegetables often.

Read books and talk to people.

Register as a member and make a reservation online.

Additional Vocabulary

• Vocabulary related to symptoms

 감기에 걸리다
(감기에 걸렸어요.)
to catch a cold

 목이 붓다
(목이 부었어요.)
to have a swollen throat

 기침이 나다
(기침이 나요.)
to have a cough

 다리를 다치다
(다리를 다쳤어요.)
to hurt one's leg

 소화가 안되다
(소화가 안돼요.)
to experience indigestion

 어지럽다
(어지러워요.)
to be dizzy

Conversation Rehearsal

(time)부터 Describing symptoms

어제부터 머리가 아파요.

I had a headache since yesterday.

일주일 전부터 소화가 안돼요.

I've been experiencing indigestion since a week ago.

며칠 전부터 기침이 나요.

I've been coughing since a few days ago.

작년부터 어깨가 아파요.

My shoulder has been hurting since last year.

-(으)면 어떡해요? Asking your doctor

잠이 안 오면 어떡해요?

What if I can't sleep?

계속 열이 나면 어떡해요?

What if I keep having a fever?

알레르기가 있으면 어떡해요?

What if I have allergies?

아침에 일어날 수 없으면 어떡해요?

What if I can't get up in the morning?

Pronunciation Tip

콧물 [콘물]

track 118

When the final consonant is pronounced as [ㄱ, ㄷ, ㅂ] and the syllable that follows begins with ㄴ, ㅁ, the final consonant [ㄱ, ㄷ, ㅂ] is pronounced as [ㅇ, ㄴ, ㅁ]. In the above example, the consonant ㅅ of 콧 is pronounced [ㄷ], but because the first sound ㅁ of 물 is connected to it, it is changed to [ㄴ]. Thus, 콧물 is pronounced as [콘물].

예 **냇물** [낸물] **햇님** [핸님]

 Coffee Break

Titles for doctors and nurses

In Korea, various titles are used. The title 선생님 is often called out of respect for the person, even if the actual job of the person is not related to teaching. Especially in the case of doctors and nurses working in hospitals, patients call them 의사 선생님 and 간호사 선생님. These titles are very common, so if you address them without adding 선생님, they may feel disrespected.

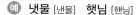

K-Quarantine: Korea's medical services and medical insurance system

South Korea's quarantine system drew the world's attention during the 2020 COVID-19 pandemic. It can be said that the state-led meticulous quarantine system showed its true value through fast and accurate diagnostic kits, widespread availability of hospital beds across the country, creative drive-through testing methods, and prompt disclosure of areas where patients contracted the virus.

Korea's high-quality medical service is another reason that contributed to Korea's quarantine success. In particular, the level of medical care in Korea is excellent enough to be recognized worldwide. Doctors are highly astounded individuals in Korea as they receive top scores in the fierce university entrance exam. In addition to general hospitals, there are many medical practitioners in each neighborhood, so people can choose hospitals easily due to easy access.

But, above all, National Health Insurance shined during the K-Quarantine. National Health Insurance is a public health insurance system that is considered a part of the social security system. Although insurance premiums vary according to income, National Health Insurance is a social security system that provides great benefits to the public. While operating state-led medical services even during the COVID-19 outbreak in 2020, the state bore the costs of the diagnosis and treatment, demonstrating the true nature of state-led medical services. Even if Koreans have mild symptoms such as a cold, National Health Insurance enables Koreans to access medical services or hospitals frequently. Senior citizens over the age of 65 pay less than 2,000 won

even if they receive treatment at a local clinic. Not only Koreans, but also foreigners who stay for more than 6 months can join the National Health Insurance system.

옷이 조금 크니까 한 치수 작은 사이즈로 주세요.

The clothing is a little big, so could you give me one size smaller?

Mei

An Employee at a clothing store

Conversation

직원	어서 오세요. 뭐 찾으세요?
메이	노란색 바지 좀 보여 주세요.
직원	여기 있어요.
메이	이거 입어 볼 수 있어요?
직원	그럼요. 이쪽으로 오세요. (*After trying it on*) 마음에 드세요?
메이	디자인이 마음에 들어요. 그런데 옷이 조금 크니까 한 치수 작은 사이즈로 주세요.
직원	알겠습니다.

Employee	Come in. What are you looking for?
Mei	Please, show me your yellow pants.
Employee	Here you go.
Mei	Can I try this on?
Employee	Of course. Please, come this way. (*After trying it on*) Do you like it?
Mei	I like the design. However, the clothing is a little big, so could you give me one size smaller?
Employee	OK.

뭐 what

찾다 to look for

흰색 white

바지 pants

입다 to wear

보다 to look

마음에 들다 to like something

옷 clothing

크다 to be large

치수 size, measurement

작다 to be small

사이즈 size

▶ **New Expressions**

뭐 찾으세요?
What are you looking for?

이거 입어 볼 수 있어요?
Can I try this on?

마음에 드세요? Do you like it?

디자인이 마음에 들어요.
I like the design.

한 치수 작은 사이즈로 주세요.
I would like this one size smaller.

▶ **Close-Up**

❶ 보다
(An auxiliary verb saying "try")

The verb 보 has the meaning of "look" as well as the meaning of "try" as an auxiliary predicate. It is usually used between verb stems in the form of –아/어 보다. In this conversation, 입어 볼 수 있어요 is used when asking an employee whether it's okay to try on something. Here, if you do not use the auxiliary predicate 보다 and write 입을 수 있어요, it has a completely different meaning of being able to wear clothes.

(Ex.) 패러글라이딩이 무서워요. 하지만 해 보고 싶어요.
I am afraid of paragliding. But I want to try it.

❷ 마음에 들다 and 좋아하다
(I like)

마음에 들다 is equivalent to "like" in English, and has a similar meaning to 좋아하다, but the usage is different. 마음에 들다 means that an object is received well at first sight, and is usually used for an object that is seen for the first time. For example, you can say 마음에 들다 if you find a design you like in a store or if you see someone you like on the street. On the other hand, 좋아하다 is an expression of liking a certain object. For example, when you are talking about a color or design you usually like, use 좋아하다 instead of 마음에 들다.

(Ex.) 이 카페에 처음 갔어요. 카페 분위기가 마음에 들었어요.
I went to this cafe with a friend for the first time. I liked the atmosphere of the cafe.

(Ex.) 저는 음악을 좋아하고 제 친구는 영화를 좋아해요.
I like music and my friend likes movies.

Flashback

• **Words for colors**

빨간색 red	파란색 blue	노란색 yellow	녹색 (초록색) green	검은색 (까만색) black	흰색 (하얀색) white	금색 golden	은색 silver
주황색 orange	하늘색 sky blue	베이지색 beige	연두색 yellow-green	분홍색 pink	갈색 brown	밤색 dark brown	회색 grey

Grammar in Focus

Grammar Chart **p.274**

-(으)니까 Explaining reasons

-(으)니까 is used to indicate that the content of the first half of the sentence is the reason for the content of the second half of the sentence. -(으)니까 is a grammar pattern that connects two sentences that indicate the reason and result in one sentence as a connecting adverb, 그러니까. In Korean, unlike in English, the clause indicating the reason of -(으)니까 is always written before the result clause. -으니까 is used with verbs and adjectives. When the stem of a verb or an adjective ends in a vowel, -니까 is used, and when the stem ends with a consonant, -으니까 is used.

오다   내일 손님이 오니까 집을 청소하세요.
Please clean the house, because guests will be coming tomorrow.

같다   가격이 같으니까 여기에 사인만 해 주세요.
Since the prices are the same, please sign here.

When expressing the reason for an event or condition in the past, combine the past tense marker -았/었- with -(으)니까 as -았/었으니까.

되다   약속이 취소됐으니까 친구한테 전화해야 돼요.
I need to call my friend because the appointment has been canceled.

사다   선물은 제가 샀으니까 신경 쓰지 마세요.
You don't need to worry about it, because I already bought a present.

> ⚠ **Be careful!**
> -(으)니까 and -아/어서 have similar meanings in that they indicate a reason, but have different uses. When using the command -(으)세요 to express the reason for an order, instruction, request, or favor, and when making a suggestion or request to the other party, -아/어서 cannot be used. Thus, you have to use -(으)니까 in such cases.
>
> [오다] 비가 오니까 우산을 갖고 가세요. (O)
> 비가 와서 우산을 갖고 가세요. (X)
> Because it is raining, take an umbrella with you.
>
> [먹다] 조금 전에 저녁을 먹었으니까 다음에 같이 식사합시다. (O)
> 조금 전에 저녁을 먹어서 다음에 같이 식사합시다. (X)
> Because I had dinner a little while ago, why don't we eat together another time?

Quiz Yourself!

1~4 Complete the conversation by choosing the correct answer.

1. A 왜 피곤해요?

B _____ 피곤해요.

① 친구가 없으니까 　　② 날씨가 좋으니까 　　③ 어제 못 잤으니까

2. A 왜 빨리 가야 돼요?

B _____ 빨리 가야 돼요.

① 시간이 있으니까 　　② 주말을 좋아하니까 　　③ 약속에 늦었으니까

3. A 왜 오늘 만날 수 없어요?

B _____ 오늘 만날 수 없어요.

① 바쁘니까 　　② 잤으니까 　　③ 만나고 싶으니까

4. A 왜 밤에 커피를 마시면 안 돼요?

B _____ 밤에 커피를 마시면 안 돼요.

① 커피가 있으니까 　　② 잘 수 없으니까 　　③ 커피가 필요하니까

5~8 Complete the sentence by using -(으)니까 with the correct answer from the following options.

여기는 비싸다	오늘은 다른 약속이 있다
아침에 길이 막히다	재미있는 영화를 하다

5. _____ 내일 일찍 출발하세요.

6. _____ 여기에서 사지 마세요.

7. _____ 다음에 식사할까요?

8. _____ 그 영화를 봅시다.

Answer **p.279**

Grammar Rehearsal

track 120

-(으)니까 -(으)세요 Explaining a reason

조금 비싸니까 싼 걸로 보여 주세요. It's a little pricey, so please, show me a cheap one.

옷이 작으니까 큰 옷으로 주세요. The clothes are small, so please, give me a larger one.

일주일이 지나면 환불할 수 없으니까 일주일 안에 오세요. Please, come within a week as refunds are not accepted after one week.

더우니까 에어컨을 켜 주세요. It's hot, so please, turn on the air conditioner.

-(으)니까 -아/어 보세요 A worker recommending something to a customer

이 색이 손님한테 잘 어울리니까 한번 입어 보세요. This color suits you well, so please, give it a try.

이런 신발이 요즘 인기가 많으니까 한번 신어 보세요. These shoes are very popular these days, so please, try them on.

이게 인기가 많으니까 한번 써 보세요. This is popular, so please, give it a try.

Additional Vocabulary

• **Vocabulary related to clothing**

가격 price

품질 quality

사이즈 (= 크기) size

색 color

교환 exchange

환불 refund

반품 returned merchandise

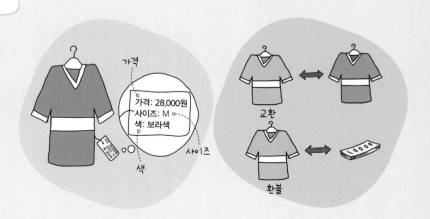

Conversation Rehearsal

(Noun) 좀 보여 주세요 Requesting a product from a worker

뭐 찾으세요?

➡ 바지 좀 보여 주세요.

➡ 운동화 좀 보여 주세요.

➡ 모자 좀 보여 주세요.

➡ 스카프 좀 보여 주세요.

What are you looking for?

➡ Please, show me your pants.

➡ Please, show me your sneakers.

➡ Please, show me your hats.

➡ Please, show me your scarves.

-아/어 볼 수 있어요? Asking approval from a worker

바지를 입어 볼 수 있어요?

운동화를 신어 볼 수 있어요?

모자를 써 볼 수 있어요?

스카프를 해 볼 수 있어요?

Can I try on the pants?

Can I try on these runners?

Can I try on a hat?

Can I try on a scarf?

Pronunciation Tip

 track 122

흰색 [힌색]

The vowel ㅢ is pronounced as [의] when used alone. However, when a consonant is used in the first sound before ㅢ, the vowel ㅢ is pronounced as [이]. In the above example, when the consonant ㅎ appears before 의 as in 희, 희 is pronounced as [히].

예 희망 [히망] 띄어쓰기 [띠어쓰기]

☕ Coffee Break
Questions about service

When asking what kind of service is available, add 되다 to the service. For example, when buying an item, ask 교환돼요? (Can I exchange it?) to see if it can be exchanged later. Similarly, when asking if a refund is possible, you can ask, 환불돼요?, If you need a gift to be wrapped, ask 포장돼요?. If the store is out of stock but it is available by placing an order, you can ask, 배달돼요? (Do you deliver?)

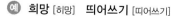

The collective culture of Korean people

Koreans are accustomed to group culture. Moreover, since Korea has a passive immigration policy, it is easy to find people with similar skin, similar clothes, and similar hairstyles. Office workers wear black, gray, or dark-colored suits. Although women are free to wear whatever they please, they wear similar clothes according to popular trends. Many people wear similar makeup because there are trendy styles. Middle and high school students wear school uniforms, daily life clothes, and sportswear in groups. Many people dye their hair, even older people, so it is rare for people to have gray hair. The roads in Korea are lined with black, gray, and white cars.

Not only that. More than 90% of Korean high school students go on to college. Because of Korea's focus on the importance of education, Korean students start attending academies around the age of ten. Since most of the students go to learning academies after school, there are also jokes that they must go to learning academies just to make friends. Women prepare for employment exams in their mid-20s, and men go to the military to get a job in their late 20s. At least before getting a job, it can be said that there is a relationship between the age of a person and the responsibilities that they carry.

Whether at school or work, Koreans feel comfortable belonging to a group. So, preference is given to people with a friendly personality who don't have a problem with joining a group. People who are too flashy are unique, but this is also the reason why they are not liked. Of course, the young generation of Korea in the 21st century values individuality. When the younger generation becomes the older generation, will they continue to value individuality?

이따가 출발할 때 연락해 주세요.

Please contact me when he leaves later.

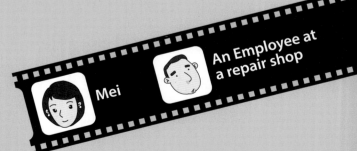

Mei

An Employee at
a repair shop

Conversation

직원	여보세요.
메이	311호예요. 수도가 고장 나서 전화했어요.
직원	어떻게 고장 났어요? 자세히 말해 주세요.
메이	물이 안 나와요. 빨리 와 주세요.
직원	그런데 수리 기사가 지금 없어요.
메이	그래요? 많이 기다려야 돼요?
직원	아니요, 수리 기사가 곧 올 거예요.
메이	그럼, 이따가 출발할 때 연락해 주세요.

Employee	Hello.
Mei	This is unit 311. I called because the water isn't working.
Employee	How did it break? Please, tell me in detail.
Mei	No water comes out. Please, come quickly.
Employee	But the repairman is not in right now.
Mei	Really? Should I wait for him for a long time?
Employee	No. The repairman should be coming soon.
Mei	Then, please, contact me when he leaves later.

호 unit

수도 tap

고장 나다 to be broken

전화하다 to call

자세히 in detail

물 water

빨리 quickly

수리 기사 repairman

기다리다 to wait

곧 soon

이따가 later

출발하다 to depart, leave

연락하다 to contact

► **New Expressions**

어떻게 고장 났어요?
How did it break?

자세히 말해 주세요.
Please, tell me in detail.

물이 안 나와요. No water comes out.

빨리 와 주세요. Please, come quickly.

많이 기다려야 돼요?
Should I wait for him for a long time?

곧 올 거예요.
He should be coming soon.

이따가 출발할 때 연락해 주세요.
Please, contact me when he leaves later.

► **Close-Up**

❶ 나오다 and 나다

The verb 나오다 refers to something coming from the inside out through a clear passage. Usually, 나오다 is mainly used with the marker 에서, which indicates the source. In the conversation, the verb 나오다 is used to express water coming out of a faucet. On the other hand, the verb 나다 refers to something that rises from the surface.

Ex. 지하철역 6번 출구에서 나오면 가게가 있어요.
There is a shop if you come out of the subway station's exit 6.

Ex. 벌써 수염이 났어요.
I already have a beard.

❷ 이따가 and 나중에

The adverbs 이따가 and 나중에 are adverbs that indicate a later point in time based on the point of speaking, and correspond to the English word "later". However, 이따가 refers to a point in the future within the same day as the point in time being said, while 나중에 refers to a distant future with an undetermined point in time, such as 언젠가. In this conversation, 어느 정도 시간이 지난 후 (after some time has passed) falls within 오늘, so 이따가 is used instead of 나중에.

Ex. 이따가 다시 전화하세요. 아마 회의가 1시간 후에 끝날 거예요.
Call me again later. The meeting will probably be over in an hour.

Ex. 우리 나중에 다시 만나요. 건강하세요.
We'll see you later. Stay healthy.

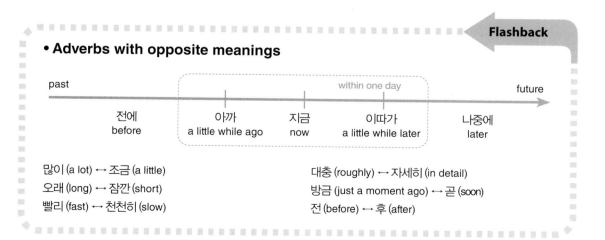

Flashback

• **Adverbs with opposite meanings**

past — 전에 (before) — 아까 (a little while ago) — 지금 (now) — 이따가 (a little while later) — 나중에 (later) — future

within one day

많이 (a lot) ↔ 조금 (a little)
오래 (long) ↔ 잠깐 (short)
빨리 (fast) ↔ 천천히 (slow)

대충 (roughly) ↔ 자세히 (in detail)
방금 (just a moment ago) ↔ 곧 (soon)
전 (before) ↔ 후 (after)

Grammar Chart **p.274**

–(으)ㄹ 때 when

–(으)ㄹ 때 is used to talk about a moment when a certain event occurs simultaneously with another action or an ongoing condition. –(으)ㄹ 때 is used together with a verb stem or adjective stem. When the stem of a verb or an adjective ends in a vowel, –ㄹ 때 is used, and, –을 때 is used when it ends with a consonant.

쉬다	피곤할 때 쉬어야 해요.	You need to take a rest when you are tired.
끄다	영화를 볼 때 핸드폰 전원을 끄세요.	Turn off your cell phone when watching a movie.
찍다	사진을 찍을 때 웃는 게 좋아요.	It is good to smile when taking pictures.
★듣다	친구 얘기를 들을 때 집중하세요.	Pay attention when listening to your friend.
★춥다	날씨가 추울 때 스키 타러 가요.	I go skiing when the weather is cold.

When stating an action or situation in the past, the past tense marker –았/었– is combined with –(으)ㄹ 때. In other words, –았/었을 때 is a combination of the past tense marker and –(으)ㄹ 때.

하다	옛날에 인도를 여행했을 때 그 친구를 만났어요.
	I met that friend when I was traveling in India a long time ago.
받다	남자 친구한테서 선물을 받았을 때 기분이 정말 좋았어요.
	It felt so good when I got a gift from my boyfriend.

! **Be careful!**

In the case of action verbs like 가다 and 오다, the meaning of the present tense and the meaning of the past tense are completely different. 갈 때 and 올 때 refer to the state of moving from one point to another, whereas 갔을 때 and 왔을 때 refer to the state in which movement from one point to another has been completed. Let's check the difference in meaning with the following example.

Ex) 회사에 갈 때 보통 지하철을 타요.
    I usually take the subway to go to work. (When you are on the way from home and have not yet arrived at work)

Ex) 회사에 갔을 때 8시 30분이었어요.
    It was 8:30 am when I went to work. (When you have already arrived at the company)

Quiz Yourself !

1~3 Complete the sentence by choosing the correct answer.

1. _____ 전화하면 안 돼요.

① 날씨가 나쁠 때   ② 운전할 때

③ 친구가 없을 때   ④ 행복할 때

2. _____ 이 케이크를 드세요.

① 커피를 마실 때   ② 수영할 때

③ 안경이 없을 때   ④ 화장실에 갈 때

3. _____ 여행 갑시다.

① 시간이 없을 때   ② 옷을 살 때

③ 어려울 때   ④ 날씨가 좋을 때

4~6 Complete the conversation by using –(으)ㄹ 때 with the correct answer from the following options.

대학교에 다니다	회사 면접을 보다	가족이 보고 싶다	일이 많이 있다

Ex. A 언제 가족한테 전화해요?

     B **가족이 보고 싶을** 때 가족한테 전화해요.

4. A 언제 정장을 입어요?

     B _____ 때 정장을 입어요.

5. A 언제 집에 늦게 가요?

     B _____ 때 집에 늦게 가요.

6. A 언제 한국어 공부를 시작했어요?

     B _____ 때 한국어 공부를 시작했어요.

Answer **p.279**

Grammar Rehearsal

-(으)ㄹ 때 -아/어 주세요   Requesting something

저한테 연락할 때 이메일을 보내 주세요.   Please, send an email when you want to contact me.

한국어로 얘기할 때 천천히 얘기해 주세요.   Please, speak slowly when speaking in Korean.

사진을 찍을 때 "하나, 둘, 셋"이라고 말해 주세요.   Please, say "one, two, three" when taking pictures.

한국 음식을 만들 때 맵지 않게 해 주세요.   Please, try not to make it spicy when cooking Korean food.

-(으)ㄹ 때 어떻게 했어요?/해야 돼요?   Asking a question

집을 구할 때 어떻게 했어요?   How did you go about finding a house?

길을 잃어버렸을 때 어떻게 했어요?   What did you do when you got lost?

문제가 생겼을 때 어떻게 해야 돼요?   What should I do if I have a problem?

한국어를 못 알아들을 때 어떻게 해야 돼요?   What should I do if I can't understand Korean?

Additional Vocabulary

• **Vocabulary related to repairs**

수리하다 (= 고치다) to repair, fix
수리 기사 repairman
수리비 repair fee
무료 free of charge
유료 fee charging
청구서 bill

Conversation Rehearsal

(time) 됐어요 Saying how much

언제 고장 났어요?

➥ 1시간쯤 됐어요.

➥ 3일 됐어요.

➥ 일주일 됐어요.

When did it break?

➥ It's been about an hour.

➥ It's been three days.

➥ It's been a week.

(price)쯤 돼요 Talking about the cost of something

수리비가 얼마나 돼요?

➥ 10만 원쯤 돼요.

월세가 얼마나 돼요?

➥ 50만 원쯤 돼요.

표 값이 얼마나 돼요?

➥ 20만 원쯤 돼요.

How much does the repair fee cost?

➥ About 100,000 won.

How much is your monthly rent?

➥ About 500,000 won.

How much is the ticket?

➥ About 200,000 won.

Pronunciation Tip

올 거예요 [올 꺼예요]

When the initial sound syllable that comes after the relative clause -(으)ㄹ is ㄱ, ㄷ, ㅂ, ㅅ, ㅈ, it is pronounced as [ㄲ, ㄸ, ㅃ, ㅆ, ㅉ]. In the example above, because of the consonant ㄹ, the ㄱ in 거예요 is pronounced as [ㄲ]. Therefore, 올 거예요 is pronounced as [올 꺼예요].

예 **할 수 있어요** [할 쑤 이써요] **할게요** [할께요]

Coffee Break

A simple problem situation expression

되다 is used to express that something works or has an effect. If there is no problem, use 돼요 and if there is a problem say 안 돼요. For example, if the washing machine breaks down, you can simply say, 세탁기가 안 돼요. Of course, you'll need to know a lot of vocabulary to describe how it's broken, but remember that when you want to express something is wrong, you can simply say 안 돼요.

A Korean culture that emphasizes hierarchical order

In Korea, there is a social atmosphere that emphasizes hierarchical order. You have to use respectful words for people who are older than you, and you can't call older people by their names. Even if that person is no more than 10 years older than you, only 3-4 months apart, or one year older, you should show respect. So, a person born in March cannot call a person who was born 3-4 months earlier and whose birth year is one year earlier by his/her name. You should regard the person as 형, 누나, 오빠, 언니.

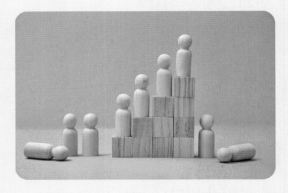

The criterion for the dividing hierarchy is not limited to age. In school, seniors and juniors are ranked by the time in which they entered the school, and in the military by the number of soldiers who entered the army. For example, if you enter college late even if you are older, you must abide by the junior-senior hierarchical culture. In a company, age, school number, or military rank are not, in itself, regarded as important. The company ranks the top and bottom according to rank. In the end, Koreans clearly divide according to a hierarchy that is important to the community they belong to.

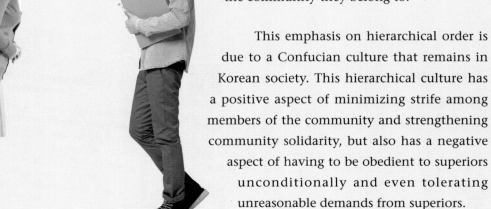

This emphasis on hierarchical order is due to a Confucian culture that remains in Korean society. This hierarchical culture has a positive aspect of minimizing strife among members of the community and strengthening community solidarity, but also has a negative aspect of having to be obedient to superiors unconditionally and even tolerating unreasonable demands from superiors.

가방을 잃어버렸는데 어떻게 해야 돼요?

I lost my bag, what should I do?

Mei

An Employee at a Lost-and-Found center

Conversation

직원	무엇을 도와 드릴까요?
메이	가방을 잃어버렸는데 어떻게 해야 돼요?
직원	어떤 가방이에요?
메이	파란색 작은 가방이에요.
직원	가방 안에 뭐가 있어요?
메이	책하고 여권이 있어요.
직원	지금 그런 가방이 없어요. 여기에 이름하고 연락처를 써 주세요. 가방을 찾으면 연락 드릴게요.

Employee	How may I help you?
Mei	I lost my bag, what should I do?
Employee	What kind of bag is it?
Mei	It's a small blue bag.
Employee	What's inside the bag?
Mei	My passport and a book are in it.
Employee	I don't have such a bag now. Please, write your name and contact information here. We will contact you if we find the bag.

▶ New Vocabulary

무엇 what

돕다 to help

가방 bag

잃어버리다 to lose

어떤 what kind

파란색 blue

책 book

그런 that kind of

이름 name

연락처 contact information

▶ New Expressions

무엇을 도와 드릴까요?
How may I help you?

어떻게 해야 돼요? What should I do?

어떤 가방이에요?
What kind of bag is it?

가방 안에 뭐가 있어요?
What's inside the bag?

여기에 이름하고 연락처를 써 주세요.
Please, write your name and contact
information here.

연락 드릴게요. We will contact you.

▶ Close-Up

❶ 어떤 (Asking about the type)

어떤 is used before a noun to ask about the characteristics or nature of a certain object. In some cases, 어떤 can be used interchangeably with 무슨, but there is a difference in meaning. 무슨 is used when asking about the kind of object, while 어떤 is used when asking about the characteristics of an object. In this conversation, 어떤 is used to request a description of the characteristics of the lost bag. If you ask using 무슨, you are asking about the type of bag – whether the bag is a backpack or purse.

(Ex.) 무슨 영화를 좋아해요?　　What kind of movie do you like?

(Ex.) 어떤 영화를 좋아해요?　　What movie do you like?

❷ 이런/그런/저런 (This kind of/that kind of)

이런/그런/저런 is used before a noun to express the state, shape, and nature of the object it is referring to. Like 이/그/저 learned in Scene 2, 이런/그런/저런 is also used depending on the distance between the speaker and the listener. 이런 is used when referring to the state of an object that is close to the speaker, and 저런 is used to refer to the state of an object that is far from both the speaker and the listener. 그런 is used to refer to the state of an object that is far from the speaker but close to the listener, and is also used to refer to the state of an object that is not visible from the listener's point of view.

Flashback

• Frequently used question words

뭐 (What): 뭐 좋아해요? What do you like?

무슨 (Which): 무슨 색을 찾으세요? Which color are you looking for?

어떤 (What kind): 어떤 사람이에요? What kind of person is he/she?

누구 (Who): 이분이 누구세요? Who is this person?

누가 (Who): 누가 사무실에 있어요? Who is in the office? (*when "who" is used as the subject of the verb)

몇 (How many): 사람이 몇 명 있어요? How many people are there? (*when counting numbers)

몇 (What): 전화번호가 몇 번이에요? What's your phone number?

언제 (When): 언제 수업이 시작해요? When does the class start?

어디 (Where): 어디에 살아요? Where do you live?

얼마 (How much): 이거 얼마예요? How much is this?

얼마나 (How long): 시간이 얼마나 걸려요? How long does it take?

얼마 동안 (For how long): 얼마 동안 한국어를 공부했어요? For how long have you studied Korean?

어떻게 (How): 어떻게 알았어요? How did you know?

왜 (Why): 왜 그렇게 생각해요? Why do you think like that?

Grammar Chart **p.274**

-(으)ㄴ/는데 Explaining a situation

-(으)ㄴ/는데 is used to explain the background or introduce a situation before asking, instructing, or making a suggestion to the other party. -(으)ㄴ/는데 is used with a verb or an adjective, and the form differs depending on whether it is a verb or an adjective. Whether the verb stem ends in a vowel or a consonant, -는데 is combined between the verb stems. When an adjective stem ends in a vowel, -ㄴ데 is used, and when an adjective stem ends in a consonant, -은데 is used.

하다	친구가 식당을 하는데 같이 갑시다.
	My friend runs a restaurant. Let's go together.

찾다	제가 지금 핸드폰을 찾는데 좀 도와주세요.
	Please help me. I'm looking for my phone right now.

아프다	머리가 아픈데 혹시 약 있어요?
	I have a headache. Do you have any medicine by any chance?

좋다	날씨가 좋은데 잠깐 밖에 나갈까요?
	The weather is nice, so shall we go outside for a while?

The stem ending syllable ㅂ of irregular verbs (for example 덥다, 춥다) is changed to 우 when combined with -은데.

★덥다	날씨가 더운데, 커피 대신에 시원한 주스를 마실까요?
	The weather is hot. Would you like to drink some cool juice instead of coffee?

When the situation or background introduces an event or state in the past, the past tense marker -았/었- can be combined with -는데. Therefore, -았/었는데 is used with the verb stem or adjective stem.

보다	그 영화를 아직 못 봤는데 같이 봐요.
	I haven't seen that movie yet, let's watch it together.

하다	어제 전화했는데 왜 전화 안 받았어요?
	I called you yesterday, but why didn't you pick up the phone?

Quiz Yourself !

1~3 Match the two sentences and complete the sentence by using -(으)ㄴ/는데.

Ex. 지금 사무실에 없어요 •

• ㉠ _____ 조금 이따가 전화해도 돼요?

1. 오늘 날씨가 안 좋아요. •

• ㉡ **지금 사무실에 없는데** 메모 남기시겠어요?

2. 지금 식사하고 있어요 •

• ㉢ _____ 길을 좀 가르쳐 주세요.

3. 길을 잃어버렸어요 •

• ㉣ _____ 다음에 같이 가요.

4~7 Complete the conversation by using -(으)ㄴ/는데 with the correct answer from the following options.

| 내일은 시간이 없다 | 한식이 먹고 싶다 |
| 식당에 갔다 | 얘기하려고 했다 | 숙제했다 |

Ex. A 숙제 주세요.

　　 B 죄송합니다. **숙제했는데** 안 가져왔어요.

4. A 왜 식사를 못 했어요?

　　 B _____ 식당이 문을 안 열었어요.

5. A 내일 만날까요?

　　 B 미안해요. _____ 다음 주에 만나요.

6. A 오늘 식사하러 어디에 갈까요?

　　 B _____ 한식당에 가요!

7. A 마이클 씨한테 얘기했어요?

　　 B 아니요, 어제 _____ 마이클 씨를 못 만났어요.

Answer p.279

Grammar Rehearsal

-(으)ㄴ/는데 (question) Asking a question to another person.

신청서를 내야 되는데 어디에
내야 돼요?

I need to submit an application form. Where should I submit it?

한국어를 잘 못하는데 어떻게
공부해야 돼요?

I'm not good at Korean. How should I study?

핸드폰을 잃어버렸는데 어떻게
해야 돼요?

I lost my phone. What should I do?

(action) **-(으)ㄴ/는데,** (thoughts/feelings) Talking about your experience to another person

산에 갔는데 경치가 정말
아름다웠어요.

I went to the mountains, and the scenery was really beautiful.

한국 음식을 먹었는데 정말
맛있었어요.

I ate Korean food, and it was really delicious.

한국어를 공부하고 있는데
조금 어려워요.

I'm studying Korean, but it's a little difficult.

Additional Vocabulary

• **Vocabulary related to one's belongings**

신분증 identification card
지갑 wallet
현금 cash
서류 document
화장품 makeup
핸드폰 cell phone
이어폰 earphones

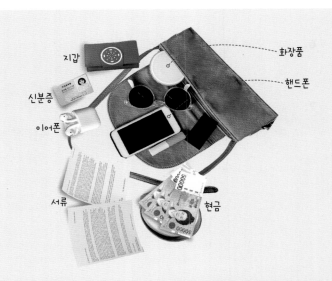

Conversation Rehearsal

track 129

색 + 크기/재료 (Noun)   Describing a bag

어떤 가방이에요?

➡ 빨간색 작은 가방이에요.

➡ 갈색 큰 가방이에요.

➡ 검은색 가죽 가방이에요.

➡ 흰색 천 가방이에요.

What kind of bag is it?

➡ It's a small red bag.

➡ It's a big brown bag.

➡ It's a black leather bag.

➡ It's a white fabric-based bag.

(Noun)이/가 있어요   Talking about what are your belongings

가방 안에 뭐가 있어요?

➡ 핸드폰이 있어요.

➡ 핸드폰하고 여권이 있어요.

➡ 여권만 있어요.

➡ 아무것도 없어요.

What's inside your bag?

➡ My cell phone is in it.

➡ My cell phone and passport are in it.

➡ I only have my passport in it.

➡ Nothing is in it.

Pronunciation Tip

연락처 [열락처]

track 130

ㄴ is pronounced as [ㄹ] before or after ㄹ. In the above example, the final consonant ㄴ of 연 is followed by ㄹ of 락, and the pronunciation of ㄴ is changed from [ㄴ] to [ㄹ] respectively. Therefore, 연락 is pronounced as [열락].

예 신라 [실라]   달나라 [달라라]

Coffee Break

Expressions that can be used in urgent situations

Everyone has a situation where they need help or assistance. Say 도와주세요 if you need help in Korean or if you want to ask someone for help when you are in trouble. In movies or TV shows, however, you may hear the words 살려 주세요 in life-threatening situations (for example, when someone is drowning or when someone is begging for their life from a criminal). If by chance, you offend a person, you can ask the offended to forgive you by saying, 한번만 봐 주세요.

Useful services

119 The center for reporting safety concerns

119 is an emergency telephone line that provides medical assistance to patients and transports them to hospitals in the case of a sudden accident, or rescues people in disasters such as fires. The 119 Center is an emergency telephone number used by all citizens of the country. You can dial 119 without an area code. Emergency calls can be reported even if there is no service or an inactivated cell phone is available. In other words, it is possible to report as long as the cell phone has a battery. When a foreigner calls 119, the staff at the 119 Center calls an external interpreting agency to receive the report through a three-way call.

112 The Center for Reporting Various Crimes

112 is the number to report various crimes. The 112 reports can be made by text as well as by phone, and the police respond to how the incident was handled by phone or text. Like 119, 112 is an emergency call, so you can dial 112 without an area code and file a report via an inactivated cell phone. When reporting to 112, the location of the incident cannot be arbitrarily tracked without clear evidence that the reporter is exposed to a crime. 112 should only be used to report crimes, and non-emergency reports such as non-criminal police complaints should be forwarded to 182.

1345 The Information Center for Foreigners

1345 is an information center provided by the Ministry of Justice to provide consultation on civil complaints and administrative information necessary for foreigners residing in Korea to adjust to life in Korea. For example, when a foreigner residing in Korea uses an administrative agency, a third-party interpretation service is provided. The telephone consultation service is available in 20 languages. From anywhere in the country, if you dial 1345 without an area code and press the language you want, a consultation will be conducted in that language. Consultation hours are limited to working hours and language availability is limited at night.

Chapter **6**

Traveling in Korea

폴 스미스 (캐나다)
Paul Smith (Canada)

Chapter 6

Traveling in Korea

Checking into a hotel

방을 예약했는데 확인해 주시겠어요?

Could you please confirm the room that I reserved?

Paul

An Employee at a hotel

폴	방을 예약했는데 확인해 주시겠어요?
직원	성함이 어떻게 되세요?
폴	폴 스미스입니다.
직원	1205호입니다. 그런데 12시부터 체크인이 가능합니다.
폴	그래요? 그럼, 지금 나가야 하는데 가방 좀 맡아 주시겠어요?
직원	알겠습니다.
폴	여기 가방 부탁합니다.

Paul	Could you please confirm the room that I reserved?
Employee	What's your name?
Paul	I'm Paul Smith.
Employee	It's number 1205. But, check-in starts at noon.
Paul	Really? I must leave now. Could you take care of my bag then?
Employee	Okay.
Paul	Here's the bag. I'll leave it in your care.

► New Vocabulary

방 room

예약하다 to make a reservation

확인하다 to check, verify, confirm

성함 name

체크인 check-in

가능하다 to be possible

나가다 to go out

맡다 to take care of something

부탁하다 to make a request

► New Expressions

예약을 확인해 주시겠어요?
Could you please confirm my reservation?

성함이 어떻게 되세요?
What's your name?

12시부터 체크인이 가능합니다.
Check-in starts at noon.

가방 좀 맡아 주시겠어요?
Then could you take care of my bag?

부탁합니다. I'll leave it in your care.

► Close-Up

❶ 성함이 어떻게 되세요?
(Asking for someone's name)

In Korean, when conveying respect, a verb or adjective is written with -(으)시-. Some nouns used frequently in daily life are replaced with other special nouns that convey respect. In this conversation, 성함 is the respectful equivalent of 이름. Thus, instead of asking 이름이 뭐예요?, respect is conveyed in the form of 성함이 어떻게 되세요?. In addition, 나이 is replaced with 연세, 생일 with 생신, and 밥 with 진지.

(Ex.) 할머니, 진지 드셨어요?
Grandma, did you eat?

(Ex.) 할아버지, 연세가 어떻게 되세요?
Grandpa, how old are you?

❷ 부탁합니다
(Politely asking the other person)

When asking someone to do something formally, first say what you want to ask followed by 부탁합니다. In the conversation, Paul asks the employee to take care of his bag and uses the expression 부탁합니다. You can use 부탁드립니다 instead of 부탁합니다 when wanting to be more polite. For example, when asking someone to call you, you can say 전화 부탁드립니다.

(Ex.) 지금 메일을 보냈습니다. 확인 부탁드립니다.
I've sent you an email now. I'd appreciate it if you check.

Flashback

• Expressing time throughout the day

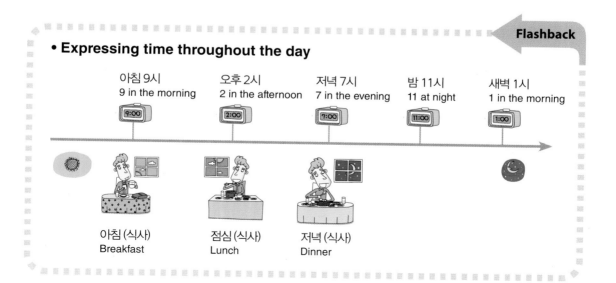

아침 9시
9 in the morning

오후 2시
2 in the afternoon

저녁 7시
7 in the evening

밤 11시
11 at night

새벽 1시
1 in the morning

아침 (식사)
Breakfast

점심 (식사)
Lunch

저녁 (식사)
Dinner

Grammar in Focus

Grammar Chart p.275

-아/어 주시겠어요? Would/Could you please...?

-아/어 주시겠어요 is used to politely ask the other person to do something for you. -아/어 주시겠어요 has the same meaning as -아/어 주세요, which we learned in Scene 1, but -아/어 주시겠어요 is a more formal and more polite way of asking people to do something for you. For example, -아/어 주시겠어요 is used when asking a favor to someone you are meeting for the first time or making a difficult request to someone you know. -아/어 주시겠어요? is used with a verb, and the tone of your voice should be raised slightly towards the end of the sentence to make the question sound more polite.

말하다	다시 한번 말해 주시겠어요?	Could you please say it again?
맡다	열쇠를 맡아 주시겠어요?	Could you please keep this key in your care?
들다	짐 좀 들어 주시겠어요?	Could you please lift my luggage?

When asking the other person for an object rather than requesting an action, add 주시겠어요? after the object.

| noun | 영수증 주시겠어요? | Could you please give me a receipt? |

When you receive a respectful request from someone, you can answer by granting the request with -아/어 드릴게요 or -아/어 드리겠습니다. -아/어 드릴게요 is a more friendly expression used in casual, less formal situations (such as meeting on the street) and -아/어 드리겠습니다 is used in formal situations (such as when an employee responds to a customer).

연락하다	A 확인되면 연락해 주시겠습니까?	Can you please contact me upon confirmation?
	B 네, 연락해 드리겠습니다.	Yes, I'll contact you.
★ 돕다	A 길을 잃어버렸는데 좀 도와 주시겠어요?	I've lost my way. Can you please help me?
	B 도와드릴게요.	I'll help you.

Quiz Yourself !

Answer p.279

1~4 Change the following sentences by using –아/어 주시겠어요.

Ex. 다시 한번 말해 주세요. → **다시 한번 말해 주시겠어요?**

1. 이 주소를 찾아 주세요. →

2. 조금 후에 연락해 주세요. →

3. 사진을 찍어 주세요. →

4. 여기에 사인해 주세요. →

5~8 Connect the first half and second half.

5. 한국 친구가 없어요. •   • ㉠ 열쇠를 맡아 주시겠어요?

6. 10분 후에 회의가 끝나요. •   • ㉡ 아침에 전화해 주시겠어요?

7. 지금 밖에 나가려고 해요. •   • ㉢ 한국 사람을 소개해 주시겠어요?

8. 아침 일찍 일어나야 돼요. •   • ㉣ 조금 더 기다려 주시겠어요?

9~12 Complete the conversation by using –아/어 주시겠어요.

9. A 연락처를 _____?
   B 네, 알려 드릴게요.

10. A 내일 저녁으로 _____?
   B 네, 예약해 드리겠습니다.

11. A 다른 것을 _____?
   B 네, 보여 드릴게요.

12. A 이것 좀 _____?
   B 네, 치워 드리겠습니다.

Grammar Rehearsal

track **132**

(Noun) 좀 –아/어 주시겠어요? Carefully asking a favor

짐 좀 들어 주시겠어요?	Could you please lift my luggage?
가방 좀 맡아 주시겠어요?	Could you please look after my bag?
택시 좀 불러 주시겠어요?	Could you please call a taxi for me?
7층 버튼 좀 눌러 주시겠어요?	Could you please press the 7th-floor button?

(Noun) 좀 더 주시겠어요? Asking for more objects

수건 좀 더 주시겠어요?	Could you please give me a towel?
반찬 좀 더 주시겠어요?	Could you please give me some more side dishes?
물 좀 더 주시겠어요?	Could you please give me some more water?
이거 좀 더 주시겠어요?	Could you please give me some more of this?

Additional Vocabulary

• **Vocabulary related to accommodations**

체크인 (입실) check-in (entering the room)
체크아웃 (퇴실) check-out (leaving the room)
조식 포함 including breakfast
조식 제외 excluding breakfast
1인실 single room
2인실 double room
다인실 a room for multiple people

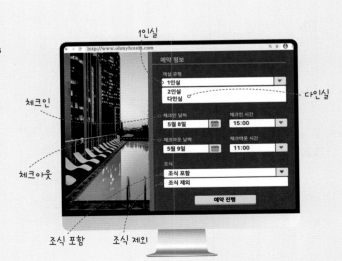

Conversation Rehearsal

track **133**

(Noun) 이/가 어떻게 되세요? When a worker is asking a customer for more information

성함이 어떻게 되세요?	What's **your** name?
직업이 어떻게 되세요?	What's **your** occupation?
연락처가 어떻게 되세요?	What's **your** contact information?
가족이 어떻게 되세요?	How many people **are in your** family?

(Request) 부탁합니다 Asking another person a favor

언제요?	When?
➡ 내일 부탁합니다.	➡ Tomorrow, please.
몇 시요?	At what time?
➡ 7시에 부탁합니다.	➡ Seven o'clock, please.
어떤 거요?	Which one?
➡ 커피 부탁합니다.	➡ Coffee, please.

Pronunciation Tip

부탁합니다 [부타캄니다]

track **134**

When the sound of the final consonant ㄱ, ㄷ, ㅂ, ㅈ is followed by an initial consonant ㅎ in the next syllable, their sounds are joined together and pronounced as [ㅋ, ㅌ, ㅍ, ㅊ]. In the above example, when the final consonant ㄱ of 부탁 joins ㅎ, it is pronounced together as [ㅋ]. Also, when the consonant [ㄱ, ㄷ, ㅂ] is followed by ㄴ, ㅁ, it is pronounced as [ㅇ, ㄴ, ㅁ]. In the above example, the consonant ㅂ is followed by ㄴ in 합니다 and pronounced together as [ㅁ]. Therefore, 부탁합니다 is pronounced as [부타캄니다].

Coffee Break

Expressing the duration of a trip with: 0박 0일

Use 0박 0일 when speaking about the duration of a trip. For example, if you depart on Monday, stay on Monday night and Tuesday night, and return on Wednesday, express this duration as 2박 3일 (3 days and 2 nights). In such cases, Sino-Korean numbers are used. Similarly, if you start on Monday, sleep three nights, and return on Thursday, you would say 3박 4일 (4 days and 3 nights). If you spend the night traveling by train or plane instead of staying at an accommodation during your trip, it is sometimes expressed as 무박 2일 (2 days without nights).

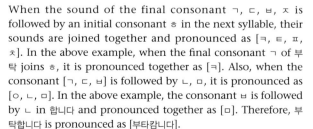

Temple stay:
Enjoy meditation at a Korean temple

Although Buddhism is not Korea's state religion, it has historical significance to Koreans. These days, you can learn more about Buddhism through temple stay: a program that opens the temple to non-Buddhists. Temple stays are held at most of the country's representative temples. There is a day program and an overnight program where you can stay at the temple. The program is conducted in the same way for Koreans and foreigners, and since most of the programs are conducted by meditating or demonstrating, foreigners can participate without any burden.

You can make a reservation by applying online. Once you arrive at the temple, you change into a Buddhist robe and begin the temple stay according to the rules of Korean temples. Even if you participate as a family, you must abide by gender separation. Men and women are separated, and each group of the same sex is camped in a large room. All the lights in the temple go out at 9:30, so you must go to bed and get up around 3:30 or 4:00 in the morning to participate in the morning prayer service. Also, photography or video recording is prohibited on the grounds, and smoking or drinking is prohibited in the temple. In this way, a temple stay begins by calming individual desires and following 금기의 규율.

There are various programs facilitated by the temple stay program. For example, you can meditate and participate in The Pre-dawn Ceremonial Service and Zen Meditation, which are representative Buddhist rituals, and have a Buddhist meal through The Meal Offering. The Tea Ceremony, Lotus Lantern Making, Rubbings, Temple Tour, Community Work, Buddhist Martial Arts, Buddhist Bead Making, etc are various events you can also experience. Since the temple allows you to experience Korean Buddhism firsthand and it is worth trying if you are a foreigner in Korea.

At the ticket booth

Buying a ticket

돌아오는 배가 몇 시에 있어요?

What time is the return ship?

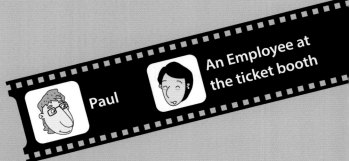

Paul

An Employee at the ticket booth

Conversation

폴	섬에 가는 배 표를 사고 싶어요.
직원	왕복으로 가실 거예요? 편도로 가실 거예요?
폴	왕복으로 주세요.
직원	몇 명 가실 거예요?
폴	한 명요. 얼마예요?
직원	왕복 표가 12,000원입니다.
폴	돌아오는 배가 몇 시에 있어요?
직원	저녁 6시에 있어요.
폴	감사합니다.

Paul	I want to buy a ship ticket to the island.
Employee	Roundtrip? Or one way?
Paul	Roundtrip, please.
Employee	For how many people?
Paul	One person. How much is it?
Employee	A roundtrip ticket costs 12,000 won.
Paul	What time is the return ship?
Employee	It's at 6 pm, dinner time.
Paul	Thank you.

▶ New Vocabulary

섬 island

표 ticket

사다 to buy

왕복 roundtrip

편도 one way

명 counter for people

돌아오다 to return, come back

저녁 dinner time (lit. dinner)

▶ New Expressions

왕복으로 가실 거예요?
Roundtrip?

편도로 가실 거예요?
One way?

몇 명 가실 거예요?
For how many people?

돌아오는 배가 몇 시에 있어요?
What time is the return ship?

▶ Close-Up

❶ 섬 and 도 (Words describing an island)

When referring to an island in Korean, it is sometimes called 섬 or read as 도. After the name, 섬 is added when referring to an island as a common noun and 도 is added when referring to an island by a proper noun (for example 제주도, 독도, etc.). When referring to a temple, after the name, 절 is added to common nouns and 사 is added to proper nouns (for example 조계사, 범어사, etc.).

(Ex.) 제가 어제 '울릉도'라는 섬에 갔다 왔어요.
I went to an island called '울릉도' yesterday.

❷ 몇 명 and 몇 시 (Asking about numbers)

When asking about numbers, use 몇 to ask questions. However, when answering, depending on the meaning, the number is answered in native Korean numbers or Sino-Korean numbers. In this conversation, the question 몇 명 is used when asking about the number of people and, therefore, is answered with native Korean numbers. However, the question 몇 시 is used when asking about the time and, therefore, is answered with Sino-Korean numbers. When answering the question 몇 번, the focus of the question is important to take into account. If the question asks for the number of times, answer with native Korean words, and if the question asks for the number's name, answer with Sino-Korean numbers.

(Ex.) A 제주도에 몇 번 갔어요?
How many times have you been to Jeju Island?
B 2(두)번 갔어요.   I went two times.

(Ex.) A 지금 몇 번 문제를 했어요?
Which question did you do now?
B 2(이)번 문제를 했어요. I did question number 2.

Flashback

• Irregular verbs II: ㄹ Omission

When a verb stem that ends in ㄹ (for example 알다, 살다, etc) is connected with an adjective stem that begins with ㄴ, ㄹ, ㅂ, ㅅ, the ㄹ is dropped in both cases.

When ㄹ is omitted		When ㄹ is not omitted	
살다: 살 + -니까 → 사니까	멀다: 멀 + -니까 → 머니까	살다: 살 + -아요 → 살아요	멀다: 멀 + -어요 → 멀어요
살다: 살 + -ㄹ 거예요 → 살 거예요	멀다: 멀 + -ㄹ 거예요 → 멀 거예요	살다: 살 + -고 → 살고	멀다: 멀 + -고 → 멀고
살다: 살 + -ㅂ니다 → 삽니다	멀다: 멀 + -ㅂ니다 → 멉니다	살다: 살 + -지만 → 살지만	멀다: 멀 + -지만 → 멀지만
살다: 살 + -세요 → 사세요	멀다: 멀 + -세요 → 머세요	살다: 살 + -면 → 살면	멀다: 멀 + -면 → 멀면

Grammar in Focus

Grammar Chart **p.275**

−는 The noun modifier

The noun modifier −는 is used to explain nouns in more detail. Unlike in English, in Korean, the noun modifier must always be placed before the noun it modifies. When the content to be modified is in the same tense as the content of the main clause, for example, in the present tense, the noun modifier −는 is combined between the verb stems regardless of whether the verb stem ends in a vowel or a consonant.

가다	제주도로 가는 비행기 표를 사고 싶어요.
	I want to buy an airplane ticket for Jeju Island (lit. that goes to Jeju island).

좋아하다	비빔밥은 제가 제일 좋아하는 음식이에요.
	Bibimbap is the food that I like the most.

있다	정원이 있는 집에 살고 싶어요.
	I want to live in a house that has a garden.

먹다	매일 아침을 먹는 사람이 건강해요.
	Those who eat breakfast every day are healthy.

웃다	저는 잘 웃는 사람을 좋아해요.
	I like a person who smiles often.

ㄹ is dropped when the final syllable of the verb stem ends with ㄹ (for example 살다, 알다) as the final syllable of the verb becomes ㄴ.

★살다	지금 사는 곳이 명동이에요.
	The place where I live is Myeongdong.

> **Be careful!**
> The following verb stems that end in [ㄱ, ㄷ, ㅂ] change in pronunciation to [ㅇ, ㄴ, ㅁ] respectively when the first syllable ends in a final consonant and is followed by the initial consonant ㄴ in the next syllable.
>
> | [ㄱ] → [ㅇ] | [ㄷ] → [ㄴ] | [ㅂ] → [ㅁ] |
> | --- | --- | --- |
> | 먹 + 는 → [멍는] | 듣 + 는 → [든는] | 입 + 는 → [임는] |
> | 닦 + 는 → [당는] | 웃 + 는 → [운는] | 돕 + 는 → [돔는] |
> | 읽 + 는 → [잉는] | 찾 + 는 → [찬는] | 줍 + 는 → [줌는] |

Quiz Yourself !

1~3 Look at the picture and complete the sentence by using –는.

1.

　매일 ＿＿＿＿＿＿＿ 친구가 진수예요.
　　　　(전화하다)

2.

　저는 1시에 ＿＿＿＿＿＿＿ 비행기를 타요.
　　　　　　(출발하다)

3.

　폴 씨가 잘 ＿＿＿＿＿＿＿ 음식이 김치찌개예요.
　　　　　　(만들다)

4~6 Complete the conversation by using –는 with the correct answer from the following options.

| 먹을 수 없다 | 명동에 가다 | 외국인이 좋아하다 | 옆에 앉아 있다 |

Ex. A **옆에 앉아 있는** 사람이 누구예요?

　 B 존 씨예요.

4. A ＿＿＿＿＿＿＿＿＿＿ 음식이 뭐예요?

　 B 삼계탕이에요.

5. A ＿＿＿＿＿＿＿＿＿＿ 곳이 어디예요?

　 B 경복궁이에요.

6. A ＿＿＿＿＿＿＿＿＿＿ 지하철이 몇 호선이에요?

　 B 4호선이에요.

Answer p.279

Grammar Rehearsal

-는 (Noun)이/가 뭐예요/누구예요/어디예요/언제예요? Describing a noun in detail

아침에 먹는 음식이 뭐예요?

What is the meal that you eat for breakfast?

이 사진에서 웃고 있는 사람이 누구예요?

Who is the person that is smiling in this photo?

매일 혼자 산책하는 곳이 어디예요?

Where is the place that you go for a walk alone every day?

고향에서 친구가 오는 날이 언제예요?

When is the day that the friend is coming from your hometown?

이거 -는 거예요? Asking for a detailed explanation

이거 어떻게 먹는 거예요?

By what means do you eat this?

이거 어떻게 하는 거예요?

By what means do you do this?

이거 뭘로 만드는 거예요?

What is this being made with?

이거 뭘로 쓰는 거예요?

What are you using this for?

Additional Vocabulary

- **Vocabulary related to expenses "비"**

교통비 transportation expense

식비 food expense

숙박비 lodging expense

- **Vocabulary related to the expenditure "금"**

상금 prize money

등록금 tuition

장학금 scholarship

- **Vocabulary related to fares "료"**

입장료 entrance fee

이용료 usage fee

수수료 fees

- **Vocabulary related to money "돈"**

용돈 pocket money

세뱃돈 New Year's money

(Noun)(이)나 (Noun) Talking about choices

어떻게 가요?

➡ 비행기나 배로 가요.

뭐 마셔요?

➡ 커피나 주스를 마셔요.

뭐 먹어요?

➡ 김밥이나 샌드위치를 먹어요.

How do you get there?

➡ I go by plane or ship.

What can you drink?

➡ I can drink coffee or juice.

What can you eat?

➡ I can eat gimbap or sandwiches.

-(으)면 어떻게 해요? Asking about if anything should happen

사고가 나면 어떻게 해요?

현금이 없으면 어떻게 해요?

날씨가 안 좋으면 어떻게 해요?

한국어를 못 알아들으면 어떻게 해요?

What do I do if I have an accident?

What do I do if I don't have cash?

What do I do if the weather is bad?

What do I do if I can't understand Korean?

Pronunciation Tip

몇 명 [면 명] / **몇 개** [면 깨] / **몇 호실** [며 토실] track **138**

Since all consonants that end with ㄷ, ㅌ, ㅅ, ㅈ, ㅊ, ㅎ are pronounced as [ㄷ], 몇 is pronounced as [면]. In 몇 명, when the consonant [ㄷ] of 몇, if followed by the ㅁ of 명, [ㄷ] changes to [ㄴ], and is pronounced as [면 명]. When saying 몇 개, the ㄱ is changed to [ㄲ] and is pronounced as [몇 깨] because of the consonant [ㄷ] of [면] in 몇. In 몇 호실, the consonant [ㄷ] of 몇 is followed by the syllable ㅎ and changes to [ㅌ]. Thus, 몇 호실 is pronounced as [며 토실].

Coffee Break

When asking about the first service and the last service

When traveling, it is necessary to check the 첫차 and 막차 times for transportation means such as buses, subways, and trains. So, when buying a ticket, ask 첫차가 몇 시예요?. Alternatively, you can check the time by asking 막차가 몇 시 예요?. On the other hand, for ships or airplanes, the first operation on that day is not referred to as the 첫차, but rather as 첫배, 첫 비행기. However, remember that we do not say that the last flight is 막차, but instead 마지막 배, 마지막 비행기.

Director's Commentary

Korea's topography

Korea is a peninsula bordered on three sides by the sea (the East Sea, the South Sea, and the West Sea). The East Sea is connected to the Pacific Ocean, so the water is deep and the coastline is calm, so you can enjoy the cool sea and sunrise. On the other hand, the South Sea and West Sea are shallower than the East Sea and have many islands, so they have complex coastlines. In particular, the southern coast boasts of unexplored scenery as it is made up of thousands of small islands to the extent that it has been called '다도해 (a sea of many islands)'. The West Sea has the world's largest tidal-flat ecosystem due to tidal differences and its shallow water depth. Apart from Chungcheongbuk-do, all regions in Korea have access to the sea and many Korean foods use seafood.

Korea also has many mountains. It is said that about 70% of the Korean peninsula is composed of mountainous regions, so there are more mountainous areas than plains. High mountains are located in the north of the Korean Peninsula and low mountains are located in the south. The Taebaek Mountains stretch long from the north to the south of the Korean Peninsula, and the Taebaek Mountains are skewed to the east of the Korean Peninsula, forming a topography that is high in the east and low in the west. Mountains are easy to find in most areas of Korea. For example, there are 26 mountains in Seoul, most of which are low at 250-300m, but there are relatively high mountains of 700-900m among them. There are many people who enjoy mountaineering in Korea. If you go to the entrance of the mountain by a subway station in Seoul, you can easily find people wearing mountain climbing clothes on the subway on weekends.

Due to the geographical characteristics of Korea, there are many mountainous areas, so the population density of flat land where people can live is high. Moreover, the population density of the metropolitan area is very high, with about 50% of the Korean population concentrated in the metropolitan area in Seoul. In fact, although Seoul is quite large as a city, the population density of Seoul is 8 times that of New York and 3 times that of Tokyo due to population concentration.

Receiving must-eat restaurant recommendations

'바다' 식당에 가 보세요.

Go to the restaurant 'Bada'.

Paul

A Korean passerby

폴	저……, 이 근처에 맛집 있어요?
한국인	맛집요? 무슨 음식을 좋아하세요?
폴	저는 한국 음식 다 좋아해요.
한국인	그럼, '바다' 식당에 가 보세요. 거기 해산물 요리가 진짜 맛있어요.
폴	여기에서 멀어요?
한국인	아니요, 가까워요. 지도로 식당 위치를 알려 드릴게요.

Paul	Excuse me, is there a must-eat restaurant in this vicinity?
Korean	A must-eat restaurant? What kind of food do you like?
Paul	I like all Korean food.
Korean	Go to the restaurant 'Bada'. The seafood dishes there are really tasty.
Paul	Is it far from here?
Korean	No, it is close by. I will show you the location of the restaurant on the map.

▶ New Vocabulary

맛집 a must-eat restaurant

좋아하다 to like

다 all

식당 restaurant

해산물 seafood

요리 dishes

진짜 really

맛있다 to be tasty

에서 from

멀다 to be far

가깝다 to be close

지도 map

위치 location

알리다 to let somebody know

▶ New Expressions

이 근처에 맛집 있어요?
Is there a must-eat restaurant in this vicinity?

저는 한국 음식 다 좋아해요.
I like all Korean food.

여기에서 멀어요? Is it far from here?

▶ Close-Up

❶ The adverb 다 (The adverb meaning "all")

The adverb 다 means "all" in English and modifies verbs or adjectives. In this conversation, 다 is a modification of the verb 좋아하다. However, since 다 is an adverb, it cannot be used before a noun to modify a noun. Therefore, when modifying a noun, 모든 should be used in place of 다 to convey the meaning of "all".

Ex. 갈비, 불고기, 삼겹살이 다 맛있어요.
Galbi, bulgogi, and samgyeopsal are all delicious.

Ex. 모든 음식이 안 매워요. All of the food is not spicy.

❷ -아/어 드릴게요 (Expressing an offer)

-아/어 드릴게요 is used when you are doing something for a person with whom you need to use an honorific expression. -아/어 드릴게요 is mainly used when answering a request or requesting someone to do something. In this conversation, the passerby used 알려 드릴게요 to politely show the location of the restaurant on a map to Paul, who inquired about the location of the restaurant. If this was a dialogue between friends, there would be no need to speak in a polite manner. Thus, -아/어 줄게요 is used between friends.

Ex. A 내일 책을 갖다드릴게요. (= 갖다줄게요)
I'll bring you a book tomorrow.

B 감사합니다. Thank you.

Flashback

• Irregular verbs III: Omission of ㄷ and ㅂ

1. The omission of ㄷ

When irregular verbs with a stem ending in ㄷ (for example 듣다, 걷다, etc.) are combined with a verb tense ending that begins with a vowel (for example 아/어요, -은, etc.), the ㄷ is changed to ㄹ. However, if a regular verb with a stem that ends with ㄷ (for example 닫다, 받다, etc.) is combined with a vowel ending, the stem ending syllable ㄷ does not change.

2. The omission of ㅂ

When an irregular verb stem (for example 줍다, 굽다, etc.) or an irregular adjective stem (for example 덥다, 쉽다, etc.) ends in ㅂ, this ㅂ becomes 우 when the verb tense ending begins with a vowel (for example -아/어요, -은, etc.). However, even if a regular verb with a stem ending in ㅂ (for example 입다, 씹다, etc.) or a regular adjective stem (for example 좁다) is combined with a verb tense ending that begins with a vowel, the ㅂ stem ending syllable does not change.

	Irregular verb	Regular verb
ㄷ	듣다: 듣 + -어요 → 들 + -어요 → 들어요 Ex. 매일 음악을 들어요. I listen to music every day.	받다: 받 + -아요 → 받아요 Ex. 친구한테서 선물을 받아요. I receive a gift from a friend.
ㅂ	쉽다: 쉽 + -어요 → 쉬우 + -어요 → 쉬워요 Ex. 이번 숙제가 쉬워요. The homework this time is easy.	입다: 입 + -어요 → 입어요 Ex. 진수는 매일 티셔츠를 입어요. I wear pants every day.

Grammar Chart **p.275**

–아/어 보세요 You should…

–아/어 보세요 is a sentence form used with a verb to invite, recommend, suggest, or advise the other person to try an action. The verb 하다 is used as 해 보세요. When a verb stem ends with a vowel ㅏ or ㅗ, –아 보세요, and –어 보세요 is added to the stem.

| 운동하다 | 매일 30분씩 운동해 보세요. 건강이 좋아질 거예요. |
| | You should exercise for 30 minutes every day. Your health will improve. |

| 가다 | 제주도에 꼭 가 보세요. 경치가 정말 좋아요. |
| | Be sure to visit Jeju Island. The scenery is really nice. |

| 찾다 | 인터넷에서 정보를 찾아보세요. 쉽게 찾을 수 있어요. |
| | You should try to search for information on the Internet. It's easy to find. |

| 먹다 | 이 떡을 한번 먹어 보세요. 정말 맛있어요. |
| | You should try this rice cake. It's really tasty. |

When the verb 보다 is combined with –아/어 보세요, it is used as 보세요 instead of 봐 보세요.

| ★ 보다 | 이 영화를 한번 보세요. 진짜 재미있어요. |
| | You should view this movie. It's really fun. |

When answering a recommendation or suggestion with –아/어 보세요, use –아/어 볼게요 to indicate that you want to try it.

| 마시다 | A 이 차가 진짜 맛있어요. 한번 마셔 보세요. |
| | This tea is really delicious. You should try it. |

| | B 네, 마셔 볼게요. | Yes, I'll try. |

| 읽다 | A 이 책이 진짜 재미있어요. 한번 읽어 보세요. |
| | This book is really enjoyable. You should read it. |

| | B 알겠어요. 읽어 볼게요. | Alright. I'll read it. |

Quiz Yourself !

1~4 Complete the sentences by using -아/어 보세요.

1. 이 식당에 한번 _____ . 음식이 맛있어요.
　　　　　　　　　　(가다)

2. 이 옷을 한번 _____ . 옷이 진짜 멋있어요.
　　　　　　　　　(입다)

3. 친구 연락을 조금 더 _____ . 친구가 곧 연락할 거예요.
　　　　　　　　　　(기다리다)

4. 이 음악을 한번 _____ . 노래 가사가 진짜 좋아요.
　　　　　　　　　(듣다)

5~9 Complete the conversation by using -아/어 보세요.

5. A 케이블카를 _____ . 경치가 진짜 좋아요.
　　 B 네, 케이블카를 타 볼게요.

6. A 이 안경을 _____ . 진짜 잘 어울릴 거예요.
　　 B 알겠어요, 안경을 써 볼게요.

7. A 이 운동화를 _____ . 진짜 편해요.
　　 B 네, 한번 신어 볼게요.

8. A 김치를 _____ . 아마 재미있을 거예요.
　　 B 네, 김치를 만들어 볼게요.

9. A 매일 공원을 _____ . 그러면 기분도 좋아질 거예요.
　　 B 알겠어요. 걸어 볼게요.

Answer p.279

Grammar Rehearsal

(Noun) 을/를 좋아하면 한번 -아/어 보세요   Recommending something

바다를 좋아하면 섬에 한번 가 보세요.   If you like **the sea,** you should **go to the island.**

생선을 좋아하면 회를 한번 먹어 보세요.   If you like **fish,** you should **try sashimi.**

커피를 좋아하면 이 커피를 한번 마셔 보세요.   If you like **coffee,** you should **try this coffee.**

한국 음악을 좋아하면 이 음악을 한번 들어 보세요.   If you like **Korean music,** you should **listen to this song.**

꼭 -아/어 보세요   Strongly recommending something

바닷가에 꼭 가 보세요. 진짜 좋아요.   Be sure to go **to the beach.** It's really nice.

케이블카를 꼭 타 보세요. 진짜 편해요.   Be sure to ride **the cable car.** It's really comfortable.

해산물을 꼭 먹어 보세요.
진짜 맛있어요.   Be sure to try **the seafood.** It's really delicious.

김치를 꼭 만들어 보세요.
진짜 재미있어요.   Be sure to make **kimchi.** It's really fun.

Additional Vocabulary

- **Vocabulary related to accommodation**
  호텔 hotel
  게스트 하우스 guesthouse
  민박 B&B

- **Vocabulary related to transportation**
  비행기 airplane
  기차 train
  버스 bus

- **Vocabulary related to sights**
  유적지 historical sites
  관광지 tourist attractions

- **Vocabulary related to food**
  전통 음식 traditional food
  지역 음식 local food

Conversation Rehearsal

track **141**

-(으)ㄹ 거예요 Talking about your expectations

맛있을 거예요. — It'll be delicious.

괜찮을 거예요. — It'll be fine.

재미있을 거예요. — It'll be fun.

문제 없을 거예요. — There'll be no problem.

제가 -아/어 드릴게요 Offering an act of goodwill to another person

한국어를 잘 못 써요. — I can't write Korean well.

➡ 제가 써 드릴게요. — ➡ I'll write it for you.

가방이 너무 무거워요. — The bag is too heavy.

➡ 제가 도와 드릴게요. — ➡ Let me help you.

사진을 보고 싶어요. — I want to see the pictures.

➡ 제가 보여 드릴게요. — ➡ I'll show you.

이 문법을 잘 모르겠어요. — I'm not familiar with this grammar.

➡ 제가 설명해 드릴게요. — ➡ Let me explain it.

Pronunciation Tip

track **142**

맛집 [맏찝]

The ㅅ in 맛 is pronounced as [ㄷ]. When the final consonant [ㄱ, ㄷ, ㅂ] is followed by an initial consonant ㄱ, ㄷ, ㅂ, ㅅ, ㅈ in the next syllable, the final consonant is pronounced as [ㄲ, ㄸ, ㅃ, ㅆ, ㅉ]. In the above example, the first consonant ㅈ of 집 is pronounced as [ㅉ] because of the [ㄷ] in 맛. Therefore, 맛집 is pronounced as [맏찝].

예 밧줄 [받쭐] 낮잠 [낟짬] 꽃집 [꼳찝]

Coffee Break

Taking pictures with Koreans

When taking photos with Koreans, say 김치 after 하나, 둘, 셋! and smile when taking a picture. This is a word that Koreans say a lot when taking pictures. When taking pictures with young Korean students, many Koreans use their index and middle fingers to make a "V" sign. Let's all say 김치~ and smile when taking a picture.

Means of transportation when traveling domestically

Let's take a look at the means of transportation that Koreans mainly use when traveling in Korea without a vehicle.

First of all, airplanes are overwhelmingly used when going to and from Jeju Island. Of course, you can travel from the southern half of the Korean Peninsula to Jeju by boat, but Koreans mainly use airplanes. In fact, there are many airplane users when going to Jeju Island to the extent that the Seoul-Jeju route was selected as the route with the most aircraft among the world's air routes. As there are many passengers, competition among low-cost airlines is fierce, and there are often discounts on air tickets. The flight time from Seoul to Jeju is only about 50 minutes. To get to Jeju by plane from Seoul, you should go to Gimpo Airport.

Train is the fastest way to get to areas other than Jeju Island. High-speed trains such as KTX and SRT reach Busan in about 2 hours and 30 minutes from Seoul and to Yeosu in about 4 hours. In addition to high-speed trains, there are regular trains that make stops along the way, but it takes 4-5 hours to get to Busan. If you reserve a ticket in advance, you can pay less at a discounted rate. In Seoul, trains going east often use Cheongnyangni Station, and trains going south often use Seoul Station or Yongsan Station.

Express buses do not have the same discount as trains, but they have the advantage of being able to depart at any time. Even if you do not make a reservation in advance, you can take a bus that departs every 30 minutes if you go to the Express Bus Terminal. In addition, since buses go to areas that cannot be reached by planes or trains, Koreans love to use express buses to travel all over the country. As for the express bus, there are regular express bus and premium express bus services, and there is also a late-night premium express bus service that operates at night. There are two express bus terminals departing from Seoul. One is the Seoul Express Bus Terminal (Express Bus Terminal Station can be found on Subway Line 3), which is divided into the Gyeongbu Line to Gyeongsang-do and the Honam Line to Jeolla-do. The other is the Sangbong Express Bus Terminal (Gangbyeon Station can be found on Subway Line 2), which mainly handles routes to Gangwon-do.

While talking to a friend

Talking about travel experiences

한국에서 여행해 봤어요?

Have you traveled in Korea?

Paul   Yujin

track 143

유진	한국에서 여행해 봤어요?
폴	네, 몇 번 여행해 봤어요.
유진	어디가 제일 좋았어요?
폴	제주도가 제일 좋았어요.
유진	그럼, 경주에 가 봤어요?
폴	아니요, 아직 못 가 봤어요.
유진	그래요? 나중에 꼭 가 보세요. 야경이 진짜 멋있어요.
폴	그럴게요.

Yujin	Have you traveled in Korea?
Paul	Yes, I've traveled a few times.
Yujin	Where did you enjoy the best?
Paul	Jeju Island was the best.
Yujin	Then, have you been to Gyeongju?
Paul	No, I haven't been there yet.
Yujin	Really? Be sure to visit later. The night view is really nice.
Paul	I will.

▶ New Vocabulary

한국 Korea

여행하다 to travel

몇 번 few times

어디가 where

제주도 Jeju Island

경주 Gyeongju

나중에 sometime in the future

꼭 definitely

야경 night view

멋있다 to be cool

▶ New Expressions

한국에서 여행해 봤어요?
Have you traveled in Korea?

몇 번 여행해 봤어요.
I've traveled a few times.

어디가 제일 좋았어요?
Where did you enjoy the best?

아직 못 가 봤어요.
I haven't been there yet.

나중에 꼭 가 보세요.
Be sure to visit later.

그럴게요. I will.

▶ Close-Up

❶ 몇
(Saying some)

몇 is used to convey an approximate of not many numbers. Therefore, 몇 번 indicates a small number of times, and 몇 명 indicates a small number of people. In Korean, 몇 is used with numbers, so 몇 번 is sometimes used in both question and answer forms.

Ex. A 제주도에 몇 번 갔어요?
　　How many times have you been to Jeju Island?
　　B 몇 번 갔어요. I've been there a few times.

❷ 꼭
(The adverb)

The adverb 꼭 is used together with –(으)세요 or –아/어 보세요 to strongly make a request or recommendation. Use the adverb 한번 to soften the request or recommendation. In the case of negatives, 절대(로) is used instead of the adverb 꼭 with –지 마세요.

Ex. 한국 음식을 꼭 배워 보세요. 진짜 재미있어요.
You should learn how to cook Korean food. It's really fun.

Ex. 한국 춤을 한번 배워 보세요. 어렵지만 재미있어요.
You should learn Korean dance once. It's difficult but fun.

Ex. 앞으로 절대 담배를 피우지 마세요. 담배가 몸에 안 좋아요.
You should never smoke in the future. Cigarettes are bad for your body.

Flashback

• Vocabulary expressing emotions

기분이 좋다
to feel good

기분이 나쁘다
to feel bad

놀라다
to feel surprised

아프다
to feel sick

행복하다
to feel happy

슬프다
to feel sad

당황하다
to feel embarrassed
(because of
an unexpected action)

졸리다
to feel sleepy

화가 나다
to feel angry

무섭다
to feel afraid

피곤하다
to feel tired

부끄럽다
to feel bashful

Grammar in Focus

Grammar Chart **p.276**

–아/어 봤다 I have done...

–아/어 봤다 is used with a verb to convey that you have experienced or tried something. The verb 하다 is used as 해 봤다. When a verb stem ends with a vowel ㅏ or ㅗ, –아 봤다 is used and for all other cases, –어 봤다 is added to the stem.

하다	A 한국 게임을 해 봤어요?	Have you tried playing a Korean game?
	B 네, 전에 해 봤어요.	Yes, I've tried one before.
먹다	A 삼계탕을 먹어 봤어요?	Have you tried Samgyetang?
	B 네, 먹어 봤어요.	Yes, I ate it before.

Use 안 to convey that you have no experience. However, to express that you want to experience something but haven't had the chance yet, use 못 with the adverb 아직.

| 가다 | A 경주에 가 봤어요? | Have you been to Gyeongju before? |
| | B 아니요, 안 가 봤어요. | |

No, I haven't been. (When expressing only the fact that I did not go)

| 가다 | A 경주에 가 봤어요? | Have you been to Gyeongju before? |
| | B 아니요, 경주에 아직 못 가 봤어요. | |

I haven't been to Gyeongju yet. (When expressing that you want to go but have not experienced it yet)

When expressing an experience or attempt with the verb 보다, use 봤어요 instead of 봐 봤어요.

| ★보다 | A 전에 한국 영화를 봤어요? | Have you seen a Korean movie before? |
| | B 아니요, 아직 못 봤어요. | No, I haven't seen one yet. |

Quiz Yourself !

1~3 Look at the picture and complete the conversation by using –아/어 봤다.

1. A 윷놀이를 _____?

   B 네, 해 봤어요. 진짜 재미있었어요.

윷놀이

2. A 한복을 _____?

   B 아니요, 못 입어 봤어요.

한복

3. A 구절판을 _____?

   B 아니요, _____.

구절판

4~6 Complete the conversation by choosing the correct answer from the following options.

　　　㉠ 어땠어요?　　　㉡ 부산에 한번 가 보세요.　　　㉢ 부산에 가 봤어요?

A 부산에 가 봤어요?

B 아니요, 못 가 봤어요. **4.** _____

A 네, 저는 지난주에 부산에 가 봤어요.

B **5.** _____

A 너무 재미있었어요.

B 저도 가고 싶어요.

A **6.** _____ 재미있을 거예요.

Answer **p.279**

Grammar Rehearsal

처음 -아/어 봤어요 Talking about first experiences

이 노래를 처음 들어 봤어요.	I heard **this song** for the first time.
이곳에 처음 와 봤어요.	I came **here** for the first time.
이 음식을 처음 먹어 봤어요.	I tried **this food** for the first time.
이 책을 처음 읽어 봤어요.	I read **this book** for the first time.

(number) 번 -아/어 봤어요 Talking about the number of experiences

제주도에 한 번 가 봤어요.	I've been **to Jeju Island** once.
자전거를 두 번 타 봤어요.	I've ridden **a bike** twice.
이 음식을 몇 번 먹어 봤어요.	I've tried **this food** a few times.
이 음악을 몇 번 들어 봤어요.	I've listened **to this music** a few times.

Additional Vocabulary

• **Vocabulary related to frequency**

1 2 3 4 5 6 7 8 9 10

1. 한 번도 안 해 봤어요. I've never done it before.
2. 전혀 안 해요. I don't at all.
3. 한 번 해 봤어요. I did it once.
4. 거의 안 해요. I rarely do.
5. 몇 번 해 봤어요. I've done it a few times.

6. 가끔 해요. I do it from time to time.
7. 여러 번 해 봤어요. I've tried it several time.
8. 자주 해요. I do it often.
9. 많이 해 봤어요. I've done it a lot.
10. 항상 해요. I always do it.

Conversation Rehearsal

(Noun)이/가 어때요/어땠어요? Asking about feelings or impressions

음식이 어때요?   How's the food?

➡ 진짜 맛있어요.   ➡ It's really delicious.

날씨가 어때요?   How's the weather?

➡ 진짜 좋아요.   ➡ It's really nice.

숙소가 어땠어요?   How was the accommodation?

➡ 진짜 깨끗했어요.   ➡ It was really clean.

이거 –지 않아요? Seeking consent from another person

이거 맛있지 않아요?   Isn't this delicious?

이거 재미있지 않아요?   Isn't this fun?

이거 이상하지 않아요?   Isn't this strange?

이거 비슷하지 않아요?   Isn't this similar?

Pronunciation Tip

track 146

제주 [제주]

Consonants ㄱ, ㄷ, ㅂ, ㅈ have different pronunciations depending on if they are the first syllable or between vowels. In the example 제주, the ㅈ of 제 is pronounced halfway between [ch] and [j]. On the other hand, the ㅈ in 주 is situated between two vowels (ㅔ and ㅜ) and is pronounced closer to [j].

예 기기 [기기] 도도 [도도] 부부 [부부]

Coffee Break

Sentences with a common question and answer

Koreans often use unspecified expressions to avoid answers. In this case, words such as 뭐, 누구, 언제, 어디 are often used. In fact, in Korean, there are many cases where the question and answer are the same, but only the intonation is different because the interrogative verb has the same form as the unspecified thing. For example, you can answer the question "뭐 먹었어요?" with "뭐 먹었어요". To the question "언제 같이 가요?", we can answer "언제 같이 가요!".

Famous Korean festivals

부산 국제 영화제 Busan International Film Festival

The Busan International Film Festival, which started in 1996, is held in early October every year for around two weeks. The Busan International Film Festival is an international film festival representing Asia and serves as a venue for Asian films to enter the global film market. The festival consists of many creative works of master directors and new directors. It is always crowded with many people, so it is better to reserve the movies you want to see through the 티켓박스(ticket box) website in advance or purchase a ticket on-site.

광주 비엔날레 Gwangju Biennale

The Gwangju Biennale is an international contemporary art exhibition representing Asia and is held every two years in Gwangju, Jeollanam-do for about two months from September to November. As well as works by established artists, pieces from event exhibitions, student works, and audience participation are major parts of the exhibition. You can request a docent (a guide with professional artistic knowledge) at the entrance of the exhibition hall and enjoy a more comfortable and informed viewing experience.

머드 축제 Mud Festival

The Mud Festival is a festival that uses mud from the tidal flats which extend along the west coast. The mud festival is usually held in July, the middle of summer, and at this time you can see young people burying mud and having fun. Both Koreans and foreigners actively participate in the mud festival and have enjoyable experiences. Koreans think mud is good for the skin, so they do not mind even if their skin becomes muddy and messy. In fact, famous K-beauty Korean cosmetic brands even have facial mask products made of mud.

Appendix

Grammar Chart ■

Adjectives │ Just as in English, there are verbs and adjectives in Korean. However, Korean adjectives act and look like verbs. Thus it's much easier to think of Korean as having two types of verbs: action verbs (to run, to do, to work, to think, etc.) and descriptive verbs (to be happy, to be sad, to be expensive, etc.). From here forward, these descriptive verbs will be identified as adjectives. These two types of verbs sometimes behave differently in certain grammar constructions, so you need to keep these two types in mind.

Chapter 1

Scene 01   –아/어 주세요 Could you please…?

Verbs	–아/어 주세요	Verbs	–아/어 주세요
하다 (to do)	(하+-여 주세요) 해 주세요	쓰다 (to write)	★(쓰+-어 주세요) 써 주세요
오다 (to come)	(오+-아 주세요) 와 주세요	모으다 (to gather)	★(모으+-아 주세요) 모아 주세요
사다 (to buy)	(사+-아 주세요) 사 주세요	누르다 (to press)	★(누르+-어 주세요) 눌러 주세요
찾다 (to find/look for)	(찾+-아 주세요) 찾아 주세요	듣다 (to listen)	★(듣+-어 주세요) 들어 주세요
읽다 (to read)	(읽+-어 주세요) 읽어 주세요	만들다 (to make)	(만들+-어 주세요) 만들어 주세요
기다리다 (to wait)	(기다리+-어 주세요) 기다려 주세요	굽다 (to roast)	★(굽+-어 주세요) 구워 주세요
외우다 (to memorize)	(외우+-어 주세요) 외워 주세요	붓다 (to pour)	★(붓+-어 주세요) 부어 주세요

Scene 02   The imperative –(으)세요 and –지 마세요

Verbs	–(으)세요	–지 마세요
하다 (to do)	(하+-세요) 하세요	(하+-지 마세요) 하지 마세요
보다 (to look)	(보+-세요) 보세요	(보+-지 마세요) 보지 마세요
찾다 (to find/look for)	(찾+-으세요) 찾으세요	(찾+-지 마세요) 찾지 마세요
앉다 (to sit)	(앉+-으세요) 앉으세요	(앉+-지 마세요) 앉지 마세요
쓰다 (to write)	(쓰+-세요) 쓰세요	(쓰+-지 마세요) 쓰지 마세요
부르다 (to sing)	(부르+-세요) 부르세요	(부르+-지 마세요) 부르지 마세요
듣다 (to listen)	★(듣+-으세요) 들으세요	(듣+-지 마세요) 듣지 마세요
만들다 (to make)	★(만들+-세요) 만드세요	(만들+-지 마세요) 만들지 마세요
굽다 (to roast)	★(굽+-으세요) 구우세요	(굽+-지 마세요) 굽지 마세요
붓다 (to pour)	★(붓+-으세요) 부으세요	(붓+-지 마세요) 붓지 마세요
먹다 (to eat)	★드시다 → 드세요	(먹+-지 마세요) 먹지 마세요
자다 (to sleep)	★주무시다 → 주무세요	(자+-지 마세요) 자지 마세요
있다 (to be/stay)	★계시다 → 계세요	(있+-지 마세요) 있지 마세요

Scene 03   Honorific –(으)세요

		–(으)세요 (Present)	–(으)셨어요 (Past)	–(으)실 거예요 (Future/guess)
Verbs	하다 (to do)	(하+-세요) 하세요	(하+-셨어요) 하셨어요	(하+-실 거예요) 하실 거예요
	보다 (to look)	(보+-세요) 보세요	(보+-셨어요) 보셨어요	(보+-실 거예요) 보실 거예요
	읽다 (to read)	(읽+-으세요) 읽으세요	(읽+-으셨어요) 읽으셨어요	(읽+-으실 거예요) 읽으실 거예요

Verbs	쓰다 (to write)	(쓰+-세요) 쓰세요	(쓰+-셨어요) 쓰셨어요	(쓰+-실 거예요) 쓰실 거예요
	부르다 (to sing)	(부르+-세요) 부르세요	(부르+-셨어요) 부르셨어요	(부르+-실 거예요) 부르실 거예요
	듣다 (to listen)	★ (듣+-으세요) 들으세요	★ (듣+-으셨어요) 들으셨어요	★ (듣+-으실 거예요) 들으실 거예요
	살다 (to live)	★ (살+-세요) 사세요	★ (살+-셨어요) 사셨어요	★ (살+-실 거예요) 사실 거예요
	돕다 (to help)	★ (돕+-으세요) 도우세요	★ (돕+-으셨어요) 도우셨어요	★ (돕+-실 거예요) 도우실 거예요
	낫다 (to be cured)	★ (낫+-으세요) 나으세요	★ (낫+-으셨어요) 나으셨어요	★ (낫+-으실 거예요) 나으실 거예요
	먹다 (to eat)	★ 드시다 → 드세요	★ 드시다 → 드셨어요	★ 드시다 → 드실 거예요
	자다 (to sleep)	★ 주무시다 → 주무세요	★ 주무시다 → 주무셨어요	★ 주무시다 → 주무실 거예요
	있다 (to be)	★ 계시다 → 계세요	★ 계시다 → 계셨어요	★ 계시다 → 계실 거예요.
	있다 (to possess)	★ 있으시다 → 있으세요	★ 있으시다 → 있으셨어요	★ 있으시다 → 있으실 거예요
Adjectives	피곤하다 (to be tired)	(피곤하+-세요) 피곤하세요	(피곤하+-셨어요) 피곤하셨어요	(피곤하+-실 거예요) 피곤하실 거예요
	좋다 (to be good)	(좋+-으세요) 좋으세요	(좋+-으셨어요) 좋으셨어요	(좋+-으실 거예요) 좋으실 거예요
	바쁘다 (to be busy)	(바쁘+-세요) 바쁘세요	(바쁘+-셨어요) 바쁘셨어요	(바쁘+-실 거예요) 바쁘실 거예요
	다르다 (to be different)	(다르+-세요) 다르세요	(다르+-셨어요) 다르셨어요	(다르+-실 거예요) 다르실 거예요
	길다 (to be long)	★ (길+-세요) 기세요	★ (길+-셨어요) 기셨어요	★ (길+-실 거예요) 기실 거예요
	춥다 (to be cold)	★ (춥+-으세요) 추우세요	★ (춥+-으셨어요) 추우셨어요	★ (춥+-으실 거예요) 추우실 거예요
	Noun이다 (to be)	(이+-세요) 친구세요 선생님이세요	(이+-셨어요) 친구셨어요 선생님이셨어요	(이+-실 거예요) 친구실 거예요 선생님이실 거예요

Scene 04 –(으)면 If...

Verbs	-(으)면	Adjectives	-(으)면
하다 (to do)	(하+-면) 하면	피곤하다 (to be tired)	(피곤하+-면) 피곤하면
보다 (to look)	(보+-면) 보면	좋다 (to be good)	(좋+-으면) 좋으면
기다리다 (to wait)	(기다리+-면) 기다리면	많다 (to be a lot)	(많+-으면) 많으면
먹다 (to eat)	(먹+-으면) 먹으면	맛있다 (to be delicious)	(맛있+-으면) 맛있으면
찾다 (to find, look for)	(찾+-으면) 찾으면	재미없다 (to be boring)	(재미있+-으면) 재미있으면
쓰다 (to write)	(쓰+-면) 쓰면	아프다 (to be sick)	(아프+-면) 아프면
부르다 (to sing)	(부르+-면) 부르면	다르다 (to be different)	(다르+-면) 다르면
듣다 (to listen)	★ (듣+-으면) 들으면	멀다 (to be far)	(멀+-면) 멀면
울다 (to cry)	(울+-면) 울면	길다 (to be long)	(길+-면) 길면
돕다 (to help)	★ (돕+-으면) 도우면	쉽다 (to be easy)	★ (쉽+-으면) 쉬우면
낫다 (to be cured)	★ (낫+-으면) 나으면	Noun이다 (to be)	(이+-면) 친구면 가족이면

Chapter 2

Scene 05 -고 싶다 want to...

Verbs	-고 싶다	Verbs	-고 싶다
하다 (to do)	(하+-고 싶다) 하고 싶다	먹다 (to eat)	(먹+-고 싶다) 먹고 싶다
만나다 (to meet)	(만나+-고 싶다) 만나고 싶다	앉다 (to sit)	(앉+-고 싶다) 앉고 싶다
보다 (to look)	(보+-고 싶다) 보고 싶다	받다 (to receive)	(받+-고 싶다) 받고 싶다
마시다 (to drink)	(마시+-고 싶다) 마시고 싶다	듣다 (to listen)	(듣+-고 싶다) 듣고 싶다
배우다 (to learn)	(배우+-고 싶다) 배우고 싶다	알다 (to know)	(알+-고 싶다) 알고 싶다
쓰다 (to write)	(쓰+-고 싶다) 쓰고 싶다	돕다 (to help)	(돕+--고 싶다) 돕고 싶다
부르다 (to sing)	(부르+-고 싶다) 부르고 싶다	낫다 (to be cured)	(낫+-고 싶다) 낫고 싶다

Scene 06 -(으)ㄹ 수 있다 can

Verbs	-(으)ㄹ 수 있다	Adjectives	-(으)ㄹ 수 있다
하다 (to do)	(하+-ㄹ 수 있다) 할 수 있다	편하다 (to be comfortable)	(편하+-ㄹ 수 있다) 편할 수 있다
보다 (to look)	(보+-ㄹ 수 있다) 볼 수 있다	좋다 (to be good)	(좋+-을 수 있다) 좋을 수 있다
먹다 (to eat)	(먹+-을 수 있다) 먹을 수 있다	많다 (to be a lot)	(많+-을 수 있다) 많을 수 있다
쓰다 (to write)	(쓰+-ㄹ 수 있다) 쓸 수 있다	아프다 (to be sick)	(아프+-ㄹ 수 있다) 아플 수 있다
부르다 (to sing)	(부르+-ㄹ 수 있다) 부를 수 있다	다르다 (to be different)	(다르+-ㄹ 수 있다) 다를 수 있다
걷다 (to walk)	★(걷+-을 수 있다) 걸을 수 있다	맛있다 (to be delicious)	(맛있+-을 수 있다) 맛있을 수 있다
만들다 (to make)	★(만들+-ㄹ 수 있다) 만들 수 있다	멀다 (to be far)	★(멀+-ㄹ 수 있다) 멀 수 있다
굽다 (to roast)	★(굽+-을 수 있다) 구울 수 있다	춥다 (to be cold)	★(춥+-을 수 있다) 추울 수 있다
낫다 (to be cured)	★(낫+-을 수 있다) 나을 수 있다	Noun이다 (to be)	(이+-ㄹ 수 있다) Noun일 수 있다

Scene 07 -아/어야 되다 have to, must...

Verbs	-아/어야 되다	Adjectives	-아/어야 되다
하다 (to do)	(하+-여야 되다) 해야 되다	따뜻하다 (to be warm)	(따뜻하+-여야 되다) 따뜻해야 되다
보다 (to look)	(보+-아야 되다) 봐야 되다	싸다 (to be cheap)	(싸+-아야 되다) 싸야 되다
먹다 (to eat)	(먹+-어야 되다) 먹어야 되다	좋다 (to be good)	(좋+-아야 되다) 좋아야 되다
마시다 (to drink)	(마시+-어야 되다) 마셔야 되다	맛있다 (to be delicious)	(맛있+-어야 되다) 맛있어야 되다
배우다 (to learn)	(배우+-어야 되다) 배워야 되다	재미있다 (to be fun)	(재미있+-어야 되다) 재미있어야 되다
쓰다 (to write)	★(쓰+-어야 되다) 써야 되다	예쁘다 (to be pretty)	★(예쁘+-어야 되다) 예뻐야 되다
부르다 (to sing)	★(부르+-어야 되다) 불러야 되다	다르다 (to be different)	★(다르+-어야 되다) 달라야 되다
듣다 (to listen)	★(듣+-어야 되다) 들어야 되다	길다 (to be long)	(길+-어야 되다) 길어야 되다
알다 (to know)	(알+-아야 되다) 알아야 되다	쉽다 (to be easy)	★(쉽+-어야 되다) 쉬워야 되다
굽다 (to roast)	★(굽+-어야 되다) 구워야 되다	가볍다 (to be light)	★(가볍+-어야 되다) 가벼워야 되다
낫다 (to be cured)	★(낫+-아야 되다) 나아야 되다	Noun이다 (to be)	(이+-어야 되다) 친구여야 되다 가족이어야 되다

Scene 08 –(으)ㄴ The noun modifier

Adjectives	–(으)ㄴ	Adjectives	–(으)ㄴ
싸다 (to be cheap)	(싸+-ㄴ) 싼	맛있다 (to be delicious)	(맛있+-는) 맛있는
피곤하다 (to be tired)	(피곤하+-ㄴ) 피곤한	재미없다 (to be boring)	(재미없+-는) 재미없는
바쁘다 (to be busy)	(바쁘+-ㄴ) 바쁜	길다 (to be long)	★(길+-ㄴ) 긴
다르다 (to be different)	(다르+-ㄴ) 다른	쉽다 (to be easy)	★(쉽+-은) 쉬운
좋다 (to be good)	(좋+-은) 좋은	어렵다 (to be difficult)	★(어렵+-은) 어려운
많다 (to be a lot)	(많+-은) 많은	Noun이다 (to be)	(이+-ㄴ) 친구인

Chapter 3

Scene 09 –(으)ㄹ까요? Shall we …?

Verbs	–(으)ㄹ까요?	Verbs	–(으)ㄹ까요?
하다 (to do)	(하+-ㄹ까요?) 할까요?	먹다 (to eat)	(먹+-을까요?) 먹을까요?
보다 (to look, see)	(보+-ㄹ까요?) 볼까요?	듣다 (to listen)	★(듣+-을까요?) 들을까요?
마시다 (to drink)	(마시+-ㄹ까요?) 마실까요?	살다 (to live)	★(살+-ㄹ까요?) 살까요?
쓰다 (to write)	(쓰+-ㄹ까요?) 쓸까요?	돕다 (to help)	★(돕+-을까요?) 도울까요?
부르다 (to sing)	(부르+-ㄹ까요?) 부를까요?	붓다 (to pour)	★(붓+-을까요?) 부을까요?

Scene 10 –(으)려고 하다 be going to…

Verbs	–아/어서	Verbs	–아/어서
하다 (to do)	(하+-려고 하다) 하려고 하다	먹다 (to eat)	(먹+-으려고 하다) 먹으려고 하다
가다 (to go)	(가+-려고 하다) 가려고 하다	찾다 (to find/look for)	(찾+-으려고 하다) 찾으려고 하다
보다 (to look)	(보+-려고 하다) 보려고 하다	듣다 (to listen)	★(듣+-으려고 하다) 들으려고 하다
마시다 (to drink)	(마시+-려고 하다) 마시려고 하다	살다 (to live)	(살+-려고 하다) 살려고 하다
배우다 (to learn)	(배우+-려고 하다) 배우려고 하다	만들다 (to make)	(만들+-려고 하다) 만들려고 하다
쓰다 (to write)	(쓰+-려고 하다) 쓰려고 하다	돕다 (to help)	★(돕+-으려고 하다) 도우려고 하다
부르다 (to sing)	(부르+-려고 하다) 부르려고 하다	붓다 (to pour)	★(붓+-으려고 하다) 부으려고 하다

Scene 11 –아/어서 because

Verbs	–아/어서	Adjectives	–아/어서
하다 (to do)	(하+-여서) 해서	피곤하다 (to be tired)	(피곤하+-여서) 피곤해서
보다 (to look)	(보+-아서) 봐서	싸다 (to be cheap)	(싸+-아서) 싸서
먹다 (to eat)	(먹+-어서) 먹어서	좋다 (to be good)	(좋+-아서) 좋아서
찾다 (to find)	(찾+-아서) 찾아서	맛있다 (to be delicious)	(맛있+-어서) 맛있어서
쓰다 (to write)	★(쓰+-어서) 써서	바쁘다 (to be busy)	★(바쁘+-아서) 바빠서
부르다 (to sing)	★(부르+-어서) 불러서	다르다 (to be different)	★(다르+-아서) 달라서
듣다 (to listen)	★(듣+-어서) 들어서	게으르다 (to be lazy)	★(게으르+-어서) 게을러서
알다 (to know)	(알+-아서) 알아서	멀다 (to be far)	(멀+-어서) 멀어서
굽다 (to roast)	★(굽+-어서) 구워서	맵다 (to be spicy)	★(맵+-어서) 매워서
붓다 (to swell)	★(붓+-어서) 부어서	Noun이다 (to be)	(이+-어서) 친구여서 가족이어서

Scene 12 The formal form -(스)ㅂ니다

		-(스)ㅂ니다 (Present)	-았/었습니다 (Past)
Verbs	하다 (to do)	(하+-ㅂ니다) 합니다	(하+-였습니다) 했습니다
	먹다 (to eat)	(먹+-습니다) 먹습니다	(먹+-었습니다) 먹었습니다
	쓰다 (to write)	(쓰+-ㅂ니다) 씁니다	★(쓰+-었습니다) 썼습니다
	부르다 (to sing)	(부르+-ㅂ니다) 부릅니다	★(부르+-었습니다) 불렀습니다
	듣다 (to listen)	(듣+-습니다) 듣습니다	★(듣+-었습니다) 들었습니다
	알다 (to know)	★(알+-ㅂ니다) 압니다	(알+-았습니다) 알았습니다
	붓다 (to swell)	(붓+-습니다) 붓습니다	★(붓+-었습니다) 부었습니다
Adjectives	편하다 (to be comfortable)	(편하+-ㅂ니다) 편합니다	(편하+-였습니다) 편했습니다
	좋다 (to be good)	(좋+-습니다) 좋습니다	(좋+-았습니다) 좋았습니다
	바쁘다 (to be busy)	(바쁘+-ㅂ니다) 바쁩니다	★(바쁘+-았습니다) 바빴습니다
	다르다 (to be different)	(다르+-ㅂ니다) 다릅니다	★(다르+-았습니다) 달랐습니다
	멀다 (to be far)	★(멀+-ㅂ니다) 멉니다	(멀+-었습니다) 멀었습니다
	어렵다 (to be difficult)	(어렵+-습니다) 어렵습니다	★(어렵+-었습니다) 어려웠습니다
	Noun이다 (to be)	(이+-ㅂ니다) 친구입니다 가족입니다	(이+-었습니다) 친구였습니다 가족이었습니다

Chapter 4

Scene 13 The comparative 보다 더 and the superlative 제일, 가장

		더	제일, 가장
Adjectives	싸다 (to be cheap)	더 싸요	제일 싸요
	좋다 (to be good)	더 좋아요	제일 좋아요
	맛있다 (to be delicious)	더 맛있어요	제일 맛있어요
Verbs	좋아하다 (to like)	더 좋아해요	제일 좋아해요
	잘하다 (to do something well)	더 잘해요	제일 잘해요
	먹다 (to eat)	더 잘 먹어요	제일 잘 먹어요
	만들다 (to make)	더 잘 만들어요	제일 잘 만들어요

Scene 14 Changing an adjective into an adverb -게

Adjectives	-게	Adjectives	-게
싸다 (to be cheap)	(싸+-게) 싸게	좋다 (to be good)	(좋+-게) 좋게
따뜻하다 (to be warm)	(따뜻하+-게) 따뜻하게	맛있다 (to be delicious)	(맛있+-게) 맛있게
예쁘다 (to be pretty)	(예쁘+-게) 예쁘게	짧다 (to be short)	(짧+-게) 짧게
바쁘다 (to be busy)	(바쁘+-게) 바쁘게	길다 (to be long)	(길+-게) 길게
다르다 (to be different)	(다르+-게) 다르게	쉽다 (to be easy)	(쉽+-게) 쉽게

		- 지만 (Present)	**- 았/었지만 (Past)**
Verbs	하다 (to do)	(하+-지만) 하지만	(하+-였지만) 했지만
	먹다 (to eat)	(먹+-지만) 먹지만	(먹+-었지만) 먹었지만
	쓰다 (to write)	(쓰+-지만) 쓰지만	★(쓰+-었지만) 썼지만
	부르다 (to sing)	(부르+-지만) 부르지만	★(부르+-었지만) 불렀지만
	듣다 (to listen)	(듣+-지만) 듣지만	★(듣+-었지만) 들었지만
	알다 (to know)	★(알+-지만) 알지만	(알+-았지만) 알았지만
	굽다 (to roast)	(굽+-지만) 굽지만	★(굽+-었지만) 구웠지만
	붓다 (to swell)	(붓+-지만) 붓지만	★(붓+-었지만) 부었지만
Adjectives	싸다 (to be cheap)	(싸+-지만) 싸지만	(싸+-았지만) 쌌지만
	좋다 (to be good)	(좋+-지만) 좋지만	(좋+-았지만) 좋았지만
	바쁘다 (to be busy)	(바쁘+-지만) 바쁘지만	★(바쁘+-았지만) 바빴지만
	다르다 (to be different)	(다르+-지만) 다르지만	★(다르+-았지만) 달랐지만
	멀다 (to be far)	★(멀+-지만) 멀지만	(멀+-었지만) 멀었지만
	어렵다 (to be difficult)	(어렵+-지만) 어렵지만	★(어렵+-었지만) 어려웠지만
	Noun이다 (to be)	(이+-지만) 친구지만 가족이지만	(이+-었지만) 친구였지만 가족이었지만

Verbs	**- 겠- / -(으)ㄹ게요**	**Verbs**	**- 겠- / -(으)ㄹ게요**
하다 (to do)	(하+-겠-) 하겠다 (하+-ㄹ게요) 할게요	먹다 (to eat)	(먹+-겠-) 먹겠다 (먹+-을게요) 먹을게요
보다 (to look)	(보+-겠-) 보겠다 (보+-ㄹ게요) 볼게요	신다 (to put on)	(신+-겠-) 신겠다 (신+-을게요) 신을게요
마시다 (to drink)	(마시+-겠-) 마시겠다 (마시+-ㄹ게요) 마실게요	듣다 (to listen)	(듣+-겠-) 듣겠다 ★(듣+-을게요) 들을게요
배우다 (to learn)	(배우+-겠-) 배우겠다 (배우+-ㄹ게요) 배울게요	만들다 (to make)	(만들+-겠-) 만들겠다 (만들+-ㄹ게요) 만들게요
쓰다 (to write)	(쓰+-겠-) 쓰겠다 (쓰+-ㄹ게요) 쓸게요	굽다 (to roast)	(굽+-겠-) 굽겠다 ★(굽+-을게요) 구울게요
부르다 (to sing)	(부르+-겠-) 부르겠다 (부르+-ㄹ게요) 부를게요	붓다 (to pour)	(붓+-겠-) 붓겠다 ★(붓+-을게요) 부을게요

Chapter 5

Scene 17   -고 and

Verbs	-고	Adjectives	-고
하다 (to do)	(하+-고) 하고	싸다 (to be cheap)	(싸+-고) 싸고
보다 (to look)	(보+-고) 보고	좋다 (to be good)	(좋+-고) 좋고
먹다 (to eat)	(먹+-고) 먹고	재미있다 (to be fun)	(재미있+-고) 재미있고
쓰다 (to write)	(쓰+-고) 쓰고	바쁘다 (to be busy)	(바쁘+-고) 바쁘고
부르다 (to sing)	(부르+-고) 부르고	다르다 (to be different)	(다르+-고) 다르고
듣다 (to listen)	(듣+-고) 듣고	멀다 (to be far)	(멀+-고) 멀고
살다 (to live)	(살+-고) 살고	길다 (to be long)	(길+-고) 길고
굽다 (to roast)	(굽+-고) 굽고	춥다 (to be cold)	(춥+-고) 춥고
붓다 (to swell)	(붓+-고) 붓고	Noun이다 (to be)	(이+-고) Noun이고

Scene 18   Explaining reasons -(으)니까

		-(으)니까(Present)	-았/었으니까(Past)
Verbs	하다 (to do)	(하+-니까) 하니까	(하+-였으니까) 했으니까
	먹다 (to eat)	(먹+-으니까) 먹으니까	(먹+-었으니까) 먹었으니까
	쓰다 (to write)	(쓰+-니까) 쓰니까	★ (쓰+-었으니까) 썼으니까
	부르다 (to sing)	(부르+-니까) 부르니까	★ (부르+-었으니까) 불렀으니까
	듣다 (to listen)	★ (듣+-으니까) 들으니까	★ (듣+-었으니까) 들었으니까
	알다 (to know)	★ (알+-니까) 아니까	(알+-았으니까) 알았으니까
	굽다 (to roast)	★ (굽+-으니까) 구우니까	★ (굽+-었으니까) 구웠으니까
	붓다 (to swell)	★ (붓+-으니까) 부으니까	★ (붓+-었으니까) 부었으니까
Adjectives	싸다 (to be cheap)	(싸+-니까) 싸니까	(싸+-았으니까) 쌌으니까
	좋다 (to be good)	(좋+-으니까) 좋으니까	(좋+-았으니까) 좋았으니까
	바쁘다 (to be busy)	(바쁘+-니까) 바쁘니까	★ (바쁘+-았으니까) 바빴으니까
	다르다 (to be different)	(다르+-니까) 다르니까	★ (다르+-았으니까) 달랐으니까
	멀다 (to be far)	★ (멀+-니까) 머니까	(멀+-었으니까) 멀었으니까
	어렵다 (to be difficult)	★(어렵+-으니까) 어려우니까	★(어렵+-었으니까) 어려웠으니까
	Noun이다 (to be)	(이+-니까) 친구일 때 가족일 때	(Noun+-였으니까) 친구였으니까 (Noun+-이었으니까) 가족이었으니까

Scene 19 -(으)ㄹ 때 when

Verbs	-(으)ㄹ 때	Adjectives	-(으)ㄹ 때
하다 (to do)	(하+-ㄹ 때) 할 때	싸다 (to be cheap)	(싸+-ㄹ 때) 쌀 때
보다 (to look)	(보+-ㄹ 때) 볼 때	좋다 (to be good)	(좋+-을 때) 좋을 때
먹다 (to eat)	(먹+-을 때) 먹을 때	재미있다 (to be fun)	(재미있+-을 때) 재미있을 때
쓰다 (to write)	(쓰+-ㄹ 때) 쓸 때	바쁘다 (to be busy)	(바쁘+-ㄹ 때) 바쁠 때
부르다 (to sing)	(부르+-ㄹ 때) 부를 때	다르다 (to be different)	(다르+-ㄹ 때) 다를 때
듣다 (to listen)	★(듣+-을 때) 들을 때	멀다 (to be far)	★(멀+-ㄹ 때) 멀 때
살다 (to live)	★(살+-ㄹ 때) 살 때	길다 (to be long)	★(길+-ㄹ 때) 길 때
굽다 (to roast)	★(굽+-을 때) 구울 때	춥다 (to be cold)	★(춥+-을 때) 추울 때
붓다 (to swell)	★(붓+-을 때) 부을 때	Noun이다 (to be)	(이+-ㄹ 때) 친구일 때 가족일 때

Scene 20 Explaining a situation -(으)ㄴ/는데

		-(으)ㄴ/는데(Present)	-았/었는데(Past)
Verbs	하다 (to do)	(하+-는데) 하는데	(하+-였는데) 했는데
	먹다 (to eat)	(먹+-는데) 먹는데	(먹+-었는데) 먹었는데
	쓰다 (to write)	(쓰+-는데) 쓰는데	★(쓰+-었는데) 썼는데
	부르다 (to sing)	(부르+-는데) 부르는데	★(부르+-었는데) 불렀는데
	듣다 (to listen)	(듣+-는데) 듣는데	★(듣+-었는데) 들었는데
	알다 (to know)	★(알+-는데) 아는데	(알+-았는데) 알았는데
	굽다 (to roast)	(굽+-는데) 굽는데	★(굽+-었는데) 구웠는데
	붓다 (to swell)	(붓+-는데) 붓는데	★(붓+-었는데) 부었는데
Adjectives	피곤하다 (to be tired)	(피곤하+-ㄴ데) 피곤한데	(피곤하+-였는데) 피곤했는데
	좋다 (to be good)	(좋+-은데) 좋은데	(좋+-았는데) 좋았는데
	바쁘다 (to be busy)	(바쁘+-ㄴ데) 바쁜데	★(바쁘+-았는데) 바빴는데
	다르다 (to be different)	(다르+-ㄴ데) 다른데	★(다르+-았는데) 달랐는데
	길다 (to be long)	★(길+-ㄴ데) 긴데	(길+-었는데) 길었는데
	어렵다 (to be difficult)	★(어렵+-은데) 어려운데	★(어렵+-었는데) 어려웠는데
	Noun이다 (to be)	(이+-ㄴ데) 친구인데 가족인데	(이+-었는데) 친구였는데 가족이었는데

Chapter 6

Scene 21 –아/어 주시겠어요? Would/Could you please...?

Verbs	–아/어 주시겠어요?	Verbs	–아/어 주시겠어요?
하다 (to do)	(하+–여 주시겠어요?) 해 주시겠어요?	쓰다 (to write)	★ (쓰+–어 주시겠어요?) 써 주시겠어요?
오다 (to come)	(오+–아 주시겠어요?) 와 주시겠어요?	모으다 (to gather)	★ (모으+–아 주시겠어요?) 모아 주시겠어요?
사다 (to buy)	(사+–아 주시겠어요?) 사 주시겠어요?	누르다 (to press)	★ (누르+–어 주시겠어요?) 눌러 주시겠어요?
찍다 (to take, shoot)	(찍+–어 주시겠어요?) 찍어 주시겠어요?	듣다 (to listen)	★ (듣+–어 주시겠어요?) 걸어 주시겠어요?
읽다 (to read)	(읽+–어 주시겠어요?) 읽어 주시겠어요?	들다 (to hold)	(들+–어 주시겠어요?) 들어 주시겠어요?
기다리다 (to wait)	(기다리+–어 주시겠어요?) 기다려 주시겠어요?	굽다 (to roast)	★ (굽+–어 주시겠어요?) 구워 주시겠어요?
외우다 (to memorize)	(외우+–어 주시겠어요?) 외워 주시겠어요?	붓다 (to pour)	★ (붓+–어 주시겠어요?) 부어 주시겠어요?

Scene 22 –는 The noun modifier

Verbs	–는	Verbs	–는
하다 (to do)	(하+–는) 하는	먹다 (to eat)	(먹+–는) 먹는
보다 (to look)	(보+–는) 보는	찾다 (to find/ look for)	(찾+–는) 찾는
만나다 (to meet)	(만나+–는) 만나는	걷다 (to walk)	(걷+–는) 걷는
마시다 (to drink)	(마시+–는) 마시는	알다 (to know)	★ (알+–는) 아는
주다 (to give)	(주+–는) 주는	입다 (to wear)	(입+–는) 입는
쓰다 (to write)	(쓰+–는) 쓰는	굽다 (to roast)	(굽+–는) 굽는
부르다 (to sing)	(부르+–는) 부르는	붓다 (to pour)	(붓+–는) 붓는

Scene 23 –아/어 보세요 You should...

Verbs	–아/어 보세요	Verbs	–아/어 보세요
하다 (to do)	(하+–여 보세요) 해 보세요	쓰다 (to write)	★ (쓰+–어 보세요) 써 보세요
가다 (to go)	(가+–아 보세요) 가 보세요	부르다 (to sing)	★ (부르+–어 보세요) 불러 보세요
먹다 (to eat)	(먹+–어 보세요) 먹어 보세요	걷다 (to walk)	★ (걷+–어 보세요) 걸어 보세요
마시다 (to drink)	(마시+–어 보세요) 마셔 보세요	살다 (to live)	(살+–아 보세요) 살아 보세요
배우다 (to learn)	(배우+–어 보세요) 배워 보세요	굽다 (to roast)	★ (굽+–어 보세요) 구워 보세요
보다 (to look)	★ (보+–아 보세요) 보세요	붓다 (to pour)	★ (붓+–어 보세요) 부어 보세요

Scene 24 –아/어 봤다 I have done...

Verbs	–아/어 봤다	Verbs	–아/어 봤다
하다 (to do)	(하+–여 봤다) 해 봤다	쓰다 (to write)	★ (쓰+–어 봤다) 써 봤다
가다 (to go)	(가+–아 봤다) 가 봤다	부르다 (to sing)	★ (부르+–어 봤다) 불러 봤다
먹다 (to eat)	(먹+–어 봤다) 먹어 봤다	듣다 (to listen)	★ (듣+–어 봤다) 들어 봤다
마시다 (to drink)	(마시+–어 봤다) 마셔 봤다	만들다 (to make)	(만들+–어 봤다) 만들어 봤다
배우다 (to learn)	(배우+–어 봤다) 배워 봤다	굽다 (to roast)	★ (굽+–어 봤다) 구워 봤다
보다 (to look)	★ (보+–아 봤다) 봤다	붓다 (to pour)	★ (붓+–어 봤다) 부어 봤다

Answers

Part 1

Unit 01
1 뵙겠습니다
2 잘 부탁드립니다

Unit 02
1 감사합니다

Unit 03
1 잘 모르겠는데요
2 그럽시다

Unit 04
1 몇 시에 만나요
2 맞아요

Unit 05
1 잘 지내셨어요
2 저도 잘 지냈어요

Unit 06
1 잘 먹겠습니다
2 잘 먹었습니다

Unit 07
1 축하합니다
2 감사합니다

Unit 08
1 여보세요
2 통화 괜찮아요

Unit 09
1 말해 주세요
2 못 들었어요

Unit 10
1 휴가 잘 보내세요
2 안녕히 가세요

Part 2

Scene 01
1 ㄷ   2 ㄹ   3 ㄱ   4 ㄴ
5 기다려 주세요
6 고쳐 주세요
7 바꿔 주세요

Scene 02
1 ①   2 ②   3 ②
4 건너세요
5 드세요
6 피우지 마세요

Scene 03
1 좋아하세요
2 가세요
3 전화하셨어요
4 오셨어요
5 드셨어요
6 보세요
7 계셨어요
8 읽으셨어요

Scene 04
1 ㄷ   2 ㄴ   3 ㄹ   4 ㄱ
5 카페, 왼쪽
6 약국, 우체국, 오른쪽
7 쪽, 왼쪽, 뒤

Scene 05
1 먹고 싶어요
2 가고 싶어요
3 보고 싶어요
4 ㄷ 만나고 싶어요
5 ㄱ 먹고 싶어요
6 ㅂ 배우고 싶어요
7 ㄹ 일하고 싶어요
8 ㄴ 보고 싶어요

Scene 06

1 ②　　2 ①　　3 ②　　4 ②

5 ①

6 읽을 수 없어요

7 만날 수 있어요

8 입을 수 없어요

Scene 07

1 ①　　2 ①　　3 ②　　4 ①

5 먹어야 돼요

6 마셔야 돼요

7 없어야 돼요

Scene 08

1 ②　　2 ①　　3 ①　　4 ①

5 비싼

6 재미있는

7 매운

Scene 09

1 볼까요

2 마실까요

3 먹을까요

4 ㄴ, ㅅ, ㄹ, ㄱ, ㄷ, ㅂ

Scene 10

1 ②　　2 ①　　3 ②　　4 ①

5 ②

6 먹으려고 해요

7 가려고 해요

8 있으려고 해요

9 찾으려고 해요

Scene 11

1 친절해서

2 몰라서

3 아파서

4 먹어서

5 내일 아침에 약속이 있어서

6 한국 사람하고 말하고 싶어서

7 핸드폰이 고장 나서

Scene 12

1 봅니다

2 먹습니다

3 마십니다

4 봤습니다

5 재미있었습니다

6 왔습니다

7 일합니다

8 시작했습니다

Scene 13

1 비행기, 자동차, 더

2 침대, 의자, 더

3 더 많아요

4 ①

5 ①

6 ②

7 ②

Scene 14

1 ㉠　　2 ㉣　　3 ㉡　　4 ㉢

5 바쁘게

6 크게

7 짧게

8 쉽게

Scene 15

1 ②　　2 ②　　3 ②　　4 ①

5 멋있지만

6 싫지만

7 맵지만

8 했지만

9 먹었지만

Scene 16

1 일어나겠습니다 / 일어날게요

2 먹겠습니다 / 먹을게요

3 읽겠습니다 / 읽을게요

4 말하지 않겠습니다 / 말하지 않을게요

5 사시겠어요

6 입으시겠어요

7 보시겠어요
8 드시겠어요

Scene 17
1 운동하고
2 춥고
3 먹고
4 마시고
5 보고
6 끝나고
7 쓰고
8 배우고

Scene 18
1 ③   2 ③   3 ①   4 ②
5 아침에 길이 막히니까
6 여기는 비싸니까
7 오늘은 다른 약속이 있으니까
8 재미있는 영화를 하니까

Scene 19
1 ②   2 ①   3 ④
4 회사 면접을 볼
5 일이 많이 있을
6 대학교에 다닐 때/다녔을 때

Scene 20
1 ㄹ 오늘 날씨가 안 좋은데
2 ㄱ 지금 식사하고 있는데
3 ㄷ 길을 잃어버렸는데
4 식당에 갔는데
5 내일은 시간이 없는데
6 한식이 먹고 싶은데
7 얘기하려고 했는데

Scene 21
1 이 주소를 찾아 주시겠어요?
2 조금 후에 연락해 주시겠어요?
3 사진을 찍어 주시겠어요?
4 여기에 사인해 주시겠어요?
5 ㄷ
6 ㄹ

7 ㄱ
8 ㄴ
9 알려 주시겠어요
10 예약해 주시겠어요
11 보여 주시겠어요
12 치워 주시겠어요

Scene 22
1 전화하는
2 출발하는
3 만드는
4 먹을 수 없는
5 외국인이 좋아하는
6 명동에 가는

Scene 23
1 가 보세요
2 입어 보세요
3 기다려 보세요
4 들어 보세요
5 타 보세요
6 써 보세요
7 신어 보세요
8 만들어 보세요
9 걸어 보세요

Scene 24
1 해 봤어요
2 입어 봤어요
3 먹어 봤어요, 못 먹어 봤어요/
  안 먹어 봤어요
4 ㄷ
5 ㄱ
6 ㄴ

Index ·····································